THE PHILOSOPHY OF NATURE

**STUDIES IN PHILOSOPHY
AND THE HISTORY OF PHILOSOPHY**

General Editor: Jude P. Dougherty

Studies in Philosophy
and the History of Philosophy   Volume 14

The Philosophy of Nature

by Ivor Leclerc

THE CATHOLIC UNIVERSITY OF AMERICA PRESS
Washington, D.C.

To
PHYLLIS and RICHARD
ROBERT, MARIAN, NATHANIEL and MARGARET

Copyright © 1986
The Catholic University of America Press
All rights reserved
Printed in the United States of America

Library of Congress Cataloging in Publication Data
Leclerc, Ivor.
  The philosophy of nature.
  (Studies in philosophy and the history of philosophy ; v. 14)
  Bibliography; p.
  Includes index.
  1. Philosophy of nature.   I. Title.   II. Series.
B21.S78 vol. 14 [BD581]   100 s [113]   85-9607
ISBN 978-0-8132-3086-3

Contents

Abbreviations	vii
Preface	ix
Acknowledgments	xi

PART I: INTRODUCTORY

1	The Philosophy of Nature	3

PART II: HISTORICAL

2	The Modern Concept of Nature	19
3	The Physical as Matter	35
4	Matter and Mind	44
5	Atomism, Substance, and the Concept of Body	57
6	Leibniz and the Analysis of Matter and Motion	75
7	Concepts of Space	91
8	The Meaning of "Space" in Kant	97

PART III: ISSUES

9	The Problem of the Physical Existent	107
10	The Physical Existent as a Compound Actuality	130
11	The Problem of Relations	139
12	Physical Existence, Matter, Activity	152

13 Compounds, Body, Change   165
14 Motion, Action, and Physical Being 180
15 Platonism, Aristotelianism, and
    Modern Science   194

Index   209

Abbreviations

AI	A. N. Whitehead, *Adventures of Ideas* (Cambridge: Cambridge University Press; New York: Macmillan, 1933).
Gerhardt	*Die Philosophischen Schriften von Gottfried Wilhelm Leibniz*, ed. C. I. Gerhardt, 7 vols. (Berlin: Wiedmann, 1875–90; rpt. Hildesheim: Georg Olms, 1965).
Gerhardt M	*Leibnizens mathematischen Schriften*, ed. C. I. Gerhardt, 7 vols. (Berlin and Halle: Wiedmann, 1849–55).
Loemker	L. E. Loemker, ed. and trans., *G. W. Leibniz: Philosophical Papers and Letters*, 2nd ed. (Dordrecht, Holland: D. Reidel Publishing, 1969).
NPE	Ivor Leclerc, *The Nature of Physical Existence* (London: Allen & Unwin; New York: Atlantic Highlands, Humanities Press, 1972).
PR	A. N. Whitehead, *Process and Reality* (Cambridge: Cambridge University Press; New York: Macmillan, 1929). Page references to these two editions given parenthetically as C and M, respectively.
SMW	A. N. Whitehead, *Science and the Modern World* (Cambridge: Cambridge University Press; New York: Macmillan, 1926). Page references to these two editions given parenthetically as C and M, respectively.

Preface

The philosophy of nature is a field of inquiry which had been a casualty of the increasing and dominant acceptance from the early nineteenth century of the conception of physics as a mechanics. This led to the doctrine that the science of mechanics alone achieved positive, i.e. certain, knowledge of nature. The implication of this is that philosophy cannot legitimately have "nature" as its object; its object could only be "science"—thus philosophy of science replaced philosophy of nature.

One consequence of the acceptance of this positivist doctrine by both scientists and philosophers has been an obscuring, indeed a blocking, of the realization of the full magnitude and extent of the twentieth-century developments in science, in particular of the most fundamental respects, namely, the ontological and metaphysical, in which those developments have affected the conception of nature. Some recognition of the philosophical implications of the scientific advances has, however, slowly been growing, and therewith an appreciation of the basic importance of the philosophy of nature and of the necessity of its restoration.

This realization has brought to the fore the primary need for the recovery of the problematic of the philosophy of nature, which had largely been lost during two centuries of neglect of the field. One way to that recovery is through an investigation of the problems in their origin and development, from the Greeks to our time—this was the course I adopted in *The Nature of Physical Existence.* The present book takes a somewhat different approach, inquiring into the issues and problems of the philosophy of nature as they face us in this century. But since these cannot be properly and adequately understood except as the outcome of a long historical development, it has been necessary to recur considerably to earlier periods, especially the seventeenth and eighteenth centuries.

Some of the chapters, particularly those comprising part II, dwell almost exclusively on analyses of the issues in the early modern period, and are thus complementary to the investigations of my earlier book, in some respects amplifying them, in others presenting the topics in somewhat different perspective. The other chapters, those of part III, explicitly investigate a number of issues and problems in the philosophy of nature which have come increasingly to the fore in our time.

The investigations comprising the chapters of this book were undertaken in the course of some two decades and were intended eventually to constitute the present volume—many of them were presented during that period in invited lectures, the form of which has for the most part been retained. The unity of the book derives from the logical coherence of the issues and their sequential investigation, as well as from the progressive development of my own thinking. This is especially manifest in the chapters of part III, which contain conclusions to which I have been led by my inquiries, and which reveal an evolving metaphysics of nature of my own.

I should like to express my gratitude to the societies and universities which have provided me occasions for presenting my inquiries and thereby opportunities for me to benefit from discussion with other scholars. I should also like particularly to express my indebtedness to my friends Milič Čapek, Joseph Earley, Hans Wagner, Leroy E. Loemker, and Albert Shalom, with whom I have had many and most helpful talks about the issues of this field.

Finally, I wish to express my very special indebtedness and gratitude to my wife.

Foxhill
Camden, Maine
July, 1984

Acknowledgments

Permission of the publishers and editors to use the following material previously published by the author is gratefully acknowledged.

"The Necessity Today for the Philosophy of Nature," *Proceedings of the XV World Congress of Philosophy*, 1973, and *Process Studies* 3 (1973).

"The Philosophy of Nature in the Seventeenth and Eighteenth Centuries." In *Akten des II. Internationalen Leibniz-Kongress*, 2. Stuttgart: Franz Steiner Verlag, 1974.

"Atomism, Substance, and the Concept of Body," *Filosofia* 18 (November, 1967).

"Leibniz and the Analysis of Matter and Motion." In *The Philosophy of Leibniz and the Modern World*, edited by Ivor Leclerc. Nashville: Vanderbilt University Press, 1973.

"Concepts of Space." In *Probability, Time, and Space in Eighteenth-Century Literature*, edited by Paula R. Backscheider. New York: AMS Press, 1979.

"The Meaning of Space in Kant." In *Kant's Theory of Knowledge*, edited by L. W. Beck. Dordrecht: D. Reidel Publishing Company, 1974. Copyright © 1974 D. Reidel Publishing Company, Dordrecht, Holland.

"The Problem of the Physical Existent," *International Philosophical Quarterly* 9, 1 (1969).

"A New Theory of the Physical Existent as a Compound Actuality." In *Akten des XIV. Internationalen Kongress für Philosophie*. Wien: Verlag Herder, 1968.

"Motion, Action, and Physical Being," *International Philosophical Quarterly* 21, 1 (1981).

"Platonism, Aristotelianism, and Modern Science," *International Philosophical Quarterly* 16, 2 (1976).

PART I
INTRODUCTORY

1

THE PHILOSOPHY OF NATURE

I

Earlier, and until about two centuries ago, there had been a main field of inquiry known as *philosophia naturalis*, the philosophy of nature. Then this field of inquiry fairly abruptly ceased being pursued. It is interesting, and as I shall show, important to us today to determine how and why this happened. It is indeed not difficult to do so, and the main features of this history can be fairly quickly sketched.

In the sixteenth century there occurred a considerable expansion of interest, especially among medical men who were leading scientists and thinkers of the day, in the philosophy of nature, which led to the momentous developments of the seventeenth century. Of particular importance in this process were the steps taken in the first quarter of the seventeenth century, for these had the consequence of the introduction of a new conception of nature, which appeared in a number of books about the year 1620, by Daniel Sennert in Germany, David van Goorle in Holland, Galileo in Italy, Francis Bacon in England, and most fully developed by the Frenchman Sebastian Basso in his *Philosophia Naturalis*, 1621. This new conception of nature was elaborated and fully explored in the course of the seventeenth century by thinkers such as Descartes, Gassendi, Thomas Hobbes, Robert Boyle, Leibniz and Newton, to name but a few of the most important. Descartes' *Principles of Philosophy* (1644) was largely devoted to the philosophy of nature. Gassendi, in a number of books, worked out the theory of material atomism. Hobbes explored an alternative in his *De Corpore*. Leibniz, in the next generation, critically and penetratingly examined the theories of his predecessors and developed his own alternative philosophy of nature in a series of monographs, articles, and letters. Newton's *Philosophiae Naturalis Principia Mathematica* was published in 1686. Although the work was mainly concerned with the "mathematical principles" of the philosophy of nature, it contained some highly significant philosophical sections, especially the Rules of Reasoning in philosophy at the beginning of book 3 and the General Scholium at the end of that book. To this must be added the "Queries" at the end of his *Opticks*. Terse though they are, these philosophical sections not only evidence the depth of Newton's philosophical reflection, but also adumbrate the philosophy of nature underlying his scientific structure. These writings on the philosophy of nature by these thinkers and others are among the most important works of the seventeenth century.

Quite early Sebastian Basso had seen very clearly that basic to the new conception of nature was a new conception of matter. In this new view, matter had come to be conceived as itself substance, in contrast to the previous conception in which matter was only the correlative of form in a substance. The consequence of the conception of matter as itself substance was an ineluctable metaphysical dualism, which had been explicitly accepted by Basso and Galileo and was then systematically developed by Descartes. After Newton the success of the new natural science had become so overwhelming that the acceptance of this dualism was no longer to be withstood, despite Leibniz's vigorous struggle against it, and in the eighteenth century and onward it reigned completely.

The outcome was that the universe was divided into two, one part consisting of matter, constituting nature, and the other part consisting of mind or spirit. The fields of inquiry were divided accordingly: natural science ruled in the realm of nature, and philosophy in the realm of mind. Thenceforth these two, science and philosophy, each went its own way, in separation from the other. In this division there was no place for the philosophy of nature. Its object had been nature, and this was now assigned to natural science. What remained to philosophy was only the epistemological and logical inquiry, which has natural *science*, but not *nature*, as its object—today usually called the philosophy of science. Philosophy of nature as a field of inquiry ceased to exist.

II

In our time, however, I wish to maintain, the situation has completely changed. The reason for this is to be found in the development of science in the past hundred years. This development has had the consequence that the conception of nature which had originated in the seventeenth century and thenceforward constituted the foundation for science down into this century has now been entirely destroyed. No other conception of nature has replaced it. We today stand in need of a new conception of nature, for this is indispensable to the conception by man of himself and his place in the universe, a conception of fundamental importance to every sphere of man's life and activity. Moreover, a new conception of nature is requisite for science itself.

Adequately to comprehend the changed present-day situation and especially the necessity of a new conception of nature for science, we must have clearly in mind the scheme of concepts in terms of which nature had been understood. These concepts are matter, space, time, and motion.

Central and basic was the concept of matter, for matter was the physical substance constituting the realm of nature and was thus the principal object of scientific inquiry. Matter was conceived by the philosophy of nature of the seventeenth century as fully "being," that is, as not subject to "becoming"; in other words, matter *is*, always, and is always *what* it is. This means that matter is completely without any capability of internal change, either by itself or of being changed by anything else. Matter in itself is entirely unchangeable.

With this conception of matter there is only one possibility for there to be change at all in the realm of nature, and this is that matter is capable of undergoing change of place. But this change of place has nothing whatever to do with matter per se, either in the sense that such change affects matter internally in any way or in the sense that matter could move itself from one place to another. In the modern philosophy of nature this change of place constituted "motion" or "movement." That is, motion could only be change of place, locomotion—in contrast to the previous conception of *motus*, "motion," which included the kinds of change like expansion and growth in size, and also qualitative change, both of which had been ruled out by the new conception of material substance as in itself changeless. But in this new philosophy, locomotion was not necessitated by matter: matter in itself does not need to change place; per se it is completely indifferent to such change. Matter, as Newton explicitly recognized, is mov*able*, but it is incapable of moving itself. This means that the concept of motion is not entailed by the concept of matter and cannot be derived from it. Accordingly, in this philosophy motion is a completely independent fundamental concept.

Equally independent are the concepts of space and time. They are not derivative from the concept of matter, since matter per se does not require either space or time. In respect to time this is relatively easy to see, since matter simply "is." That the concept of space similarly is not entailed by matter is frequently not appreciated because of the strong tendency nowadays to confuse the concepts of extension and space, an error of which Descartes, Leibniz, Newton, and also Kant were not guilty. Space and time are required, not by matter per se, but because the new science of physics in the seventeenth century was a mechanics, that is, a mathematical investigation of the locomotion of pieces of matter. For this, measurability was requisite, which meant that places and velocity had to be capable of determination. It is this which was provided by space and time, for they, as Newton said in his famous Scholium, are essentially places: "For times and spaces are, as it were, the places as well of themselves as of all other things. All things are placed in time as to order of succession; and in space as to order of situation. It is of their essence or nature that they are places; and that the primary places of things should be movable, is absurd."

By the end of the seventeenth century nature was in general conceived as a mechanism, which meant that nature could in principle be completely understood in terms of the motion, i.e., locomotion, change of place, of pieces of matter, usually referred to as "bodies." This concept of body is important, as we shall have occasion to see. In the philosophy of nature which was generally accepted by scientists after the end of the seventeenth century, the concepts of matter, substance, and body were identified.

Even before the end of the seventeenth century it was becoming clear that some revision of this scheme of matter, space, time, and motion was necessary. To Leibniz and Newton it was clear that a pure kinetics, as attempted by Huygens, as well as a phoronomy, as held by Descartes, were untenable. Leibniz and Newton both introduced the concept of force, and in the eighteenth century physics became a dynamics. This entailed that the concept of force take the place of motion in the scheme; motion could be conceived as derivative from force.

The concept of force led to the conception of the interaction of bodies and the attempt to conceive force as derivative from bodies, an attempt to which the notion of gravitational force presented grave difficulties, as Newton had long before clearly seen. In a letter to Bentley he wrote:

It is inconceivable, that inanimate brute matter, should, without the mediation of something else, which is not material, operate upon and affect other matter without mutual contact, as it must be, if gravitation, in the sense of Epicurus, be essential and inherent in it. And this is one reason why I desire you would not ascribe innate gravity to me. That gravity should be innate, inherent, and essential to matter, so that one body may act upon another at a distance through a vacuum, without the mediation of any thing else, by and through which their action and force may be conveyed from one to another, is to me so great an absurdity, that I believe no man, who has in philosophical matters a competent faculty of thinking, can ever fall into it.[1]

That in the eighteenth and nineteenth centuries the attempts were nevertheless made to conceive force as derivative from bodies does not necessarily indicate that the thinkers in question were, to use Newton's words, lacking in a competent faculty of thinking, but rather that implicitly a quite different conception of body was being introduced.

A most important development was that the concept of force led to the field concept in the nineteenth century. I shall quote C. F. von Weizsäcker's excellent brief exposition of this development:

The concept of the field arose in the study of the forces acting between bodies which was pursued in the hope of overcoming the dualism of body and force. Action at a distance seemed to be rigidly and immutably "affixed" to bodies. Then Faraday taught us to understand the field as a reality independent of bodies, with its own independent dynamics. Scientists thereupon attempted to explicate the field as a peculiar body extended throughout all space, the "ether", and thus to at last fulfill the ideal of the seventeenth century. Special relativity put an end to this hope. Besides, the concrete form of electrodynamics remained dualistic in its distinction between "ponderable matter" and the "electromagnetic field". The distinction matter-field is nothing but the old distinction body-force in a new guise.[2]

If we now consider the general theory of relativity, it becomes clear how very far contemporary physics is from the basic concepts of the eighteenth century. Again I shall cite von Weizsäcker:

general relativity emerged from field theory and therefore has no room for action at a distance. In merging the field of force with space it makes the latter into a physical object in the full sense of the word, an object that produces effects and can in turn be acted on. . . . Einstein was consistent in trying to overcome the remaining dualism of matter and space by regarding matter, too, as a property of space—particles, for example, as singularities of the metric field.[3]

III

Little indeed remains in this of the former scheme. Although the words *matter*, *space*, *time*, and *motion* continue to be used, they now

1. Richard Bentley, *Works of Richard Bentley*, ed. Alexander Dyce (London: Francis Macpherson, 1838), 3:211–12.
2. C. F. von Weizsäcker, *Die Einheit der Natur* (München: Karl Hanser Verlag, 1971), 147; English trans. by Francis J. Zucker, *The Unity of Nature* (New York: Farrar, Straus, Giroux, 1980), 116.
3. Ibid., 118.

have completely different meanings. Take the concept of space. In the general theory of relativity it has become, as von Weizsäcker has said, a "physical object in the full sense of exercising action and suffering effects." But what exactly does "physical object" mean? If it means "the object of physics," then this is not anything new or special, for space has, since the seventeenth century, always been an "object" of physics. But this is not what is meant here, for von Weizsäcker said, "a physical object *in the full sense of exercising action and suffering effects.*" Clearly what he means here is a substance, a *res*. That is to say, in this theory space has become the physical existent or substance. Einstein himself saw how close this position is to that of Descartes with his one *res extensa*. In the philosophy of Newton, however, space was definitely no substance; for Newton there was only one substance, matter. In Einstein's theory, on the contrary, space has become substance, and not only one substance among others, but the true physical substance, from which matter is derivative.

To see how Einstein arrived at this position it is necessary to take into consideration a particular development after Newton. In the eighteenth century, space was conceived by increasing numbers as some kind of existent, a conception which Kant correctly completely rejected as an *Unding*. Nevertheless, space continued implicitly to be conceived as some kind of existent or substance. One important reason for this is that after Kant there no longer existed the discipline, the philosophy of nature, to subject this conception to critical scrutiny. Thus it has come to be possible for Einstein in this century to conceive space not simply as a substance but as the true physical substance. The question must, however, be raised whether Einstein's true physical substance is to be conceived as "space" at all. Certainly his physical existent or substance is extended, but not everything which is extended is to be identified with space. Further, in the classical eighteenth-century doctrine of space, space was conceived as a container, *in which* the physical material substances exist and move, itself, however, neither affecting the substances nor being affected by them. But this conception of space has been completely abolished by Einstein. What he calls space is no more a container than is Descartes's *res extensa*. And further, Einstein's space both affects and is affected by matter. With that complete difference in conception, how appropriate is it to continue to use the term "space" in the contemporary theory, and can it be done without danger of confusion? It seems to me that much confusion has indeed ensued.

In Einstein's theory we also have a concept of matter completely different from that of the earlier philosophy of nature. In the latter conception, as we have noted, matter was a full being, in itself unchangeable. Not only in Einstein's theory but in general in contemporary physics, what continues to be spoken of as "matter" is something which, by contrast, is "in becoming," an existent which is *active*, producing effects by its acting and itself suffering effects, these effects being internal changes in the entities affected. It is clear that in the contemporary theory we do not find the concept of matter as formerly understood. More precisely stated, nothing of the previous conception of matter remains in contemporary physics; every feature of matter as formerly understood has been completely abandoned.

To continue to refer to these entities as "matter," as "particles" (i.e., of matter), can have serious consequences. I shall take only one example, but it is an important one. We have noted that in the earlier philosophy of nature the concepts of matter and body were equivalent. Macroscopic bodies are composites of a mass of material particles which, right down to the smallest atomic (indivisible) particles, are still bodies. Consequently, in classical physics it was completely indifferent whether, in experiments concerning the laws of motion, bodies of (say) 10 kilograms, or 1 kilogram, or 1 milligram are used. The laws of motion hold for all bodies, however large or small. Consequently, although the laws of motion are not empirically verifiable with individual atoms, it is consistent to assume the laws, empirically verified with compound bodies, as equally applying to the final constituent bodies, the atoms, and therefore that the routes of individual atoms in motion are exactly determinable. Now, since about 1900 it has been established not only that what had been taken to be atoms, i.e., not divisible, are in fact compounds but also that the classical laws of motion do not hold for the subatomic constituents, which display variations in their motion, so that their paths are determinable only by statistical probability. In fact, all the laws of subatomic physics are statistical probabilities.

This difference in respect of laws of motion could be significant of a fundamental difference in the kinds of entities respectively involved. The presupposition has, however, continued that the newly discovered constituents must themselves be material bodies—they are spoken of as "particles" or "elementary particles," that is, of matter. For "particles" (little parts) are parts of something, and the something of which they are parts is body or matter. This presupposition is strengthened by the adjective *elementary*, for an "element" means a final, not further divisible constituent, it being not further divisible not because it is impossible to divide it but because further division would result in its ceasing to be a "part," that is, of the same kind as, that of which it is a part. Accordingly, an elementary particle of matter must be matter; an elementary particle of a body must itself be a body. Thus, the very terms used carry the presupposition of the subatomic constituents as bodily; that is, they are implicitly conceived as having the properties and characteristics of bodies.

IV

But this presupposition is definitely open to question. We have here a philosophical problem. A macroscopic body is a composite, but so is any microscopic body, down to that which is still called an "atom." The question has to be raised whether the constituents of a composite body *necessarily* have to be conceived as being bodies. Stated generally, is it necessary that the constituents be "parts," i.e., of the same kind, having the same character or property, as that of the composite? That there is no necessity in this had been clear to Leibniz in the seventeenth century—and also to Aristotle in antiquity. Leibniz strongly opposed the assumption and developed a theory of body, and matter, as composite, with the constituents entities of a very different kind, explicitly nonmaterial. But despite Leibniz the presupposition has ruled down to the present day. It seems to me that in contemporary science, not only in physics but also in chemistry, biochemistry, biophysics, and in biology, the continued implicit acceptance of this presupposition is having restrictive consequences.

For if the subatomic constituents are not particles, little parts, i.e., little material bodies, but are nevertheless implicitly conceived as having bodily characteristics, in particular as having as a basic feature that of locomotion, change of place, it would not be surprising if difficulties ensue. For example, corporeal locomotion is continuous, but in contemporary physics quantum characteristics, i.e., discontinuity, are well established. But the presupposition nevertheless continues that the motion of the subatomic constituents is essentially locomotion, change of place—subatomic physics is dominantly a quantum *mechanics*.

But if the presupposition entailed in the terminology of "elementary particles" be rejected, and we accept the possibility that in the subatomic realm we have entities of a quite different kind, then a number of important consequences open up. It could then be the case, for example, that locomotion pertains properly only to compounds, bodies, and that the changes involved in the constituents are something quite different and far more complex. Thus, if it be taken that the subatomic entities are not in themselves unchangeable— which surely is one definite outcome of contemporary physics—but rather that they are *acting* entities, then clearly we have a kind of change, i.e., that which is involved in "acting," which is not reducible to, or derivative from, change of place, locomotion—though change of place could be derivative from it. Thus locomotion could be analyzed as an abstract, derivative feature, essentially pertaining to bodies. The kind of change, motion, in the subatomic realm would be something else. In this realm A. N. Whitehead, in *Science and the Modern World* (chapter 8), distinguished a kind of change which he termed "vibratory organic deformation" in addition to that which is "vibratory locomotion," but, as he later came to see, even these are derivative from a kind of change, motion, which is still more fundamental. Clearly it is necessary that the whole concept of motion be entirely rethought.

The main point I am concerned to make is that considerations such as these are of direct relevance to science. This means that it becomes of the highest significance to know what kinds of entities we are concerned with, for the inquiry into the kind of change is not possible in dissociation from the question of the kinds of entities. It is to be noted, too, that contemporary physics displays an interesting contrast to the earlier, so-called classical physics in respect of the entities with which it is concerned. In the earlier physics all the entities were alike, material bodies. They could differ in size, structure, and composition, but they were of one single fundamental kind, matter. But contemporary subatomic physics has revealed a number of entities of different kinds. This makes the question of the nature of the entities with which it is concerned all the more acute. And this raises the further issue, namely, by what procedure the answers to these questions as to the nature of the entities and the nature of motion are to be arrived at.

In respect of this, one thing must be clearly recognized. This is that these considerations and questions transcend the realm of science; with them we are in the realm of philosophy—admittedly, philosophy which is very close to science, but philosophy nevertheless, whether it be engaged in by scientists themselves or by those who are primarily philosophers. In other words, we have philosophy here which once again has nature as its object. In our time, I wish to maintain, the development of science has come to require of philosophy as one of its most important tasks the resumption of the inquiry into nature.

V

With regard to this task, however, philosophy today faces singular difficulties. First, for the past two centuries philosophy has not had nature as its object at all, with the result that the entire problematic, the range of issues involved as well as that of method, has been lost. A second kind of difficulty is constituted not simply by philosophy's having been for two centuries essentially a philosophy of mind or spirit; the difficulty is contained in what emerged into clarity when this kind of philosophy reached its maturity with Kant's *Critique of Pure Reason*, namely, that on its basis the *Ding an sich* remained inaccessible, unknown and unknowable, on the other side of the great metaphysical divide. But it is precisely the physical *Ding an sich* which is required to be the primary object of the philosophy of nature.

How then in the circumstances today is philosophy to proceed to take up its task of making nature again an object of its inquiry? How is the problematic of the philosophy of nature to be recovered? Certainly there can be no single way, and many should be attempted. One way is to approach it from the side of natural science, that is, trying to get at the philosophical problems as they are seen to arise in scientific inquiry. This is the way followed by some thinkers, for example, Whitehead in a series of books, *The Principles of Natural Knowledge*, *The Concept of Nature*, and *Science and the Modern World*; by Milič Čapek in his *The Philosophical Impact of Contemporary Physics*; and by C. F. von Weizsäcker in his recent *Die Einheit der Natur*, as well as other books of his—this list is intended as illustrative, not exhaustive. A survey of the attempts following this way reveals an appreciable difficulty in being able to disentangle the philosophical from the scientific issues and to move further than merely formulating the contemporary scientific developments in rather general, as opposed to specifically scientific, terminology. Whitehead's success in recovering the problematic of the philosophy of nature has been the most considerable, but his writings unfortunately have been far from easy to understand, moving as they were not only in unfamiliar territory but in an unfamiliar terminology, the latter devised in an attempt to free himself from inherited presuppositions, at first epistemological and later also metaphysical. By the time he wrote *Science and the Modern World*, he had come to see that the basic issue was that of the physical existent, how it was to be conceived. The contemporary scientific development had made completely untenable the conception of the physical existent as in itself changeless, individually self-complete, each physical existent in no intrinsic relationship to any other. The very contrary emerged as the case; the physical existents act and suffer effects. This for Whitehead brought the philosophical problem of relations to the fore:

It must be remembered that just as the relations modify the natures of the relata, so the relata modify the nature of the relation. The relationship is not a universal. It is a concrete fact with the same concreteness as the relata. The notion of the immanence of the cause in the effect illustrates this truth. We have to discover a doctrine of nature which expresses the concrete relatedness of physical functionings and mental functionings, of the past with the present, and also expresses the concrete composition of physical realities which are individually diverse.[4]

But this could not be achieved without explicitly tackling as fundamental the problem of the nature of the physical existent. This is what Whitehead undertook in his major and most difficult work, *Process and Reality*, subtitled *An Essay in Cosmology*, the term "cosmology" there being a synonym for "philosophy of nature." This work contains his most extensive and most profound analysis of the problems of the philosophy of nature. It should be emphasized, what is sometimes liable to be overlooked, that Whitehead's recovery of the problematic of the philosophy of nature would not have been possible without his having gone back extensively to earlier philosophy, especially Greek and that of the seventeenth century.

This suggests another way of approach to the philosophy of nature, complementary to the one we have been discussing, that is, from science. This alternative way, one which I have followed in *The Nature of Physical Existence*, is to seek to recover the problematic of the philosophy of nature through a study of the philosophy of nature in past periods, particularly those in which it has been vigorous. The sixteenth and seventeenth centuries are of especial value in this respect. Not only was this a period of fundamental change like that in which we are living, but it was one in which the thinkers advancing the new conceptions particularly well understood the problems at issue. For they had to develop their theories in opposition to the dominant Aristotelianism. Although they rejected the particular Aristotelian doctrines, they gained from their detailed study of Aristotle a singularly good grasp of the fundamental issues involved in the philosophy of nature. This way of approach, especially by the inquiry into the sixteenth- and seventeenth-century thought, has two other advantages. One is that by securing a thorough understanding of that period from which the entire modern development in science and philosophy derives, we shall be in a better position to assess the present. Secondly, such an inquiry can be of appreciable value too in disentangling the philosophical and the scientific issues, respectively, and by distinguishing them, clarifying their interconnection.

4. *AI*, 201.

VI

I should like here briefly to discuss one issue, especially prominent in the seventeenth century, which seems to me to be of particular significance for the present. This is the problem of the status of the mathematical and its connection with the physical. I have here used the adjectives "mathematical" and "physical" as nouns in the attempt to avoid implicit presuppositions. I have posed the problem as that of the status of "the mathematical," not of "mathematics." "Mathematics" is the name of a particular science, a branch of systematic inquiry. The question can be raised as to the object or objects of mathematics, and various answers to that are possible and have been maintained. The point I wish to bring out is that the answer to that question involves the problem of the physical. That is, the philosophy of nature is necessarily implicated.

The seventeenth century was a time when the importance of mathematics for the inquiry into nature, the physical, impinged with particular force. This was the outcome of a development which had its roots in the late medieval revival of Neoplatonism, in which Nicolaus of Cusa played a determinative role. From him derived the conception of the universe as a mathematical structure, which was taken up by Galileo and a number of other thinkers in the seventeenth century. But the entire issue had to be subjected to close scrutiny, which it was by thinkers like Descartes, Gassendi, Hobbes, Leibniz, and Newton among the chief. The issue can be most satisfactorily put as the question of the status of the mathematical. Galileo, and Descartes following him, identified the mathematical and the physical. For Descartes the physical existent was *res extensa*. This was not an existent which, in addition to other properties, was also extended—as was the case in Gassendi's matter. For Descartes the very essence of the physical *res* was extensiveness; it existed as extensive; its extensiveness constituted its being. That is, this *res* in essence was geometrical extensiveness and nothing else. Descartes conceived the other existent, *res cogitans*, as the mental counterpart of the physical extensiveness; *cogitatio* in its purest form was mathematical, that is, it was the conceiving, the mental grasping, of what in the other *res* was the extended mathematical. This is why for him the knowledge of pure mathematics was the knowledge of the essence of physical existence. It was not at the level of pure thought, therefore, that the metaphysical dualism presented Descartes with difficulties in respect of mathematical knowledge of the physical.

What constituted a real difficulty for his contemporaries and thinkers of the following generations was that Descartes's identification of the physical and the mathematical made material atomism impossible. Gassendi and Newton both saw that the only way to save material atomism was to separate the mathematical entirely from the physical. But that made acute the problem of how there can be mathematical knowledge of the physical if the physical be entirely devoid of mathematical features. Gassendi did not see this problem very clearly. Newton and Leibniz, however, did, and both produced complicated and subtle solutions. Newton's was to ground the mathematical in God's activity in respect of matter. Leibniz rejected this way as a *deus ex machina*, but his own theory of a preestablished harmony did not strike his contemporaries as all that different.

In the eighteenth century two alternatives were developed. The first, not philosophically very coherent, was to regard space as the object of geometry. The second was the revolutionary doctrine of Kant, conceiving mathematics as grounded in the mind, a mental construction. The former doctrine continued in favor in the nineteenth century and was thought to be strengthened by linking it with field theory. The entire position, however, was undermined by the discovery of non-Euclidean geometries. So Kant's position came into increasing acceptance and today is dominant. But the fundamental difficulty with this doctrine is that according to it the object of mathematical investigation, in mathematical physics, for example, must itself be a mental construct. The physical existent remains on the other side of the metaphysical gulf, unknowable.

This century has seen great prominence given to the problem of the foundation of mathematics. Most of this inquiry is rooted in the basic Kantian position of mathematics as a mental construct. In this tradition too stood the great work of Bertrand Russell and Whitehead, *Principia Mathematica*. Whitehead was to have written the fourth volume of the work, on geometry. It never got written, at least not as a part of that work. For Whitehead had come to see the need to face the crucial issue of how geometry applies to the physical, as Victor Lowe has pointed out. This meant the necessity to get into the philosophy of nature, recovering its problematic, the long road leading finally to *Process and Reality*, which has developed a new position bringing the physical and the mathematical once again into close relationship.

This problem of the connection between the physical and the mathematical is one not merely of philosophical interest; it is one of the greatest relevance and importance for science, more particularly at the present time, which is why Whitehead, himself a scientist, made this problem central to his endeavor.

I have given Whitehead some prominence in this paper, not because I am concerned to propagate his particular doctrine—I have myself come to some appreciable differences from him—but because he has seen most clearly the need in our time for the philosophy of nature, particularly for science, and because he has gone furthest in recovering the problematic of the philosophy of nature and has produced the first major philosophy of nature in response to the changed situation resulting from the scientific developments of the recent period. But, just as in the seventeenth century, other such philosophical schemes will need to be produced. However, as in the seventeenth century the various later theories were not produced independently of each other but came to be developed by working through, and in divergence from, the first great attempt at a philosophical structure built upon a profound insight into the problems at issue, namely, that of Descartes, so in our time the new efforts which are required in the philosophy of nature will need to come to terms with the pioneering work of Whitehead.

PART II
HISTORICAL

2

THE MODERN CONCEPT OF NATURE

I

In the early seventeenth century there was getting under way the movement of thought which has come to be known as modern science. Toward the end of the first quarter of the century it was beginning to be appreciated that basic to the new movement was a new conception of nature. For the next century and more, the leading philosophers struggled with this new conception of nature, to get clear about exactly what it entailed and what its implications were for the conception of man and his place in the universe, implications which were soon seen to be of the profoundest consequence for the entire range of human life. It was the conception of nature which was the fundamental issue; the basic problem was how nature was to be conceived. Accordingly, *philosophia naturalis*, the philosophy of nature, was the primary preoccupation of the age.

There has in this century occurred a change in fundamental conceptions which seems to me no less momentous than that of the early seventeenth century. There is occurring, in other words, a profound change in the conception of nature. In this respect our age is interestingly similar to that which constituted the beginning of the modern era. But there is also a very striking dissimilarity between these two ages, in this respect: Whereas in the seventeenth century, philosophers were deeply aware of the change that was occurring and were seeking to clarify it—in the only way in which it can be clarified, namely, through the cultivation of *philosophia naturalis*, the philosophy of nature—in the twentieth century this field is receiving singularly little attention from philosophers. Indeed, today even the very phrase "philosophy of nature" is apt to have a rather antiquated, even perhaps obsolete, ring. It is accepted in reference to the context of seventeenth-century thought, but to what extent is it so in reference to the present-day situation? What *is* the "philosophy of nature"? Evidently the phrase means the philosophical inquiry into nature. But what is meant by "nature"? The word has today largely ceased having any significance as a philosophical concept. In the course of the last couple of centuries there has occurred a loss, very nearly complete, of the connotation which the term had in earlier times. I wish to contend that it is of singular importance, and urgency, that we recover that earlier connotation, for we are faced again, as was the seventeenth century, with a range of problems and issues which are the particular subject matter and concern of the philosophy of nature. These problems and issues go beyond the specifically scientific ones, and scientists at the frontiers of their inquiry are running up against them. The need of our time is for a systematic investigation of these problems comparable to that which occurred in the seventeenth century.

I have here begun by focusing attention on the term "nature." With respect to the question, what is nature?, what is meant by "nature"?, we have before us not a mere issue of a dictionary definition; we are concerned with a philosophical issue. That is to say, the question can be answered only in philosophical terms, and this means in terms of philosophical theory. Thus, to say that in the seventeenth century there occurred a change in the conception of nature is to say that there occurred a change in the basic philosophical theory in terms of which "nature" is conceived. And to say that there occurred a *change* in philosophical theory implies an antecedent theory from which there had been a departure. That antecedent theory cannot be simply disregarded in trying to understand the new theory. It seems to me one of the gravest errors endemic to modern, and especially recent, thought that it tends to proceed on the supposition that the antecedent theory can be disregarded. Thus, it has been widely supposed that Descartes, for example, and Galileo made a fresh start in disregard of antecedent thought. The consequence of this supposition has been a widespread failure properly to understand Descartes, and Galileo.

II

The antecedent theory in respect of nature which is relevant to us here is one which was essentially derived from Aristotle, through Avicenna and Averroës. It is best for clarity to go back to Aristotle himself. For Aristotle, *physis*, "nature," pertains to a being, an existent, which has in itself the source of its *kinesis*, "change," more particularly the process of change which is its becoming, its growth and development. A natural being stands in contrast to an artificial thing. An artifact cannot be, exist, in virtue of itself; its being is dependent upon an artificer, and the latter must be a natural being, that is, one whose very being, existence, is not derivative. Thus, for Aristotle *physis*, "nature," and "being" are very closely connected concepts. Hence when we ask What is the *nature* of something? we are asking about the *being* of the thing, namely, *what* that is whereby the thing *is*. For Aristotle the paradigm case of a natural existent is a living being, a man, a horse, a tree. A physical or natural being in Aristotle's analysis is essentially involved in a process of becoming, *genesis*; it *is* not except in becoming. That is to say, for Aristotle the being, the existence, of all physical or natural beings involves an inner process of change which is their becoming. The becoming of a natural being is a constant process of actualization of its potentiality. This process of actualization is ultimately analyzable in terms of *eidos*, "form," and *hyle*, "matter." Actualization is the *energeia*, "enacting," of *eidos*, "form," "definiteness." The concept of *hyle* is an essentially correlative one; that is, *hyle* is not understandable on its own, apart from form, but only in reference to form. It is that which has the capacity to be formed, the potentiality for form. For Aristotle *eidos*, "form," and *hyle* are not themselves beings, existents, but are the ultimate *archai*, "sources," of being. The primary beings are the natural or physical existents, and they are or exist as each a particular conjunction of the two sources; that is, each exists as a formed matter.

Nature used as a collective noun meant the totality of natural or physical existents. This totality is no mere arithmetical sum; rather, it is a whole constituting a *cosmos*, "order," which is an order of relatedness of the plurality of physical existents. The physical existents in this ordered relatedness have to be conceived, Aristotle maintained, as involving the conjoint operation of a fourfold determination—traditionally referred to, perhaps somewhat misleadingly, as the "four causes." Aristotle held that the analysis of each physical existent requires its consideration in respect of (1) that out of which it comes to be, (2) that from which as a source it comes to be, (3) that form or definiteness which determines it as this existent and not another, and (4) that for the sake of which it comes to be, that is, that which determines the reason for its existence.

This is a very brief summary of Aristotle's conception of nature. It is necessary to have at least this before us to have some appreciation of what it was which was rejected by the seventeenth-century thinkers; we get a better understanding of their position by seeing it in contrast with that which they rejected. The reasons for this rejection constitute a somewhat complicated and rather long story. For our purposes it will not be necessary to go into detail here; some points will be mentioned later.

What was earliest and most prominently rejected in the Aristotelian theory was its identification of physical existents, that is, what it designated as veridical instances of such existents, namely, entities such as men, horses, plants. The early seventeenth-century thinkers fully agreed with Aristotle that a primary physical existent must necessarily be a unitary entity; that is, it must not be composite, constituted of other existents. For if it were so constituted, it could not be primary; in that case the constituents would have to be regarded as the primary existents. In the first quarter of the seventeenth century there had come a growing conviction, especially among the medical men, who were also physicists and chemists, that a human or animal body is not one single, unitary entity, but is, rather, composite. It followed that a man or an animal could not be taken as an instance of a primary physical existent; it is the ultimate constituents which would have to be identified as the true primary existents.

III

The problem which then arose was that of the characterization of the constituents as the true physical existents. I will detail two influences on the early seventeenth-century thought in respect of this problem.[1] The first was the inheritance of the outcome of some sixteenth-century inquiries, especially those in respect of the problem of the elements, and this led the seventeenth-century thinkers to the second influence, namely, to look into the conceptions of the ancient school which Aristotle had so strongly attacked, the school of Leucippus and Democritus, which was so evidently the contrary of the Aristotelian position. The combination of the atomist conception with some important sixteenth-century developments of thought resulted in the seventeenth-century development of the conception of material atomism.

The modern doctrine of atomism is significantly different from the ancient one. They are alike in identifying the primary physical existents as the final, not further divisible (*atomos*) constituents of compounds. The difference between them was that in the modern position these atoms were conceived as "material." The point is that in this conception of the atoms as "material" we have something genuinely new: a new philosophical conception. The entire novelty of the modern period is grounded ultimately in the novelty of the conception of "matter."

---

1. See chap. 10, below.

It is in this conception of "matter" that is to be found the greatest divergence from Aristotle and the most fundamental aspect of the seventeenth-century rejection of the Aristotelian conception of the physical existent. The thinker who earliest most clearly saw this was the French medical man Sebastian Basso, who published his view in a strongly polemical book *Philosophia naturalis adversus Aristotelem Libri XII*, which appeared in Geneva in 1621. A number of others were not far behind Basso, and the new doctrine of material atomism rapidly swept across Europe.

The novelty of the doctrine consisted in the first instance in the conception of *matter* per se as the physical existent. To appreciate this point it is necessary to bear in mind that from Aristotle, right down through the sixteenth century, matter had continued to be an essentially correlative concept; it was the correlative of form, and not any existent in its own right. In other words, matter was that which is formed to constitute an existent; matter was not conceived as itself an existent independent of form. The crucial early seventeenth-century development was to separate matter from form, to view it as independently existing, and to identify this separately existing matter as the primary physical existent.

IV

Now, what was involved in this conception of the physical existent as matter? That is, how is matter to be conceived? How is it to be characterized? In regard to this issue a diversity of views soon developed, but in one basic respect they were all in agreement. This constituted the second major divergence of the modern conception of the physical existent from the Aristotelian conception. Aristotle had held, it will be recalled, that a physical existent is essentially involved in a process of *kinesis*, "change," that is, in an inner process of becoming. Contrary to this, the modern conception of the physical existent is that it is essentially devoid of any inner process of change, of becoming. It simply *is*, fully, what it is. In other words, matter was conceived as fully actual, in itself changeless. The Platonic conception of true being, *to ontos on*, as changeless and in contrast with becoming had completely triumphed. Of course the Parmenidean inheritance had come also via Democritus.

From this conception of matter as fully actual, in itself changeless, there followed a necessary implication which was also accepted by all adherents of the modern conception of the physical existent. This is that all the varieties of change which Aristotle had distinguished and ascribed to the physical existent—qualitative change, expansion and contraction, growth, generation, change of place—must be rejected as pertaining to matter as the physical existent, with the exception of the last, change of place. That is, the only respect in which change is possible for a material existent is in respect of place. All other change must ultimately be analyzable in terms of change of place, which is to say, of locomotion.

This entails that all explanation must be in terms of matter and locomotion. That is to say, science, i.e., knowledge, of the physical must be in terms of matter and motion—since there is no other *kinesis*, "motion," possible except that in respect of *locus*, "place," the term *locomotion* could be contracted to simply *motion*. In other words, physics, the science of nature, is a kinetics. Thus, the modern science of physics, like the Aristotelian, is grounded in *kinesis*, "motion." But as between the two the concept of *kinesis*, "motion," is very different. For Aristotle *kinesis*, "motion," pertains to the physical existent as an inner process of change, of becoming; for the modern doctrine *kinesis*, "motion," pertains to the physical existent only in respect of change of place. In these two conceptions of *kinesis*, "motion," we have the root difference between the conceptions of "organism" and "mechanism."

The modern conception of motion is grounded in the modern conception of the physical existent as matter. There is involved in this, it was soon realized, a major problem. With Aristotle's conception of the physical existent, he could consistently analyze locomotion as derivative from, as consequent upon, the process of becoming of the existent. That is to say, Aristotle can account for the occurrence of motion in terms of the *nature* of the physical existent. But in the modern doctrine that is not possible. The physical existent conceived as in itself fully actual and changeless internally does not at all entail motion, change of place. The most that can be said is that it is *movable*, that is, able to be moved. In other words, it cannot be said of the physical existent conceived as matter, as Aristotle could of his physical existent, that it has the source of its motion in itself. Motion, therefore, in the modern doctrine is necessarily a factor ontologically distinct from the physical existent. How, then, was it to be accounted for? Most thinkers of the seventeenth century saw no alternative but to have recourse to God as the principle, the source, of motion. Leibniz vigorously criticized this as committing the fallacy of a *deus ex machina*. Leibniz had the deepest insight of his time into the problem, and presented a solution with which we shall deal a bit later. For a number of reasons, however, Leibniz was not accepted in respect of this problem, and in the eighteenth century the way out that was adopted was to regard motion simply as an ultimate, along with the other ultimates of matter, space, and time, and not to bother further with the philosophical problem of their ontological status. Evading philosophical problems, however, is not solving them, and nemesis follows sooner or later. We are paying for this in the twentieth century.

V

So far we have dealt only with the respects in which there was agreement among thinkers regarding the characterization of the physical existent as matter. We have seen also that some thinkers at least had identified the physical existent, in the true sense, with the ultimate constituents of compounds. This means that matter is, exists as, ultimately indivisible particles. To say that they are indivisible is to say that they are extensive and have a certain bounded shape. In other words, they are minimal bodies. They are the micro-bodies of which all macro-bodies are composed. The point here is that matter per se is bodily. This means that the physical existent is essentially bodily, corporeal.

Aristotle's *Physics* being well known at the time, it is not surprising that difficulties in regard to this conception of the physical existent as atomic body were brought to the fore. The concept of body entails extension, and an atomic body implies that the extension is continuous, for there were no interstices of void since it was precisely the absence of these which constituted the body atomic, not divisible. But just here was a fundamental difficulty, for the concept of continuity implies divisibility, indeed, infinite divisibility. Thus, the conception of an atomic body involves a contradiction, as Aristotle had maintained.

The reaction to this was various. Some, such as Daniel Sennert, the prominent medical man contemporary with Basso, held that for the purposes of scientific research it was not necessary to maintain that the constituents were atomic; it was sufficient merely to maintain that macro-bodies are composed of smaller bodies as their constituents and not to raise the philosophical issues. This became the attitude of the majority, the attitude which subsequently came to characterize "positivism."

For others, however, the philosophical problems were not so easily to be evaded. Galileo, for example, as a mathematician was quite clear that continuity implies divisibility and, indeed, infinite divisibility. He accordingly drew the logical conclusion, namely, that the material constituents must be infinitely small, and therefore that they must be *atomi non quanti*, "atoms without extension." They are therefore none other than mathematical or, rather more precisely, geometrical points. But how then can these *atomi non quanti* be regarded as "material"? To this, Galileo's answer was that they could since the very essence of matter is that it is mathematical. In this we have one of the most important characterizations of the physical existent: in its essential nature it is mathematical. This position entails, it is clear, the identification of the physical and the mathematical. But Galileo's position was up against another of Aristotle's arguments, namely, that a finite extent could not be constituted of unextended points, even an infinite number of them. Galileo replied that Aristotle was wrong about this because an extended thing is not other than a geometrical extent; in other words, extended matter is not something different from geometrical extendedness, and there is an infinity of points in any geometrical extent.

The other main attempt of the seventeenth century to maintain a consistent conception of material atomism was that of Gassendi. He accepted that the physical existents are atomic material bodies. Physical existents are corporeal, but their character as "matter" is constituted, not by geometrical extendedness as in the doctrine of Galileo, but by a solid fullness. That is, solidity is the essential character of matter. There are no degrees involved in this conception; matter is that which fully occupies an extent; there cannot be degrees of occupation, more matter here and less there. Matter is none other than the full occupation, and consequently matter is necessarily atomic. For where there is not full occupation, there is the very contrary of matter, the void. Gassendi sought to overcome Aristotle's argument concerning divisibility by this conception of the essence of matter as solidity. He agreed that any given geometrical extent is infinitely divisible, but this mathematical divisibility was in thought only, and did not pertain to physical actuality. Gassendi's position thus entailed separating the mathematical from the physical. But the question has to be faced whether the mathematical can be thus separated from the physical. For is not the solid atom geometrically extended? Furthermore, is not Gassendi's void also extended? So, geometrical extension is fundamental in Gassendi's universe and cannot be relegated to the conceptual in separation from the physical. That is to say, Gassendi cannot avoid according the mathematical a peculiarly fundamental status in the universe. But then a basic philosophical problem has to be faced: what is here the ontological status of the mathematical? That is, what kind of being has the mathematical? Galileo had said that the mathematical *is* as the essence of the physical. But this was not open to Gassendi, since for him geometrical extension pertains also to the void. But therewith the ultimate contradiction of Gassendi's position comes out, that which Aristotle had insisted is ineluctably involved in the atomist doctrine. Matter, as the physical existent, is that which is, which exists. The void, then, is that which is not. But, as Aristotle said, it is not possible for there to be an extent of nothing. The conception of an extent of non-existence involves a contradiction. The only way to save the position is to regard the void, equally with matter, as constituting physical existence. But this entails that geometrical extendedness, that is, the mathematical, is the essence of the physical—precisely the position which Gassendi had started off by denying.

VI

At that time Descartes was the thinker who was clearest that the ultimate philosophical issue which had to be faced is that of the ontological status of the mathematical and its relation to the physical. Very much alive to the difficulties involved in the other two positions, Descartes formulated an alternative which would avoid them. Accepting the new seventeenth-century doctrine that matter per se is to be regarded as the physical existent, he agreed that matter is necessarily extensive. This implied that the essence of matter must be geometrical extendedness. To identify the essence of matter as anything else, such as solidity, inevitably ran into contradictions. Thus, Descartes agreed with Galileo in identifying the mathematical and the physical. In other words, the mathematical *is* as the essence of the physical.

But geometrical extensiveness implies infinite divisibility, and thus matter or the physical existent cannot be atomic; Galileo's *atomi non quanti* were a *reductio ad absurdum*. Descartes boldly drew the logical conclusion: matter, the physical existent, is one; in his terms, there is one *res extensa*.

Descartes saw that this entailed another difference with his contemporaries with regard to the conception of matter as the physical existent. We have seen that the other thinkers had not only identified matter as the physical existent but had also regarded matter as bodily. It was this latter view that Descartes rejected. Matter per se cannot be corporeal; corporeality must be ontologically distinguished from matter. Corporeality must not be identified with matter; it must be derivative from matter. Descartes had an ingenious solution to this problem, which was that bodies derive from matter through motion. That is to say, bodies come into existence through portions of the one *res extensa* moving differentially with one another. Thereby bodies are "material," that is, geometrically extensive, without themselves being the primary physical existents. For Descartes there is a plurality of bodies, but only one primary physical existent, matter. The science of physics accordingly, Descartes agreed with his contemporaries, is the science of bodies in motion, that is, kinetics, or phoronomy. The science which concerns itself with the *nature* of matter is not physics but "first philosophy" or "metaphysics," and the problems of the latter science do not concern physics. That is, physics does not have to concern itself with the question of how bodies come into being; it can start with the datum of bodies in motion and proceed to their mathematical investigation.

VII

Descartes's philosophy of nature, because it was able to resolve the basic philosophical difficulties facing the other positions, gained a prominent adherence for a time. It emerged, however, that it too had fundamental difficulties of its own. Another factor at the time was that the successfully advancing science of physics as the science of bodies in motion militated toward the conception of bodies, and ultimately micro-bodies, as the physical existents, despite the philosophical difficulties which we have seen to beset that conception. An additional factor was that the new physics was the mathematical investigation of the motion of bodies, and this made acute the philosophical issue of the ontological status of the mathematical. For if the mathematical were identified with the physical as by Descartes, then the entire enterprise of physics would be intelligible. However, this was at the cost of the validity of the concept of atomism and of the physical existent as corporeal.

Newton finally produced a way out of the dilemma. He accepted the conception of material atoms as the true physical existents: "All these things being consider'd, it seems probable to me, that God in the Beginning form'd Matter in solid, massy, hard, impenetrable, movable Particles, . . . and that these primitive Particles being Solids, are incomparably harder than any porous Bodies compounded of them; even so very hard, as never to wear or break in pieces; no ordinary Power being able to divide what God himself made one in the first Creation."[2] But what then of the problem of the ontological status of geometrical extension? To ascribe it to the material existents per se would entail the rejection of atomism and thus the acceptance of Descartes's position of a single *res extensa* and therewith also the denial of the corporeality of the physical. To Newton it was clear that geometrical extensiveness could not be ascribed to matter as its essence. His solution was to ascribe geometrical extensiveness instead to God, and

---

2. Newton, *Opticks* (New York: Dover, 1952), 400.

therewith to spirit in contrast with matter; in his doctrine, God is spirit extended everywhere. Moreover, God as spirit is active; that is to say, he is active everywhere, and always. Where God is active, and when, constitute the ultimate absolute places and times. Place, or space, and time, were for Newton not some kind of independent existents. Space, or place, is *where* God is active; that is, space *is* not in itself, but it *is* only as an attribute of God's activity. It was Newton's followers (not including Samuel Clarke) who did not take the trouble properly to understand his philosophy, who maintained the conception of space as itself some kind of absolute existent, which later Kant rejected totally as an *Unding*. Newton's position is that he ascribed geometrical extensiveness to God, to spirit, and not to matter, to the physical. Matter becomes, or acquires the feature of, extensiveness *derivatively* by its occupation of place. Thereby Newton has an alternative to Descartes in respect of the intelligibility of physics as the mathematical investigation of the motion of material bodies. Moreover, Newton therewith has a foundation for the *measurability* of bodies and of motion; this is constituted by the absolute places, which enables Newton to have an unambiguous definition of distance, and accordingly of motion as the change from one absolute place to another. In Descartes's position, place is unavoidably a relative notion, and thus the concept of motion as the change of place must remain imprecise for Descartes.

Newton's gains were immense, and it is not surprising that his system had the immediate and profound impact it did have. Newton's theology certainly appealed to few, but it was thought that it could be dispensed with and still leave the essentials of Newton's position intact. To a certain extent this is true. The position which was adopted from Newton and which remained the dominant position for the next two centuries was that there are four ultimates: material bodies, space, time, and motion. But what is entailed in saying that there are four ultimates? In what sense *are* they? What sort of being do they have? Is matter alone to be identified as the physical existent, as it was by all the thinkers we have been considering, including Descartes? But then what sort of being is space, and what time? Are they to be excluded from nature, from the physical? And if they are, not only is there the problem of what kind of being they conceivably can be, but the additional problem of their relationship to the physical. Thus, once more the problem of the ontological status of the mathematical and the problem of the relation of the mathematical and the physical become acute.

In the eighteenth century the situation became a great deal worse because of the new doctrine of Kant's *Critique of Pure Reason*, which gave an entirely new status to the mathematical: it is the product of human mental construction. How, then, does it relate in any significant way to the physical? For Kant it cannot relate to the *Ding an sich*, but to the object, which is itself an outcome of mental construction. But which is now the physical existent, the *Ding an sich* or the constructed object? I cannot pursue this question further here. I shall merely point out that we today are the inheritors of the situation bequeathed by Kant. Most thinkers, scientists and philosophers, are caught in that situation, for the influence of Kant in the course of the thought of the last two centuries is pervasive, even where it is not recognized. As far as our topic is concerned, namely, the philosophy of nature, the consequences have been devastating; herein, in part, lie the roots of the loss of the concept of "nature" as a philosophical concept of significance.

VIII

I should like in conclusion to go back a bit and consider another seventeenth-century thinker who is of the greatest importance for our topic, the philosophy of nature. More deeply than any thinker of the age, Leibniz penetrated into the problems and issues involved. The intellectual tide was against him, however, and his contribution was largely lost to his contemporaries and subsequent thought. It can, however, be of very considerable significance to us today.

Leibniz saw that the fundamental issue is that of the physical existent, its identity and its philosophical description or characterization. Leibniz subjected the modern doctrine of the physical existent as matter to the acutest analysis it has received, at that time or later. The one feature of matter on which all adherents of the doctrine were agreed, as we have seen, is that in some sense matter is essentially extensive. That is, extension was ascribed to matter as a fundamental attribute. By a penetrating analysis, into the details of which I cannot here enter,[3] Leibniz showed that this is untenable. Extension cannot consistently be conceived as an *attribute* of any single existent. On the contrary, he maintained, on a consistent analysis extension must be seen as a *relation* between existents. Not till this century has this point been seen again with real clarity, by Whitehead, who arrived at this recognition quite independently of Leibniz. Thus Whitehead has said: "The inclusion of *extensive quantity* among fundamental categoreal notions

---

3. This is dealt with more fully in chap. 6, below, sect. VII.

is a complete mistake."[4] And: "For Descartes the primary *attribute* of physical bodies is *extension*; for the philosophy of organism the primary *relationship* of physical occasions is *extensive connection*."[5]

Leibniz analyzed all the other attributes which had been ascribed to matter—solidity, impenetrability, and so on—and displayed them all as equally untenable. In short, what Leibniz had demonstrated was that the conception of the physical existent as "matter" is philosophically completely unsound. But Leibniz's analysis has been largely disregarded. Now physical science itself, as a result of developments during the last hundred years, has abandoned that seventeenth-century conception of matter. What conception of it do we now have instead? In regard to this there reigns the greatest obscurity. Nor indeed can the situation be otherwise till there is a concerted philosophical inquiry into the nature of the physical existent.

With reference to this question of the nature of the physical existent, there is much to be learned from Leibniz, especially with regard to what is at issue, the problems which have to be faced.

We have seen that from the Greeks there has been a basic connection between the nature of the physical existent and extension, and we have just seen Leibniz's radical analysis of extension as a relation. There is also a basic connection between the nature of the physical existent and *kinesis*, "motion." In respect of this, Leibniz argued, the modern doctrine of the physical existent is likewise fundamentally defective. Motion, we have seen earlier, is not to be accounted for or understood in terms of matter, and Leibniz had strongly rejected the dominant view of the status of motion as involving the fallacy of a *deus ex machina*. Further, merely to accept motion as an ultimate, as was being increasingly done, is simply to fail to face up to the fact that the modern doctrine is involved in fundamental incoherence.

Leibniz put the issue as follows: "after trying to explore the principles of mechanics itself in order to account for the laws of nature which we learn from experience, I perceived that the sole consideration of *extended mass* is not enough but that it is necessary, in addition, to use the concept of *force*."[6] Newton was also urging the necessity of the concept of force. How, then, was it to be introduced? Newton introduced this by God's activity. This view was unacceptable to Leibniz; it was but another instance of a *deus ex machina*. Leibniz argued that this concept can consistently and coherently be introduced only by

4. *PR* (C), 135; (M), 148.
5. *PR* (C), 408; (M), 441.
6. Gerhardt, 4:478; Loemker, 454.

32   THE PHILOSOPHY OF NATURE

grounding it in the nature of the physical existent, as indeed Aristotle had done.

Now, this is possible only if we reject the prevalent conception of the physical existent as simply actual, that is, in itself changeless, without any internal process of becoming. We have to recognize with Aristotle that the physical existent must be in-act, it must be an *acting* entity, and that the concept of "force" required in physics is to be grounded in this acting of the physical existent.

Further, the acting of the physical existent cannot be simply in reference to itself; that would leave each existent as essentially isolated as were the material atoms. Leibniz maintained that the acting of the physical existent is that of *perception*, and perception is essentially a *relation* to an *object*; there is no perception without an object perceived. Again we see that *relation* is fundamental with respect to the physical existent.

Now with regard to motion, since the concept means change of place, there is necessary the philosophical analysis of "change" and of "place." Place, Leibniz agreed with Descartes and Aristotle, cannot be an actual physical existent; it must therefore be conceived with reference to actual physical existents. Leibniz maintained that it could not have any meaning with reference to any physical existent simply as such; that is, it cannot pertain to a single existent in isolation. The concept has significance only when a plurality of existents is taken into account. Then the "place" of each is "where" it is relatively to the others. Once again the concept of *relation* is fundamentally involved. Motion accordingly can be analyzed as a change, resultant from the *acting* of the existent, manifesting itself in the *relations* of a plurality of existents to each other as an alteration of relative places. Thus, the concept of motion in the science of physics—which is concerned with the analysis of bodies in motion—is not a primitive or ultimate concept, but a complex, "further analyzable" concept, as Leibniz was wont to express it, a concept which is derivative from the *acting* and the *relations* of the physical existents.[7]

Likewise, Leibniz maintained, the concept of "body"—that which is involved in the science of physics as the science of bodies in motion—has to be rejected as primitive and ultimate, as it was maintained to be in the prevailing doctrine of material atomism, which held, as we have seen, that the material atoms are essentially bodily. All the features which are ascribed as the attributes of body—extension, solidity, hard-

---

7. A fuller discussion of this issue will be found in chap. 6, below.

ness or impenetrability—are not strictly *attributes* at all but must be analyzed as *relations*. Thus, there can be no simple body, as the atomists conceived it; a body is necessarily a plurality, and the features of body are the relations between the physical existents which are the constituents. Again we see the fundamental status of *relations*.

One implication of this analysis is that to treat the science of physics positivistically, that is, to regard it as providing ultimate positive knowledge, is an error. The concepts of physics are not ultimate; they are derivative. This means that we cannot properly *know* what the empirical inquiry has produced without going beyond it and interpreting its findings in terms of the ultimate concepts in which the physical existents are understood.

Recognizing this is of the greatest importance in this century. The conception of material atomism has been abandoned. Instead of atoms of inert matter, thinking is now in terms of "centers of energy." But what is "energy"? Is this the concept of an *existent* or an *attribute* or an *activity* or what? Further, the entities which modern physics has disclosed are evidently related. But to speak of them as "entities" raises the philosophical question, what sort of "entities" are they? In other words, what kind of *being* are we concerned with here? For the word "entity" means a "being"—but, as Aristotle constantly insisted, "being is used in many senses." This pushes us back to the basic issue of the nature of the physical existent, that which *is*, which *exists*, in an ultimate sense. Are electrons, protons, etc. to be identified as veridical instances of primary physical existents, or are they themselves derivative, composite for example? Further, how are the relations between them to be conceived? But relations are relations between something and something. So once again we are back at the problem of the existents which are related. I shall not enter further into this topic here,[8] but I shall mention just one point, which is that Leibniz had made quite clear that there is a basic connection between the concept of *relation* and that of *possibility* or *potentiality*. Thus, what is involved here is the entire fundamental problem of the connection between actuality and potentiality, and particularly the issue of what ontological status is to be accorded to potentiality. Closely connected with this issue is that of the connection of the physical and the mathematical, and therewith the problem of divisibility and indivisibility, and the problem of the finite and infinite. Leibniz dealt penetratingly with this entire range of issues. They have become acute again in our time.

8. It is treated at some length in chap. 12, below.

I am not claiming that Leibniz has provided all the answers—very far from that; we have to work these out for ourselves in the context of present-day scientific research. But I am saying that we can learn a vast amount from Leibniz about the basic issues, and the problems we have to face. No one had a deeper insight into these than he had.

3
THE PHYSICAL AS MATTER

I

My concern with the philosophy of nature in the seventeenth century will be with a view to the light it might shed on the issues we are having to face in this century. For in one respect the two eras are interestingly similar. The seventeenth century saw the birth and flourishing of what is now commonly called modern science, which was grounded in a new conception of nature. In the twentieth century there has occurred a change in fundamental conceptions which seems to me to be no less momentous than that which arose in the seventeenth century.

But there is also a most significant difference between the two ages. In the seventeenth century it was appreciated that the fundamental change was in respect of the concept of nature, and accordingly *philosophia naturalis* was a primary preoccupation of the time. In the twentieth century, by contrast, this field of philosophical inquiry is singularly neglected. In our day even the word "nature" is in use chiefly only in derivative senses. The basic sense has been virtually lost. It is this sense, however, which is philosophically important, and, I wish to urge, no less so now than in the seventeenth century.

The fundamental issue of *philosophia naturalis*—and that which primarily concerned the thinkers of the seventeenth century—is the problem, what is nature? That is, what is that which naturally exists, that existent which constitutes nature? Alternatively put, what is the primary physical existent?—the term *physical* being synonymous with *natural*. Another formulation would be, what is the nature of that existent with which the science of physics is basically concerned? This formulation not only relates the science of physics with "nature" but it also implies that the phrase "nature of" in respect of this existent means "that whereby this existent *is* and is *what* it is." With this formulation we begin to see what kind of answer this question requires, what it is in terms of which that question must be basically answered.

36 THE PHILOSOPHY OF NATURE

Let me illustrate this in seventeenth-century thought. The answer of the seventeenth century to this question of the physical existent—the answer which determined the entire subsequent development of the science of physics (i.e., of nature), and also of many others, down into this century—this answer was that the physical existent is *matter*.

This answer constituted a radical divergence from antecedent thought, in a number of respects. In the first place, from Greek times till then, the concept of "matter" was the correlative of "form" as that which is formed, that which takes on form. Matter was not something capable of separate existence; it could exist at all only as formed. In itself, matter was entirely lacking in definiteness—all definiteness was due to form. In the seventeenth century the crucial step was taken of conceiving matter as existing separately, identifying this separately existing matter per se as the physical existent. In this we have a genuinely new philosophical conception. The entire novelty of the modern period is grounded ultimately in the novelty of this conception of matter as the physical existent.

It was soon appreciated, however, that merely to identify matter as the physical existent is not sufficient. There is the problem of how matter as the physical existent is to be conceived, grasped, understood. What is the "nature of" matter, that whereby it is what it is, namely matter, and can be known as such? This was the issue with which the thinkers of the seventeenth century grappled. Their strivings brought to the fore a number of basic problems, all interconnected, that have to be resolved in answering the question of the nature of the physical existent.

II

The earliest response to this issue, and the answer which became most widely accepted, was that the essence of matter is corporeality. Here arose a second main divergence from antecedent thought, and from Aristotle in particular. Not any and every body is to be identified as a primary physical existent, for at that time many thinkers had come to the conviction, contrary to Aristotle, that all bodies with which we are ordinarily familiar, including human and animal bodies, are aggregate composites and not single unitary entities, so that it was the ultimate constituents which would have to be identified as the primary physical existents. This is the doctrine of corporeal material atomism.

This conception, however, was soon seen to involve serious difficulties. It is vulnerable to Aristotle's argument that a continuous quantity implies infinite divisibility, thereby rendering the conception of atomic body a contradiction. A different characterization than merely corporeality was needed for matter. The concept of corporeality as such is not ultimate; bodies are extensive, and so extensiveness is more fundamental.

Galileo put forward one of the most important alternative conceptions of matter. He identified geometrical extensiveness as the essence of matter. Since this extensiveness is infinitely divisible, Galileo accepted the implication that the ultimate constituents must be *atomi non quanti*. This entails not only the rejection of corporeal atomism but also the serious difficulty that thereby bodies become completely unintelligible.

Gassendi presented a conception of matter intended to save the intelligibility of bodies. The essence of matter, and thus of body, he held to be solid fullness. Gassendi, in contrast to Galileo, attempted to separate the mathematical from the physical, ascribing the mathematical to mind. This could not be successful, however, for not only are his solid full atoms necessarily extensive, but so also is the void. Thus, extendedness, and thereby the geometrical, is as fundamental for his as for Galileo's position. But this contradicts corporeal atomism.

Descartes had an ingenious solution to these difficulties. Accepting the essence of matter as extension, and thereby the identification of the mathematical and the physical, Descartes maintained that bodies can be consistently conceived as derived from matter by motion. There is one single, continuous matter, one *res extensa*, but by virtue of motion, parts of matter move differentially, and it is these differentially moving parts which constitute different bodies. This position rejects atomism entirely, and also the corporeality of matter. Bodies have an ontologically derivative status.

III

Another basically important respect in which the modern conception of the physical existent diverged from antecedent thought and from Aristotle in particular, was on the concept of *motion*. For Aristotle *kinesis*, "motion," was the internal process of change involved in becoming, in the actualization of potentiality, and could be distinguished into kinds, qualitative alteration, quantitative alteration, and *phora*, "change of place." In the new conception, the physical, matter, is in itself fully actual, just what it is, and thus not involved in any internal process of becoming. The only kind of motion possible for matter is change of place. Since *locomotion* is the only possible *motion*, these terms came to be synonymous.

With this came a new conception of physics as the science, i.e., knowledge, of nature. In the modern conception, as in the Aristotelian, physics is grounded in *kinesis*, "motion." But there is a fundamental divergence in respect of how motion is conceived. For Aristotle *kinesis*, "motion," pertains to the physical as an inner process of change, of becoming. Accordingly, to "know" the physical is to understand the "nature of" its process of becoming. That is, the science, knowledge, of physics is in terms of the process of actualization. This means that for Aristotle physics is inseparable from metaphysics.

For the modern doctrine, on the contrary, *kinesis*, "motion," pertains to the physical existent only in respect of change of place. Thus the science, knowledge, of physics is in terms of the motion, i.e., change of place, of bodies. The science of physics is thus a pure kinetics, or phoronomy. This still entailed a connection between physics and metaphysics, however, as Descartes was quite clear; but it did not make the science of physics *dependent upon* metaphysics, as the Aristotelian position did. For Descartes the science which concerns itself with the "nature of" matter is "first philosophy" or metaphysics, which reveals the nature of matter to be geometrical extendedness. Thereby is also provided the ground for the validity of physics as the mathematical analysis of bodies in motion. The science of physics itself has no concern with the nature of bodies or of motion. Its knowledge, the understanding it provides, is purely in terms of mathematical analysis. Thus, with the modern conception of the physical as matter and of motion as purely locomotion, the science of physics can proceed in independence of metaphysics.

This did not mean, however, that metaphysics is *irrelevant to* physics, for Descartes, or for Newton. For any understanding of what physics is concerned with, and any interpretation of the mathematics, takes the thinker implicitly or explicitly to metaphysics. Newton was clear that the metaphysical problems were not to be evaded or ignored. Crucial, for example, is the problem of the status of the mathematical and its connection with the physical. Newton, like an increasing number of thinkers, diverged from Descartes in maintaining corporeal atomism. But this entailed that the mathematical could not be identified with the physical. Newton's solution was to ascribe geometrical extendedness to God, that is, to spirit as opposed to matter. God is spirit, he held, extended everywhere. Moreover, God as spirit is active; he is active everywhere, and always. With this conception Newton achieved two important things. In this activity of God everywhere and always Newton found the principle, source, of motion. Secondly, in this conception of God's activity he also found the solution to the problem of the relation of the mathematical and the physical. *Where* God is active, and *when*, constitute the ultimate absolute *places* and *times*. Place, or space as the totality of places,[1] and time, were not for Newton some kind of independent existents; space, for example, is not some kind of extended entity. It is God who is extended, it is God to whom extension pertains as a primary attribute, and matter acquires extensiveness, and measurability, derivatively by its occupation of place. Thereby Newton had an alternative to Descartes in respect of the intelligibility of physics as the mathematical investigation of the motion of bodies. And since his places and times are absolute, as opposed to Descartes's as relative, motion and measurement are precise for Newton, whereas for Descartes they suffer an inevitable imprecision. A basic problem arises, however, whether the extension of matter can indeed be consistently conceived as thus derivative.

IV

The profoundest critic of this modern doctrine of physical existence, of nature, was Leibniz. More deeply than any other he penetrated the problems and issues involved. My concern with Leibniz here will be primarily to find what we can learn from him about those issues and problems, with a particular view to the situation we face in our own time.

Leibniz saw very clearly that the basic issue must be that of the nature and identity of the physical existent. He accordingly subjected the conception of the physical existent as matter to the acutest scrutiny it has ever received.

The most widely accepted conception of matter as the physical existent was, as we have seen, that matter is essentially extensive. By a penetrating analysis, into the details of which I will not enter here,[2] Leibniz showed that this is philosophically untenable. Extension cannot consistently be conceived as an *attribute* of a single existent. On a consistent analysis, he maintained, extension must be seen as a *relation* between a plurality of existents. Not since the early Kant has this again been seen with real clarity till by Whitehead in this century, who arrived at this recognition independently of Leibniz. As Whitehead has

---
1. See chap. 7, below; also *NPE*, 217–19.
2. See chap. 6, below, sect. VII.

stated it: "The inclusion of *extensive quantity* among fundamental categoreal notions is a complete mistake."[3] In amplification of this I quote another short statement: "For Descartes the primary *attribute* of physical bodies is *extension*; for the philosophy of organism the primary *relationship* of physical occasions is *extensive connection*."[4]

The majority of thinkers, we have seen, conceived matter not simply as extensive but also as bodily. Leibniz analyzed all the attributes ascribed to body—e.g., solidity, impenetrability—and displayed them all as equally untenable. These features must all be seen as derivative, and not as pertaining to the primary physical existents.

There remained the other basic feature of the physical existent as matter, namely, that it is fully actual, in itself without any internal process of becoming, and that accordingly the only possible change is change of place, locomotion. With this doctrine, however, Leibniz maintained, the concept of motion is philosophically unintelligible. All adherents to the doctrine were involved in the incoherence of a *deus ex machina* to account for motion. The only way, he held, that motion can be coherently explained is by finding the source of motion in the nature of the physical existent. We have to recognize with Aristotle, Leibniz argued,[5] that the physical existent must be in-act, and that this entails an inner process of actualization of potentiality. Motion can then consistently be understood as derivative from the acting of the physical existent. On this basis, too, the concept of "force," which Leibniz agreed with Newton is requisite in the science of physics, can be philosophically understood.

But the concept of motion as change of place necessarily involves the concept of extension between places, and extension, Leibniz had shown, is not to be understood as an *attribute* of *an* existent but as a *relation* between existents. Now this not only means that the concept of relation is a basically important one in physics, but it also makes acute the philosophical problem of understanding relations. What is the nature of relations? What kind of entity do we have in relations? Leibniz was clear that a relation is not to be understood as itself a physical existent or some kind of quasi-physical existent. Relations must be grounded in the nature of the physical existents, which means that they are to be understood in terms of the acting of physical existents. This implies that the acting must be relational, that is, it must be an act of relating physical existents to each other. This fundamental act of relating Leibniz maintained to be *perception*. This conception, how-

3. *PR* (C), 135; (M), 148.
4. *PR* (C), 408; (M), 441.
5. See Leibniz, "A New System of Nature," in Gerhardt, 4:478; Loemker, 454.

ever, of the nature of the acting of physical existents resulted in certain grave difficulties in the Leibnizian system. One of these is that it rendered relations *phenomenal*, and this necessitated Leibniz's doctrine of preestablished harmony—which his contemporaries felt to be one of the biggest stumbling blocks to the acceptance of his system.

For us, however, it is important not to lose sight of what is fundamentally valid in Leibniz's analysis. This is that relations must be grounded in the acting of the physical existents. This means that their acting must be a relating. Further, this relation must in a fundamental sense be an *extensive* relation.

V

But the conception of "extension" here brings to the fore the problem of the connection between the mathematical and the physical. In maintaining relation as extensive is there entailed an identification of the mathematical and the physical, and therewith the consequences and difficulties we have seen earlier?

We have here, Leibniz saw, an extremely complex problem. When an existent by its act relates itself to another, there is involved more than simply the act of relating. That act presupposes the agent as "here" with reference to the other as "there." It is true that the "here" and "there" are in some respect relative to the existents in question, but not in the sense that "here" and "there" are the *product* of the acting. On the contrary, they are *presupposed by* the relating—as Kant in his critical position came to see, having earlier held a position contrary to that of Leibniz in respect of this issue.[6]

What, however, is entailed in saying that the "here" and "there" are *presupposed by* the act of relating? What kind of status can the "here" and "there" have as so "presupposed"? Kant, in his critical doctrine, has given one answer to this question, an answer which has come to be immensely influential on subsequent thought down to the present, namely, that the "here" and "there" have the status of a subjective form of perception. One consequence of this is that the mathematical, too, has to have the status of the mental. But how then does the mathematical relate to the physical? Implied in this is the more general problem of how there can be *knowledge* of the physical. On the Kantian position there cannot be; the *Ding an sich* is unknown and unknowable. Kant's attempt to save the situation by the tour de force of according nature also the status of a mental construct cannot succeed.

6. Cf. *NPE*, 278–83.

The basic trouble is that Kant's position is grounded in an ontological dualism; consequently, the physical remains ineluctably on the other side of the dichotomy, unknowable.

Leibniz's answer to the question of the status of the "here" and "there" as presupposed by the relational acting is very different from that of Kant. Leibniz maintained that the "heres" and "theres," i.e., places, constitute an "order of possible coexistence."[7] To say that they constitute an "order" is to say that in some basic respect they are "structured." But what is the ontological status of that "order" or "structure"? What kind of being is accorded it? Leibniz maintained explicitly that its status is that of *possibility*: it is an "order of *possible* coexistence." Whitehead's doctrine is interestingly similar. He speaks of this order as an "extensive continuum": "This extensive continuum expresses the solidarity of all possible standpoints throughout the whole process of the world. It is not a fact prior to the world; it is the first determination of order—that is, of real potentiality—arising out of the general character of the world."[8] Both thinkers maintain the position that the status of this order is that of *possibility* as opposed to *actuality*. This is a distinction of signal importance.

We have here a significant alternative to antecedent modern ones for the comprehension of the connection between the mathematical and the physical. Nature, the physical, is not to be understood in terms solely of actuality but, as Aristotle had insisted, of both actuality and potentiality, *energeia* and *dynamis*. The physical is the actualization of potentiality. "What" is actualized is a determinate definiteness, and that definiteness in abstraction from the actualization is a "possibility." The mathematical pertains to possibility as a definiteness for actualization. This, contrary to the positions of Descartes and Galileo, is not to *identify* the mathematical with the physical. On the basis of this position, which Leibniz shares with Aristotle and Whitehead, the science of physics as the mathematical analysis of the physical, of nature, is consistently and coherently intelligible.

Leibniz's position entailed a conception of the science of physics importantly different from that of his contemporaries, which came to constitute the so-called classical modern physics. In the latter view, physics, as the mathematical analysis of bodies in motion, was thought to provide positive and definite knowledge of the physical. Twentieth-century developments have given renewed point to Leibniz's criticism of that conception. Bodies, Leibniz showed, are derivative entities,

---

7. Leibniz, "Reply to Bayle," in Gerhardt, 4:568; Loemker, 584.
8. *PR* (C), 92; (M), 103.

and composites, which are not to be identified as the primary physical existents. Further, it is not logically valid to ascribe features displayed by composites to the constituents individually. This applies even to the "laws of motion," which were thought to be empirically verified. Now in this century the "laws of nature" have turned out to be, as Whitehead has put it, "mainly the statistical averages resulting from confused aggregates."[9] In addition, contemporary research has revealed a number of constituent entities of significantly different kinds, which implies a situation basically different from that of the classical modern physics with its fundamental supposition of a homogeneity of all physical existents—they were all alike, matter.

But with a heterogeneity of constituents, the issue of the *nature of* those entities becomes of great consequence. This is the more so in view of contemporary research finding them to be basically "active," and involving some kind of relational "field." To conceive these entities as particles undergoing locomotion is to carry over modes of thinking appropriate to the material atomism which has been abandoned. What is manifestly required in the present situation is that there be undertaken again the kind of fundamental inquiry into the nature of the physical existent and all the issues this involves which engaged the thinkers of the seventeenth century. The science of physics now once more needs to go into partnership with *philosophia naturalis*. When this becomes effective, I venture to predict, there will come a new and fruitful conception of "natural knowledge."

9. *SMW*, 139.

4
MATTER AND MIND

I

Renaissance thought is of special interest and value with respect to the philosophy of nature for a number of reasons. It was from developments in this period that modern science and philosophy arose in the seventeenth century, and it was those developments which ultimately determined the conceptions of body and mind in the modern period. Secondly, there is a significant analogy between that time and ours, in that then, as now, serious inadequacies had begun to evidence themselves in the dominant schemes of thought. By a study of that earlier period we can not only gain an insight into the grounds of the dominant modern conceptions of mind and body, the basis upon which they were erected, but that study will also help us to achieve an appreciation of the ultimate issues involved in the present-day situation with respect to the mind-body problem. The latter point is the more significant because the course of modern thought has led to a neglect of a range of issues which were alive to the thinkers of the earlier time. For example, to those thinkers it was much clearer than it tends to be today that the mind-body question is not satisfactorily to be dealt with in separation from the wider problem of how the physical or nature in general is to be conceived, and that this problem involves a number of more ultimate philosophical issues, those which Aristotle had spoken of as constituting "first philosophy"—later termed "metaphysics"—that is, the issues which are more general than (and thus *meta*, "beyond") those specifically arising in "physics," the inquiry into nature per se.

A marked feature of the Renaissance was that it brought a resuscitation of Neoplatonism, which was to be increasingly influential and finally determinative of the new science and philosophy of the seventeenth century. But although this meant the rejection of much of the Aristotelianism of the antecedent Scholastic epoch, Renaissance thought nevertheless retained a definite impress of Aristotle. The thirteenth-century rediscovery of Aristotle had brought an enormous clarification of the problems at issue throughout the entire range of philosophical inquiry, and even when later, as in the sixteenth and seventeenth centuries, many of Aristotle's particular theories came to be rejected, his analyses of what was at issue, of the problems to be tackled, remained determinative.

In regard to our topic, Aristotle had brought out one problem which is quite fundamental, and the recognition of this persisted into the seventeenth century. This is the problem as to what exactly we are dealing with in "mind" and "body," what kind of entities we have here. The point is that in some sense both are "entities," that is, they both "are" or "exist"—the word *entity* is formed from the verb to *be* and means something which "is." But, Aristotle had insisted, everything which "is," *is* not necessarily in the same respect.[1] Thus, although we can validly say that mind "is" and body "is," this does not imply that each "is" in precisely the same sense. We can illustrate the issue by the following example. We can say of the red bird popularly called the "cardinal" that it "is," meaning that the bird "exists." But we can also say of the *red* that it "is" or "exists." But the sense in which the bird "is" is different from that in which the red "is." The bird is a self-subsistent individual, and it "is" or "exists" as a self-subsistent individual. This is not the case, however, with the red: the red is not a self-subsistent individual, but is an entity which "is" or "exists" only as a "property" or "quality" of a self-subsistent individual such as a cardinal—the red "is" or "exists" only as qualifying or inhering in an entity which is a self-subsistent individual. That is to say, in respect of "is" there is a difference of status as between the bird and the red. This difference of status could be expressed by saying that the bird is a "subject" whereas the red is a "property" or "quality" of a subject. It is the problem as to this status respecting "is" or "being" (often referred to as "ontological status," from the Greek *on*, "being") which Aristotle raised as the primary problem with regard to mind and body, respectively. Are we dealing here with two self-subsistent entities? Is that their ontological status? That is, are we to maintain that mind "is" as a self-subsisting individual, and that body, too, "is" as a self-subsisting individual? Or is it the case that only one of them has this status? Or that neither of them has this status? If one or neither has the status of a self-subsistent individual, then what kind of "being" do they respectively have?

---

1. Aristotle, *Metaphysics*, 5.7.1017a 7–1018a19.

II

Aristotle's reasoning on this issue had a considerable impact on thinkers from the thirteenth century onward, for antecedently in the Christian tradition the status which had been accorded to mind or soul was that of a self-subsistent existent, on the main ground that this was necessitated by the Christian doctrine of the immortality of the soul. Philosophically, this conception of the ontological status of soul as a self-subsistent existent had gone back through Neoplatonism to Plato. In the thirteenth century, thinkers such as Thomas Aquinas saw that Aristotle in his *De anima* had brought out an appreciable complexity of issues involved in the analysis of *psyche*, "soul," many of which constituted serious difficulties for the traditional, the Augustinian, doctrine.

Properly to appreciate the import of Aristotle's criticism it is essential to bear in mind some of the main features of the connotation of the term *psyche* deriving from the history of thought. In origin, the word *psyche*—and also *anima*, the word by which the Greek term was rendered in Latin—had a connection with breath, and in earliest recorded usage, that of Homer, *psyche* meant the "breath of life," conceived as the vital principle, the source of life. Later however, since life entailed motion, *psyche* came to include what in the archaic period had been ascribed to a separate faculty, the *thymos*, namely, the principle of motion and emotion. In addition, *psyche* came also to include what had earlier been ascribed to two other distinct faculties, on the one hand sensation and thought from *nous*, and on the other the appetitive drives. The unification of all these faculties in the concept of *psyche* is well illustrated in Plato's theory, e.g., in the *Republic*.

But with this development a problem had arisen and become acute. Earlier, the terms *nous* and *thymos*, as well as *psyche* itself, had been names of "functions" in a human being, but the result of their being absorbed into *psyche* was that *psyche* came to be thought of as one entity, in contrast with another entity, *soma*, "body."[2] The problem was the basic philosophical one concerning the ontological status of *psyche*; and it had become acute because of the tendency to contrast *psyche* and body, and to identify *psyche* with the human being per se. Plato's response to this problem was to conclude that *psyche* had to be accorded the status of a self-subsistent existent, and body likewise of a different self-subsistent existent.

Plato did not consistently recognize some of the most important

---

2. Archaic thought had no term for "body" as a whole, only of the distinct parts; the word *soma* then meant a dead body, a corpse or cadaver.

consequences of this ontological option, but they became clear in later thought, as did also the difficulties involved in it. Sensation, for example, presents a difficulty, for sensation evidently involves bodily organs; in addition, feeling and emotion (especially such as pain, hunger, sex) are also evidently connected with the body. In terms of the ontological separation of soul and body, sensation, feeling, emotion have to be conceived as psychic and not somatic; that is, they are psychic functions and occurrences, corresponding to particular somatic states and conditions. Significant of the magnitude of these difficulties is that, contrary to this theory of soul-body separation, the tendency persisted strongly throughout the medieval period to acknowledge the powerful ability of the body to affect the soul—mostly in an 'evil respect.

III

Since we are interested in the Aristotelian criticism of this position as it impinged on Scholastic thought, and through that on the Renaissance, it is necessary to take into account first the determinative influence of Neoplatonism on this mind-body issue, for this had considerably strengthened the Platonic position. Further, the respect in which it did so was of great importance in the Renaissance.

This influence of Neoplatonism derives from the basic feature of the philosophical position of Neoplatonism, namely, its doctrine of a One, single, transcendent principle or source and origin of all the plurality of existence[3]—in contrast to the conception of both Plato and Aristotle of three *archai*, principles or sources, namely the Forms, the recipient of Form (what Aristotle had termed *hyle*, "matter"), and the Divine. It was this doctrine of a single transcendent principle, identified with the Divine, as the sole source which constituted the transformation of the Platonic philosophy into what we know as Neoplatonism—this was the achievement of Plotinus.

In the Neoplatonic scheme the first derivative from the One is *nous*, "mind, intelligence, thinking." For Plotinus, thinking is the enaction (*energeia*) of being, and therefore *noema*, "thought," that which is known, the object of thinking (namely the plurality of Platonic Forms) is identified with being. Thus, *nous* is the primary being, manifesting a plurality of beings, the Forms. From *nous* proceeds *psyche*, "soul"—a

3. This doctrine did not start with Plotinus; it is to be found in thinkers in the preceding two centuries, more especially in the Alexandrian Jewish theologian-philosopher Philo, contemporary with Jesus Christ.

universal soul which is pluralized into individual souls. The function of soul is not thinking, knowing; the function of soul is governing and ordering. The universal soul governs and orders all things, and individual souls govern and order particular things. Thus, the individual souls are individual Forms of natural things, acting in things, governing them. That is, the Forms, as souls, are the principles of agency of things, which is to say, the principles of the "being" of things. This correlation of being, form, acting, soul is a most important feature of Neoplatonism.

In this Neoplatonic scheme, matter is no being at all; it stands at the opposite pole to being, a not-being. And consequently body, correlated with matter, is per se devoid of any principle of activity. It is Form, as soul, which is the principle of acting of body. This doctrine thus vastly strengthened the Platonic position that sensation, feeling, and emotion are to be conceived as psychic and not somatic. This means that sensation, for example, is psychic activity; that is, in sensation there is not a bodily activity, *affecting* soul, the soul passively responding to that bodily efficacy; in sensation it is the soul alone which acts, sensing a particular bodily state. In this relation the body is essentially passive; that is, somatic states can only be passive, and it is in reference to these that soul acts sensibly, i.e., sensing.

IV

The consequence of the rediscovery of Aristotle was that for thinkers like Thomas Aquinas it brought sharply into question the accepted Neoplatonic doctrine, transmitted through Augustine, that the operations and attributes of *psyche* or *anima*, "soul," belong to it alone, essentially in independence of any association with body. The problem of the relationship of soul and body came into renewed prominence, and thinkers took a new look at the prima facie evidence that somehow the bodily states affect, that they "force themselves on," the soul, e.g., in pain, anger, hunger, which too are feelings and sensations.

Aristotle provided an analysis and view of the relationship which could take account of such evidence and much else besides which had tended to be ignored. If we do not presuppose the body to be sheerly passive, without inherent activity, we come to recognize the considerable range of the effects the body has on soul. Not only does it become clear that soul would not feel anger or pain, etc. but for some effect on it of the body, but the same holds also for the sensation of color, sound, taste, etc. If the eye be not functioning, there is no sensation of sight in the soul, which means that by a bodily functioning, that of the eye, there is an effect on the soul. That is to say, sensing is not an activity and affection of the soul alone, but of a conjoint functioning of body and soul. Further, it might seem that, in the case of intellection at least, we have an operation which is that of the soul alone, but here equally the connection with and dependence upon the body is evident. For when we have knowledge of some natural existent, that existent must be mediated to the soul by the instrumentality of the body; unless that were the case, the soul could not have knowledge of that particular individual existent; it could have knowledge only of purely universal entities, such as are the data of pure mathematics.

Such considerations[4] made thinkers receptive to Aristotle's positive doctrine of soul and body. These evidences of the interrelatedness of soul and body made the conception of soul and body as two ontologically distinct entities, two self-subsistent individuals, highly unsatisfactory. Aristotle had rejected the Platonic conception of the relationship of soul and body as being analogous to a sailor in a ship; that is, he rejected the conception of the two as ontologically distinct, and of the soul alone as being active. On the contrary, Aristotle maintained, the natural being or existent is one integral organism; it is this total organism which is the ontologically distinct and self-subsistent existent. Such an existent is alive and active, and, in the higher types, sentient; in man there is also intelligence. In respect of such a being, when "body" is spoken of, this refers to one aspect of the total being; and likewise when "soul" is spoken of, this refers to the being in another aspect. The soul is the principle, source, of life, motion, sentience, and intelligence in the total being; and body is that which is animated, moving, and sentient. But soul is not only the principle, source, but also the completion, the actualization, of the moving, sentience, etc. By contrast with this actualization, the body is potentiality for motion, sentience, etc.

Let us illustrate this by the sense of vision. The eye, as bodily, is not vision, but the potentiality for vision. Nor is the eye as body the source of vision; this source is soul, determining that part of body as eye, i.e., as potentiality for vision. The eye is thus the potentiality to be affected by an object, and vision is the actualization of that affection. In general, therefore, in its relationship with an external object the organism is in the first instance passively receptive of an effect, and then is active in actualizing that affection. This means that the entity which is an object to the perceiving subject is itself active, producing an effect on the

---

4. See, e.g., Thomas Aquinas's *Commentary on Aristotle's De anima*, lectio 1 and 2 to bk. 1, chap. 1.

subject; and the subject is acted on, which is to say "patient." But the percipient subject, as patient, i.e., as receiving, is not perceiving; this reception, as passive, i.e., as being acted on, is potential perception. Perceiving per se is an acting, that is an actualizing of potentiality; that is, it is by acting that there is an actual perception.

It is to be noted that it is a particular strength of this Aristotelian theory that in terms of it perception of external objects becomes explicable. In the Neoplatonic theory, on the contrary, it remains inexplicable how perception, which is a feature in the soul, can correspond to and be true of a bodily object. For that bodily object can in no respect *affect* the soul, which in the Neoplatonic theory has no passivity, i.e., capacity of being acted on. This was to become a grave problem in the modern period with the resuscitation of Neoplatonism; in particular, it became a great difficulty in the seventeenth century, a difficulty which has indeed continued to beset thought down to the present day.

The Aristotelian theory remained in dominant acceptance through the sixteenth century, that is, through the Renaissance, and indeed into the seventeenth century. Among its adherents there continued a controversy arising from the problem of the reconciliation of this theory with the Christian doctrine of the immortality of the soul. Since on this theory soul is not a self-subsistent existent, but is the form of the body, it cannot survive the dissolution of the bodily organism. However, in one passage Aristotle had spoken of "active intellect" as not entailing bodily matter and accordingly as "separable," and as such "immortal" and "eternal."[5] This passage is capable of various interpretations. The Christian thinkers construed it as meaning that *psyche*, "soul," as *nous*, "intellect"—in contrast to soul as the principle of life, motion, and sentience—is not dependent upon body and is thus potentially capable of survival of death. Many thinkers, down into the sixteenth and seventeenth centuries, following the great Arab commentator on Aristotle, Averroës, maintained that the "active intellect" is not individual and particular in each single man but is an identical principle in all men—entailing that while it survives, there is no individual immortality of individual souls, a conclusion strongly opposed by those believing in individual immortality.

It is not important for our purposes to pursue this controversy. It was gradually eclipsed by the growing acceptance of Neoplatonism, which had been resuscitated in the fifteenth century, and which was integral to the intellectual renaissance of the sixteenth century. This

---

5. Aristotle, *De anima*, 430a17–19.

was to be the fundamental line of thought which determined the origin and subsequent shape and development of modern science and philosophy.

V

Renaissance Neoplatonism was not a return to the Christian Neoplatonic tradition of Augustine; the Renaissance thinkers went back to Plotinus. What is of particular significance in this is that it involved a renewal of emphasis on the conception of a world soul—in Augustine the Plotinian world soul had been replaced by the Holy Spirit. Among the Renaissance thinkers the world soul, while retaining a definite connection with God, was accorded a different status, pertaining to the derivative or created universe rather than to the Godhead. The world soul is pluralized in the multitude of individual souls. And further in this doctrine, every physical existent whatever has its soul; it is ensouled. In the Neoplatonic theory, as we have noted, the individual souls are the forms of things, i.e., "what" they are, and thus that whereby they "are" or exist; souls are the principles of the activity and of the being of things. So all things had to be ensouled in order to be. From Nicolaus of Cusa, one of the chief resuscitators of Neoplatonism, this conception of the world soul and of all things as ensouled was accepted by the great majority of thinkers in the line of development the outcome of which was the new science and philosophy of the seventeenth century: Agrippa of Nettesheim, Paracelsus, Girolamo Fracastoro, Gironimo Cardano, Julius Caesar Scaliger, Bernardino Telesio, Francesco Patrizzi, Giordano Bruno, Johannes Kepler, among the chief.

That in this theory, as in the Aristotelian, the soul is the form of things and body is matter, does not mean that the two positions are not different in respect of the conception of soul and body. On the contrary, they are fundamentally different, and this difference was to be all-important for the seventeenth-century development. This difference concerns the ontological status respectively of soul and body. In the Aristotelian theory soul and body are not ultimately self-subsistent entities, but in the Neoplatonic theory of the Renaissance this is precisely what their status is, self-subsistent entities. First, in this theory, soul—the world soul and the individual souls—is conceived as "being," derivative from God. Thus, the individual souls are pluralizations of the one being, the world soul, and are thereby ontologically distinct from body. Secondly, Renaissance Neoplatonism had inherited a trend which had started in the late thirteenth century to conceive "matter" as having an essence of its own whereby it is matter, an essence not derivative from form—in contrast to the Aristotelian conception in which matter is per se devoid of any kind of determinateness whatever. This trend implied according matter the ontological status of a distinct existent. Thus, the Neoplatonic theory of the Renaissance entailed a definite ontological dualism of soul and body, though it was held that in the realm of nature bodies existed only as ensouled.

VI

The growing acceptance of Neoplatonism in the sixteenth century had as its consequence an increasing attack on Aristotelianism, and one line of this attack was to have momentous consequences for the future. Prominent in this were thinkers who were medical men, but it was not restricted to them. This attack was on the Aristotelian conception of the total organism as a single, ontologically distinct, self-subsistent existent. The view which these thinkers were developing was that, on the contrary, an animal organism, and in particular a human being, was more adequately to be conceived as made up of a vast plurality of minute constituents. The whole was thus not a single physical existent in the strict sense; the whole was merely an aggregate. It was the ultimate constituents which were to be regarded as the true physical existents.

This new development of thought in the late sixteenth and early seventeenth century arose out of work by medical men especially on the theory of the elements and the theory of chemical combination. Hippocrates had stressed the importance for medicine of the knowledge of nature for the understanding of the human body—and in the late Hellenistic period the chief students of nature were medical men, whence they came to get the designation of *physicus*. The knowledge of nature was essential because it was the elements of nature which entered into the composition of the body, in particular combinations. Thus, the theory of the elements and of chemical combination were early of great importance and continued to be so in the Middle Ages and onward, after the reintroduction to the West of these fields from the Persian Avicenna, himself a medical man, and whose book on nature continued to be a main textbook for medical training into the seventeenth century.

Paracelsus, in the sixteenth century, introduced a new theory of the elements in place of the traditional fire, air, water, and earth. Paracelsus held the true elements to be sulphur, mercury, and salt, and that these were in themselves changeless, and not capable of changing into one another, as was the case with the elements of the traditional theory. His doctrine fundamentally affected the theory of chemical combination. From Aristotle chemical combination had been distinguished, on the one hand, from coming-into-being and ceasing-to-exist and, on the other hand, from mere aggregation. The new theory of changeless elements entailed that both coming-into-being and ceasing-to-exist, and also chemical combination (which had been conceived as a kind of changing of constituents), were impossible. All which was possible was aggregation of the constituents, and changing patterns of aggregation. This entailed then, too, that an animal or human body had to be fundamentally an aggregation; it could not be an integral one, an ultimate single physical existent, as maintained by the Aristotelian theory.

This revolutionary conclusion was reached by a French medical man, Sebastian Basso, just before the turn of the century, but so revolutionary a doctrine does not rapidly catch on; besides, it was recognized by orthodoxy, especially by the Church, as dangerous doctrine, and a ban was placed on its propagation in Paris, as well as on the teaching and the public discussion of the writings of ancient thinkers, such as Democritus, which were contrary to the Aristotelian position. Thinkers interested in the new line of thought had to meet in secret; foremost among such groups in Paris was one gathered around Sebastian Basso. But by the end of the second decade of the seventeenth century the new line of thought began to evidence itself in publication in various parts of Europe. In 1619 Daniel Sennert, professor of medicine at the University of Wittenberg, published his *De Chymicorum cum Aristotelicis et Galenicis consensu ac dissensu*, and in the next year appeared Francis Bacon's *Novum Organum* in England and a book by David Gorlaeus[6] in Holland also attacking the Aristotelian position and advocating the new doctrine of atomic physical existents. Basso's *Philosophia naturalis adversus Aristotelem libri XII* appeared in 1621, published in Geneva.

Basso had seen the implications of this new line of development more clearly than had any of his contemporaries and carried it a good deal further than they did. He saw that what was fundamentally involved in it was an entirely new conception of physical existence. In this conception the physical was body, and body alone. This meant that body was conceived as shed of soul, and thus of form, and was

---

6. David Gorlaeus, *Exercitationes Philosophicae quibus universa fere discutitur Philosophia Theoretica*, (1620).

constituted only of matter. Matter, that is to say, was now for the first time in history given fully the status of a self-subsistent existent, it alone, separated from soul, being the physical. Thus, in this position Renaissance Neoplatonism, with its ontological dualism of body and soul, was carried to its furthest consequence of the complete separation of body and soul, which is to say, into the complete bifurcation of the universe. Up till then it had been held that there was one physical existent, albeit a composite of two ontologically distinct entities—that is, the physical or nature included both body and soul. In the new position the physical was constituted of body, i.e., matter, alone; soul belonged to an entirely distinct and different realm.

VII

It was into the intellectual ferment, scientific and philosophical, of Paris, in which this Basso circle was prominent—from Basso's book we get a good impression of the kind of discussion which occurred—that Descartes came in 1625, staying till about 1628. Greatly stimulated by the discussions of the Paris circles—those of Basso, of Gassendi, and others—Descartes's philosophical thought rapidly flowered and matured; by the time of his departure he had achieved in some detail the foundations of his own philosophy of nature,[7] which he had ready for publication under the title of *Le Monde* in 1633—he did not, however, publish the work because of the condemnation of Galileo by the Inquisition. But in the next decade, in a different form, there appeared Descartes's system of the universe bifurcated into the physical as a *res extensa* and a distinct realm of *res cogitantes*, souls, minds, spirits, this being the first full elaboration of the modern philosophical position which was to be determinative of thought, scientific as well as philosophical, down into the present century.

Among scientists, however, it was not Descartes's system which proved most influential, but the theory of material atomism, that which had been originated by Basso and the earlier generation of late Renaissance thinkers; and it was this conception which triumphed toward the end of the century with Newton. But in either form, the fundamental philosophical position which has dominated the modern period is that which conceived the universe as bifurcated into a realm of material existents and a distinct realm of mental or spiritual existents. The radical break with the antecedent Aristotelianism constituted by

7. Letter to Mersenne, Dec. 18, 1629.

this new philosophy of a bifurcated universe has been much stressed. But the significance of this new position as a development of Renaissance Neoplatonism has been neglected. When this is recognized, however, we not only obtain a more complete understanding of the modern position as a whole but in particular also of the mind-body problem.

As a whole the modern doctrine is fundamentally Neoplatonist; it is late Renaissance Neoplatonism in a new development. It maintained the Neoplatonic ontological dualism and carried it through to a dichotomy of the universe into two reals or existents. The consequence was that the physical as matter had the basic features of the Neoplatonic conception of matter, except that it was regarded as per se a fully self-subsistent existent. But being fully self-subsistent did not entail that matter was thereby *active*. On the contrary, in the Neoplatonic scheme acting pertained to soul or form alone, so that matter had to be what it always had been in the Neoplatonic doctrine, namely, purely passive potentiality. In the seventeenth-century position, therefore, whether that of Descartes or of material atomism, matter was passively extensive, in itself changeless, merely mov*able*, i.e., capable of being moved from one place to another. The "motion" of matter, and thus body, is not properly and accurately *acting*—speaking of "bodily activity" is analogous to speaking of "sunrise and sunset" after the acceptance of Copernican astronomy. This means that body, as matter, cannot affect mind or soul.

In the modern theory the conception of mind or soul is correspondingly also basically Neoplatonic. That is, it is mind or soul (*Geist*), which is properly *active*. In some cases, such as sensation or perception, the mental action is in reference to body—by contrast to other mental actings, such as pure thought, in which this bodily reference is absent. But in this relation with the body and entities beyond, it is not the external object which *produces* the color in the eye, for example, or the eye which produces the color in the mind; for in the modern theory the external object is not per se colored, nor is the sense organ. The color originates in the mind, in its activity in reference to certain motions of matter in the organ and beyond. The situation is exactly the same as that of a sharp object piercing the body; in this, the object does not transmit a quality, pain, from itself into the body, it being in itself wholly devoid of the qualitative. It is the mind which acts, feeling pain—it is significant that the verb to *feel* is etymologically basically an active verb.

The main point I am concerned to bring out is that in reference to the mind-body problem the fundamental bequest of the Renaissance to the modern period has been the Neoplatonic ontological dualism and the consequent dichotomy of mind and body. It is this feature of our philosophical inheritance which in our day most urgently requires critical scrutiny.

5

ATOMISM, SUBSTANCE, AND THE CONCEPT OF BODY

I

Fundamental to and determinative of thought in the seventeenth century were two revolutionary developments in the sixteenth century. One was the new scientific theory of the elements according to which the elements were regarded as absolutely unchanging in nature. The other was the new philosophical theory of matter, in which matter was no longer conceived as a principle, the correlative of form, but as itself an independent actual existent, as self-subsistent stuff. These two theories were very compatible, and the elements were readily subject to interpretation in terms of this philosophical theory: they were identified as the primary instances of matter. By the end of the first quarter of the seventeenth century two implications of this interpretation had become clear.

The first was that if the elements be material stuff, this implies that they must all be of one ultimate kind. When this was accepted, it was recognized that the still widely held conception of a number of fundamentally different kinds among the elements, which were accordingly qualitatively differentiated, was a survival of the Aristotelian concept of substantial form. On the conception of one ultimate kind of stuff qualitative differentiation becomes otiose. Quantitative differentiation between the elements (i.e., in terms of size and shape) alone remains and is indeed completely sufficient to distinguish between them.

A second implication which was drawn from the foregoing philosophical interpretation was that which became formulated as the theory of material atomism. The new theory of the elements involved a distinction between the elements as ultimate simples and all other entities as compounds made up of the elementary simples. The concept of a compound implies that there must ultimately be simples or minima as the constituents, and so the simple minima were justifiably designated "atomic," i.e., uncuttable, thereby making it clear that the entities in question are not themselves compounds, but must be what are the ultimate constituents of compounds. Philosophically considered, these atoms are thus manifestly fundamental, and it is they which are primarily to be identified as matter.

This development, which had occurred in a number of thinkers, among the chief of whom were Sennert, Gorlaeus, and Basso, is clearly manifested also in Galileo, who indeed carried it further with his emphasis on mathematics. He had taken over the essential Cusanian doctrine of the universe as mathematical. In addition to the physical and chemical considerations adduced by previous thinkers for the unchangeability of the elements, Galileo brought forward the further, and compelling, reason that the unchangeability is a prerequisite also for mathematical handling. Qualitative elements changing into each other are not amenable to mathematical treatment, whereas it was precisely this amenability which was the tremendous advantage of the new theory of unchangeable elements. From the mathematical point of view it is sufficient if the elements have size and shape and that they move. In this new theory the quantitative features are necessary, and the qualitative features can be dispensed with. In Galileo's trenchant statement:

> Nevertheless I say, that indeed I feel myself compelled by the necessity, as soon as I conceive a piece of matter or corporeal substance, of conceiving that in its own nature it is bounded and figured in such and such a figure, that in relation to others it is large or small, that is in this or that place, in this or that time, that it is in motion or remains at rest, that it touches or does not touch another body, that it is single, few, or many; in short by no imagination can a body be separated from such conditions; but that it is white or red, bitter or sweet, sounding or mute, of pleasant or unpleasant odour, I do not perceive my mind forced to acknowledge it necessarily accompanied by such conditions.[1]

This conclusion that the primary physical existents have quantitative features only clearly raised the problem of the ontological status of the qualitative features. The answer to this problem, which during the seventeenth century quickly came into dominant acceptance, was one which Galileo also explicitly stated, earlier than most. Galileo, like his predecessors who had attacked and abandoned the Aristotelian theories of changing elements and of substantial forms, was strongly under Neoplatonic influence. From Plato through early Neoplatonism and much Christian theology and philosophy there had persisted down the ages the tradition which regarded the sensory as less "real." This doctrine came to the fore again in Renaissance

---

1. Galileo Galilei, *Opere, Edizione Nazionale*, 4:333, trans. E. A. Burtt in *The Metaphysical Foundations of Modern Science* (London: Routledge & Kegan Paul, 1932), 75.

Neoplatonism, and it was in terms of this that Basso had concluded that the homogeneous character which body presents to the senses is merely apparent, and that chemical combination is *mistio ad sensum* only. Galileo too accepted this doctrine, and it was in accordance with it that he made his distinction, in the foregoing passage, between the quantitative characters which are inherent in the elements and the qualitative characters which only apparently belong to them. Since the qualities are not really in the elements, the Neoplatonic theory suggested the readiest alternative as to their status, namely, that the qualities must be ascribed to the perceiver or experiencer: "Hence I think that the tastes, odours, colours, etc., on the side of the objects in which they seem to exist, are nothing else than mere names, but hold their residence solely in the sensitive body; so that if the animal were removed, every such quality would be abolished and annihilated."[2]

In addition to the foregoing there was a further step of great philosophical import which was taken by many thinkers, one which was to be of enormous consequence for the whole of seventeenth-century thought. This was the identification, implicit or explicit, of matter with body. The grounds of this identification lie primarily in the physical theory of the elements. According to this theory every macroscopic body is divisible into certain elementary constituents. These elements, most thinkers agreed with Sennert, must be of the same nature as the compound bodies; they are merely simple, as opposed to compound, bodies. In other words, the elements are to be conceived as small bodies, *corpuscula*. Now, what this clearly involves is that in arriving at a conception of the nature of the elements, the characters of macroscopic bodies, those whereby they are distinguished as *bodies*, were transferred to the elements. This procedure, implicit in most thinkers, was made fully explicit by Newton in the third of the "Rules of Reasoning" which preface book 3 of this *Philosophiae Naturalis Principia Mathematica*:

> We no other way know the extension of bodies than by our senses, nor do we reach these in all bodies; but because we perceive extension in all that are sensible, therefore we ascribe it universally to all others also. That abundance of bodies are hard, we learn by experience; and because the hardness of the whole arises from the hardness of the parts, we therefore justly infer the hardness of the undivided particles not only of the bodies we feel but of all others. That all bodies are impenetrable, we gather not from reason, but from sensation. The bodies which we handle we find impenetrable, and thence conclude impenetrability to be an universal property of all bodies whatsoever. That all bodies are movable, and endowed with certain powers (which we call

2. Ibid.

the inertia) of persevering in their motion, or in their rest, we only infer from the like properties observed in the bodies which we have seen. The extension, hardness, impenetrability, mobility, and inertia of the whole, result from the extension, hardness, impenetrability, mobility, and inertia of the parts; and hence we conclude the least particles of all bodies to be also extended, and hard and impenetrable, and movable, and endowed with their proper inertia. And this is the foundation of all philosophy.[3]

It is evident that if the elements be conceived according to this procedure as corporeal, and if matter be identified with the elements, then matter must be conceived as corporeal. Thus was the theory of corporeal atomism arrived at.

Now, the point I am particularly concerned to bring out is that this procedure whereby the elements or atoms are conceived as corporeal involved an obliviousness to one most important philosophical implication of the new physical theory of the elements. This implication is most readily seen by contrasting the new theory of the elements with the Aristotelian theory which it replaced.

In the Aristotelian theory, when there is a combination ($\mu\acute{\iota}\xi\iota\varsigma$) of elements to form a particular body, there takes place a change of the substantial forms of the elements into one single substantial form, that of the body in question, by virtue of which this body is one single homogeneous substance. If this substantial change did not occur, the body would not constitute a real combination ($\mu\acute{\iota}\xi\iota\varsigma$) but would merely be a compound ($\sigma\acute{\upsilon}\nu\theta\varepsilon\sigma\iota\varsigma$). A compound cannot be a single substance, for to be a true substance it would have to have a single substantial form—it is for this reason that "no substance is composed of substances."[4] Thus in a compound the true substances are the constituents.

Now, in the new theory of the elements the elements do not change but remain identically what they are. Consequently, in this theory when the elements come together to constitute a body, there is no combination ($\mu\acute{\iota}\xi\iota\varsigma$) in the Aristotelian sense. That is, the resultant body is not one single homogeneous entity. It only appears to be so; it really is but an aggregate or group of the constituent entities. In other words, in this theory the body is what Aristotle had designated a compound ($\sigma\acute{\upsilon}\nu\theta\varepsilon\sigma\iota\varsigma$). This was explicitly accepted by the protagonists of the new theory; it was this which basically distinguished their theory from the rejected Aristotelian theory.

But the full implications of the new theory of body were only slightly

---

3. I. Newton, *Philosophiae Naturalis Principia Mathematica*, trans. Andrew Motte, rev. Florian Cajori (Berkeley and Los Angeles: University of California Press, 1934), 398.
4. Aristotle, *Metaphysics* Z, 1041a5 (Ross trans.): οὔτ' ἐστιν οὐσία οὐδεμία οὐσιῶν.

or partially appreciated. In the Aristotelian theory a body is conceived as one single, and thus ultimate, entity; it is an οὐσία or substance. In the new theory body really is but an aggregate, which is to say that the true actual existents are the constituent elements. In other words, the constituent elements are the ultimate entities or substances. This means therefore that body, the aggregate, is not a substance. The new theory accordingly strictly entails a difference in ontological status between the elements on the one hand and body on the other. That is to say, we have here two different kinds of being; the being of the body as an aggregate is a different kind of being from that of the constituent substances. The latter are the true substantial beings, whereas body is derivative and not a proper substance. That there must be this difference in kind of being is what Aristotle had clearly seen when he rejected the view that a compound could be a substance. In holding that a compound body is an aggregate, the new theory was committed to this ontological difference between the constituent elements and the resultant aggregate. This is indeed but a formulation in explicit ontological terms of a central thesis of the new theory of the elements, namely, that body is not one homogeneous substance as Aristotle had maintained.

The theory of material atomism, which came into increasing and, by the end of the seventeenth century, almost universal acceptance was developed in obliviousness to the foregoing philosophical implications. For that there is an ontological difference between body and its constituent elements or atoms means that the character, indeed, the fundamental nature of body and the constituent atoms, respectively, must be different. Since body is basically an aggregate, the characters or features distinguishing it as body must be the characters of an aggregate, and these must thus of necessity be different from the characters of the individual constituent substances. When this ontological difference is recognized, it is evident that the procedure exemplified by Newton of understanding the nature of the atoms in terms of the features of body, that is, the procedure of transferring to the atoms the characteristics which are peculiarly those of body, must be an invalid procedure. This means, in the first place and generally, that the conception of the atoms as small bodies, i.e., the conception of corporeal atomism, is unacceptable. Since on this general theory of body, body as an aggregate is of a different kind and status from that of the constituent atoms, the characters whereby body is body cannot be ascribed to the atoms.

In the second place, this ontological difference seriously affects the concept of matter. For it means that matter can be identified either with the atomic constituents or with body, but not with both. That is, if the elementary entities or atoms be the primary instances of matter, then body, qua body, with its characteristic features, cannot as such be matter. Thus, the characters which Newton singled out, namely, extension, hardness, impenetrability, mobility, and inertia, as the fundamental characters of body, cannot, in view of this ontological difference, also be the characters of matter, as Newton maintained. This doctrine, which was adhered to by most thinkers, and also affected some who rejected it as we shall see, is manifestly invalid.

The valid alternatives are therefore to identify matter either with the elements or with body. There is thus manifestly a fundamental problem as to how matter is to be conceived, and some among the seventeenth-century thinkers recognized that this is so, with the consequent development of a number of different theories of the nature of matter. The majority of these thinkers identified the fundamental physical existent as matter; one only, namely, Leibniz, took the second alternative and identified matter with body alone. For most of the former group, physical existence was fundamentally constituted by a plurality of atomic entities, which were accordingly conceived as the essential instances of matter. But there was another possibility, that espoused by Descartes, namely, the conception of one homogeneous matter, with plurality being derivatively introduced. We shall start with an examination of the pluralistic conception, of which there were two main varieties.

II

One of the theories which identified matter with the atomic elements, that of which Galileo was the main representative, conceived matter (and therewith the atomic elements) as in its essential nature mathematical. The other, whose earliest and chief exponent was Gassendi, conceived matter, and thus the atomic elements as having the fundamental nature of solid stuff.

Galileo was strongly convinced by the new physical theory according to which macroscopic bodies are compounds, made up of certain elements. The elements are in motion, and all appearance of qualitative variety is reducible in physical actuality to different patterns of the moving particles and more particularly to their different velocities. Galileo equally strongly accepted the philosophical theory which regarded the nature or being of the physical existents as that of matter.

Now, since the elements are ultimately all of one kind, namely, material, and there is a plurality of elementary entities which are in motion, this raises the philosophical problem of how the individual entities are differentiated and distinguished from each other. Since they move, they must in some fundamental respect be separate from each other. But if the particles are all matter, how is this separation and distinction to be understood? That is, what is there in matter, as matter, whereby this separation and distinction is to be conceived?

It had been precisely to have such a principle in terms of which to secure the differentiation and distinction between a plurality of entities all of the same fundamental kind that ancient atomism had accepted the doctrine of the void. And in the sixteenth and seventeenth centuries, with the acceptance of the theory of a single ultimate matter, the concept of the void was again resuscitated in an attempt to provide the required principle of distinction. Galileo, however, agreed with the majority of his contemporaries and immediate predecessors that the void conceived as an extended nothingness is entirely untenable, that the very concept of it is a contradiction. Hence, a different principle was required in terms of which the particles are to be distinguished from each other.

We have a solution to this problem, Galileo maintained, when the fundamental nature of matter is seen to be mathematical, that is, when it is recognized that the essential feature whereby matter is matter is its mathematical character. Accordingly, one ultimate and essential attribute of matter is its geometrical extension. Now, in the first place, extension implies continuity, which means that the parts of extended matter are continuous with each other, which is to say that there can be no gaps of nonmatter or void between them. In the second place, extension implies infinite divisibility. This means that there can be particles of any variety of sizes and shapes. And thirdly and most important, by virtue of this divisibility there can be no minimum extension beyond which divisibility is not possible. It is necessary therefore to admit atoms of infinite smallness. Galileo's conception of matter as essentially mathematical comes out with particular clarity in this theory of infinitely small atoms.

This theory of infinitely small atoms provides Galileo with an alternative to the void, in two respects. First, if it be accepted that there can be bodies of any variety of size and shape, the differences of shape will inevitably leave interstices between them. Only if one admits atoms of infinite smallness will it be possible to fill those interstices without any remainder. Secondly, Galileo maintained that this theory of infinitely small atoms enabled him to account for motion. For if the atoms be infinitely small, extended matter can be completely fluid, i.e., to have no rigidity anywhere, thus rendering an infinite variety of motions possible.

The solution to the problem of how, in Galileo's theory, the distinction and division between entities is to be understood is that every body is, qua extended, infinitely divisible, and this divisibility implies division. This means that Galileo repudiated the Aristotelian doctrine that bodies could be divisible without being actually divided, that is, the doctrine that "divisibility" means "potential division." Consistently with the new theory of matter as changeless, Galileo held that the Aristotelian distinction between "potentiality" and "actuality" must be regarded as invalid. Accordingly, if a body be divisible, it is ipso facto divided. It follows that there is division into infinitely small atoms—which is to say that division is in the end into *atomi non quanti*. It is evident that therewith Galileo explicitly assimilated physical atoms to geometrical points. In this assimilation he was indeed with complete consistency developing the implications of the fundamental nature of matter or the physical existent as mathematical. Thus, the distinction and division between the entities in question is secured by their ultimate nature as mathematical, i.e., as geometrically extended, since this implies infinite divisibility and thus actual division.

But this doctrine involves basic difficulties. First, Galileo's infinitely small atoms are not themselves extended—they are *atomi non quanti*. Now, no finite extension can be made up of the juxtaposition of extensionless points, as Aristotle had pointed out. Galileo countered this argument by insisting that such extensionless atoms could make up a finite extension if there were an infinite number of them. This argument, however, is fallacious; it confuses infinite divisibility with composition. If each of the constituents of a finite extension be discrete and definite, then there must be a definite, i.e., finite, number of them. In other words, no finite whole can be made up of an infinite number of constituents if the constituents be discrete and definite. On the other hand, a whole can be held to be infinitely divisible only because that divisibility does not imply actual discrete and definite divisions. With his identification of the physical or material with the mathematical, Galileo had no way at all to avoid or overcome this difficulty.

This difficulty is of special import for the theory Galileo was seeking to maintain, namely, that body is a composite. For the foregoing argument makes clear that with his theory of infinitely small atoms Galileo is unable to account for corporeality at all; an infinite number of *atomi non quanti* cannot by juxtaposition make up a body.

But there is, secondly, another basic difficulty involved in Galileo's doctrine of matter as mathematical. This is that it presupposes that there is no fundamental ontological difference between the composite body and the constituent atoms. Galileo clearly assumed that there is no such ontological distinction and difference; a composite body is, ontologically considered, of the same kind as the elements or atoms, for they are all equally matter. In this theory bodies are to be distinguished from atoms only by their greater quantity, i.e., size. The fundamental difficulty is that his atoms turn out to have no size. A way out of this difficulty, as we shall see, was found by Leibniz, but it was based on an explicit recognition of the ontological distinction between the constituents and the compound body.

In view of this ontological difference Galileo is entitled to identify matter either with his atoms or with the compound bodies but not with both, as he did. But if he were to identify it with his infinitely small atoms, he would thereby forfeit the character of extension, which he took to be a quite fundamental character of matter.

Bruno had also maintained a theory of mathematical atomism. His atoms, however, were physical bodies, so that he thereby avoided Galileo's difficulty of being able to have compound bodies. But Bruno purchased this at the price of denying the fundamental feature of geometrical extension, namely, infinite divisibility.

The work of these two thinkers thus brought to light not only the issues at stake but also the fundamental problems and difficulties facing the theory which identifies the mathematical and the physical. They did not exhaust the possibilities, however; as we shall see, Descartes brought forward an alternative, but this involved the rejection of atomism. If the atomic theory be accepted, however, it is manifest that the difficulties facing Galileo and Bruno are inevitable. We have now to examine whether the atomism of Gassendi, which does not identify the physical and mathematical, avoids these difficulties.

III

Like Bruno and Galileo, Gassendi was convinced of the truth of atomism. He saw that the insuperable difficulties in which these two thinkers were involved were the consequence of their identification of the physical and the mathematical. The way to avoid those difficulties, he accordingly held, is to distinguish clearly between the mathematical and the physical, and indeed to separate them. Gassendi's attempt was to maintain the theory of corporeal atomism, from which Galileo had deviated, by explicitly rejecting Galileo's conception of the essential character of the atoms as mathematical. The essential nature of the atom, in his doctrine, is that it is solid bulk.

In his early period especially Gassendi participated vigorously in the contemporary rejection of Aristotelianism. It was however not, as with others, in Neoplatonism that he sought an alternative; he went for this to Epicurus. Thus, for the grounding and developing of his theory Gassendi returned to the atomism of Democritus. In this lies the reason for his big and important difference from his predecessors and contemporaries.

The rise of the atomic theory in the early seventeenth century, as we have noted, had brought to the fore the problem of the void. And as we have also seen, there was a definite consensus against the tenability of the concept of the void as a sheerly vacant extent, that is, of an extent of nothingness. Gassendi was very clear, however, about the difficulties which face the theory of atomism in finding a principle in terms of which atoms can be distinguished from each other. Galileo's mathematical conception of atomism completely fails, as we have seen, to provide a solution to this problem.

The fundamental difficulty is that if all physical being is the being of the atoms, and if the atoms be all of one kind, and moreover if they are unchanging in their being, what can there possibly be whereby individual atoms are separate and distinguished from each other? The conception of the atoms as solid stuff is faced with this problem no less indeed than is the mathematical conception of the atoms. But although this presents an insuperable difficulty to the mathematical conception, there is a way out, Gassendi held, for the theory of atoms of solid stuff.

This way out is, however, not to be found in the conception of solid stuff, as such. That conception certainly provides no principle in terms of which one part of the solid stuff can be separate from another. There can be no principle of separation or individuation, Gassendi held, other than that which had been asserted by the ancient atomists, namely, that there must be something which is the complete contrary in nature to that of the physical existents in order to separate them. Since the nature of physical existence is that it is solid, full stuff, the contrary of this is the void, that is, the non-full, the non-stuff.

It is therefore on this ground, that is, to have a principle in terms of which atoms are able to be distinct and separate from each other, that Gassendi, contrary to the view of his contemporaries about the void, upheld the metaphysical necessity of the concept of the void.

In Gassendi's doctrine the ultimate principles in terms of which the world is to be conceived are therefore the absolute full and the absolute void. The absolute full means the absolutely solid, which thus excludes the contrary principle. Accordingly, the atoms are absolute solids because they do not have any interstices of void. That is to say, they are atoms, i.e., not further divided into parts, not because further divisibility is in no respect possible, but because by reason of their absolute solidity they are not divided and cannot be divided, since such division could come about only by there being void extents between the solid parts. It is particularly in respect of this issue of divisibility that Gassendi's insistence on the distinction between the mathematical and the physical becomes pertinent. Geometrically considered, the atoms are certainly divisible, and indeed ad infinitum. But physically they are not divided, and physically they are not further divisible. In making this distinction Gassendi was therefore rejecting the conception of the nature and status of mathematics derived from Cusanus and maintained among others by Galileo, namely, that mathematics is an actual defining feature of physical entities whereby they are physical. For Gassendi the mathematical features are intellectual abstractions, the product of mental activity.

The absolutely solid atoms are bodily since they have extension and size (*magnitudo*). Whence they can be called *corpuscula*. Gassendi thus explicitly accepted the conception of corporeal atomism. Magnitude is sheer quantity of stuff, and this implies extension, *partes extra partes*. It also implies shape (*figura*). There can be no reason in solidity as such for the atoms to be all of one size and shape, or even of a few specific sizes and shapes. There must therefore be an indefinite number of atoms of an indefinite variety of sizes and of shapes—not an infinite number or an infinite variety, however, as the ancient atomists had maintained; a finite though very large number and variety suffices to account for the observed differences between macroscopic bodies.

Besides magnitude and shape the atoms also possess weight. This is constituted by and reducible to the inner power or *impetus* whereby the atom moves. This power or *impetus* derives from God at the creation of each atom, and since it is the donation of God, this *impetus* is constant and unchangeable, whatever the direction of motion.

This power or *impetus* is not a power of internal becoming. Each atom is created by God a fully complete being, in itself therefore unchangeable. The only change possible by virtue of this power is change of place, that is, locomotion. And this is fully sufficient for physics and chemistry. Gassendi's, therefore, is a kinetic atomic theory in terms of which all change in macroscopic bodies is reducible to changes of place of the atoms.

Gassendi's argument has brought out, as is now clear, that the conception of matter as atoms of solid stuff necessitates not only the acceptance of the void as the principle of individuation, but also the rejection of the conception of the mathematical as the essential nature of matter. This position has indeed rigidly to exclude the mathematical from matter, for if the mathematical be intrinsic to matter, there is no way to avoid infinite divisibility and thus the *atomi non quanti* of Galileo, a conception, as we have seen, which is inconsistent with the conception of atoms of solid stuff. To maintain this separation of the mathematical from the physical, Gassendi explicitly conceived geometry to be a speculative science, having its truths within itself; geometry is thus not to be carried over into the physical, material, or sensible. Gassendi explicitly grounded his justification of this on Plato's distinction between the intellectual and the sensible.[5]

But this separation of the physical from the mathematical involves Gassendi in difficulties no less great than those from which he sought to escape by asserting this separation. In the first place, if geometry or mathematics belongs to the intellect and not to matter, there arises the problem of how, on this basis, geometry relates to matter at all. This is a problem of much greater seriousness and of much profounder difficulty than is commonly acknowledged. The difficulties inherent in this conception of the status of mathematics did not impinge on Gassendi because he in fact maintained this conception in only a part of his thought. He was unable to maintain it consistently for the reason that he was precluded from doing so by his conception of matter as solidity. And with this we come to the second main difficulty in which Gassendi was involved in his attempted separation of the physical and the mathematical.

The need for this separation was in order to be able to maintain the concept of atomism. To do so Gassendi had conceived the essence of matter as solidity, as opposed to Galileo's mathematical conception. But the solid atom is extended, and to be extended is to be ipso facto geometrical. It is an evasion to say that it is geometrical only in thought; if the atom is actually extended, it is actually geometrical. And if it is actually geometrical, the atom is actually divisible.[6] The conclusion is

---

5. Cf. P. Gassendi, *Opera Omnia: Syntagmatis Philosophici*, pt. 2, bk. 3, chap. 5 (Lyons, 1658; rpt. Stuttgart-Bad Cannstadt: Frommann Verlag, 1964), 1:265: "Responderi deinde potest Geometricam ex se scientiam esse speculativam, neque ideo usum curare, sed habere solum pro fine conclusionum suarum veritatem, voluptatemque ex eo perceptam, quod tam evidenter, ac certo, cum sint adea mirabiles, consequantur: unde & visum est, quantum Plato refugerit, ut in materiam Physicam, seu sensibilem traducatur."

6. Gassendi does not have Aristotle's alternative of "potential divisibility," since his conception of the atom as fully actual excludes all potentiality.

clear; therewith Gassendi is himself inextricably involved in the difficulty of Galileo's position from which he had sought to escape.

This difficulty is not in the least diminished by the fact that Gassendi is not to be regarded as having, by his conception of solid atoms as extensive, simply implicitly slipped back into Galileo's theory of identifying the physical and the mathematical. Gassendi's position is more complicated than that. Certainly in his doctrine the physical is identified with solidity, not with the geometrical, and that this solidity must be admitted to be geometrically extensive does not imply that thereby Gassendi has identified the physical with the geometrical. For in Gassendi's doctrine it is not *only* solid matter, i.e., the physical, which is geometrically extensive, but equally so is the void, i.e., the non-physical. The outcome of this is that for Gassendi the universe as a whole, qua extensive, must be geometrical, and he accordingly requires a different principle to distinguish the physical from the non-physical. He needed this distinction, it will be borne in mind, to secure atomism. But now it is manifest that he could not succeed in this attempt to secure atomism, since to reject the geometrical as *constituting* the physical does not imply denying that the physical is geometrical at all, as he supposed when he distinguished the physical from the geometrical and assigned the latter to the mind. Now, if the physical be geometrical at all, this is sufficient to ensure that the physical must be infinitely divisible, and this contradicts Gassendi's corporeal atomism. Accordingly, Gassendi's atomism in the end involves the same fundamental difficulty as do the atomistic theories of Bruno and Galileo.

IV

The foregoing examination of the theories which identified matter with atomic elements has shown that this conception finally founders on the rock of the mathematical character of matter. The thinker who saw this most clearly was Descartes, and he fully accepted the implications. The universe is extensive and therewith ineluctably mathematical. Therefore the attempt to conceive matter as atomic must be abandoned. Descartes accordingly identified matter with mathematical extensiveness as such. That is to say, for him the essential character of matter, i.e., the character whereby it is matter, is extension.

With this abandonment of the conception of matter as in its fundamental nature atomic there is no need for Gassendi's distinction between the physical and the non-physical, and therewith the metaphysical difficulty of admitting a non-physical extensive entity, the void, does not have to be faced. On the contrary, Descartes could fully accept the Aristotelian argument that the void is an untenable conception.[7] The physical is matter, and this is the sole extended existent. That is, with the identification of matter with extension there can be only one *res extensa*.

Descartes's theory, as fully as those of Bruno and Galileo, accepts the Cusanian doctrine of the universe as mathematical. His theory indeed has some features of close similarity to that of Bruno. Matter, for Descartes, as for Bruno, is uniformly extended and homogeneous throughout—extendedness as such can be of only one kind, and cannot differ in parts. This extended matter is boundless, there being nothing in extendedness as such to require bounds, and there being no other existent whereby it could be limited. Descartes expressly spoke of this extension as "indefinite"[8] rather than, with Bruno, as "infinite," reserving the latter term as properly applying to God alone.[9] The essentially mathematical character of this existent makes it evident that it is infinitely divisible, and this clearly makes atomism an untenable theory.[10]

But this mathematical character of matter as extended also implies that there can be no reason in matter as such for one part of matter to be distinguished from another. As Bruno had maintained, matter qua mathematical "has all the species of figures and dimensions, and because it has all, has none of them."[11] In other words, matter qua mathematical has dimensionality, but no particular dimensions here and there, since the parts are not as matter distinguished from each other. Different parts of matter must therefore be distinguished from each other in terms of some principle other than that constituted by the character of matter as such as geometrically extended. When this principle is operative and parts of matter become differentiated and distinguished from each other, these parts will have particular dimensions. Their particular *dimensions* will derive by virtue of their being parts of matter; but their distinction into *parts* cannot derive from the character of matter as such.

This other principle, Descartes maintained, is motion. Motion, it is evident, can in no respect be derived from matter as extension. Descartes, like Gassendi, saw clearly that the sixteenth-century theory

---

7. Descartes, *Principles of Philosophy*, pt. 2, princ. 16.
8. Cf. ibid., pt. 2, princ. 21.
9. Descartes, *Reply to Objections*, I; *The Philosophical Works of Descartes*, 2, trans. E. S. Haldane & G. R. T. Ross (New York: Dover, 1955), 17.
10. Cf. *Principles*, pt. 2, princ. 20.
11. Giordano Bruno, *De la causa*, trans. J. Greenberg, in *Bruno's Philosophy of the Infinite* (New York: King's Crown Press, 1950), 151.

of motion as an inherent feature of matter had to be rejected. The only alternative which seemed open to him was that motion had to be introduced into the extended universe from without: God, Descartes accordingly held, sets the different parts into motion, and it is by this motion that the different parts of matter become distinguished from each other.

It is these differentially moving parts of matter which constitute bodies, of whatever size. Descartes's doctrine does not identify matter with body in the sense that matter as such is corporeal. Matter as such is extension; a body comes into existence when a part of matter moves differentially from other parts. This theory therefore introduces an ontological distinction between the fundamental existent, matter, and body; the latter is clearly a derivative entity. This distinction between the fundamental existent and body is analogous to that necessitated by the atomistic theory. But whereas on the latter theory body is a compound entity, this is not so on Descartes's theory. Body is merely a particular moving part of matter or *res extensa*.

With his theory Descartes is able consistently to avoid the difficulties of conceiving the physical as mathematical which in different ways beset the atomistic theories of Bruno, Galileo, and Gassendi, and the consequent incoherences in which they became involved. For Descartes there is, for example, no difficulty about the infinite divisibility of matter, either that of *res extensa* as such or that of the parts of it which are bodies.

Descartes's theory, however, is involved in a different incoherence. It is one which is indeed in some respects analogous to the others, for it arises with the need of a principle whereby the parts of matter, i.e., bodies, are to be distinguished from each other, a need he shares with Galileo and Gassendi. Since matter as such in Descartes's conception of it is no more able to furnish such a principle than in the conceptions of Galileo and Gassendi, this principle has to be supplied from outside matter. This principle for Descartes, as we have seen, is motion, which derives from God. The objection to this is twofold, as Leibniz argued. First, Descartes's theory is incoherent in that it introduces principles in arbitrary disconnection from each other. There is no reason in matter as he conceived it (i.e., as geometrical extension) that it should be in motion at all; the concept of extension not only does not entail motion, but it in no way requires it. Secondly, Descartes introduces this principle of motion by a *deus ex machina*.

It is manifest, therefore, that Descartes's conception of matter, though it avoids the difficulties of the atomistic theories of matter, in the end like them founders on the rock of the mathematical. In the case of the atomistic theories it was that the mathematical, or more precisely the geometrical, contains no principle whereby matter can be constituted into atomic particles; in Descartes's case it is that the geometrical contains no principle in terms of which parts can be distinguished to constitute bodies.

This examination has now made clear that these fundamental difficulties are involved in any theory according to which the ultimate physical existent is as such geometrically extended. This applies equally, for example, to Hobbes's fluidity theory of matter, which, like the theory of Galileo, tries to combine the corporeal and mathematical conceptions, and which is no more successful for basically the same reasons that Galileo's conception fails. What is fundamentally at issue here is the problem of the nature and status of mathematics, and its relation to the physical. This will become clearer when we see in contrast with the former theories of the nature of matter another which is very different, namely, that of Leibniz.

V

There was one thinker who saw that the difficulties in which his contemporaries were involved were in a fundamental respect rooted in a failure to recognize and maintain the ontological difference between body and its constituents which is implied in the conception of body as a compound. This thinker was Leibniz.

Leibniz agreed with those, the majority, of his contemporaries who characterized body as having the features of extension, impenetrability, and inertia, that is, those who conceived these as the essential features of body. As he said in his paper on "Whether the essence of body consists in extension": "I still agree that every body is extended and that there is no extension without body."[12] Further, he also agreed with those who, whether explicitly or only implicitly, identified these characters as also the basic features of matter. The error, however, in which these thinkers had fallen was that because of not recognizing the ontological distinction between body and its constituents entailed by the general theory they accepted, they then fallaciously ascribed these features also to the constituent atoms.

Leibniz accordingly took the alternative route and identified matter explicitly with body only, and conceived the constituents as necessarily having a completely different nature. Since matter or body is ex-

---

12. *Journal des Savants*, June 18, 1691 (P. P. Wiener, trans., *Leibniz Selections* [New York: Scribners, 1951], 151).

tended, the first implication is that the constituents cannot be likewise extended.[13] But this did not mean accepting Galileo's doctrine that they must be geometrical points. The requirements of entire ontological difference are fully met by conceiving the constituents as units of experience, of thought.

The philosophical task Leibniz then faced was to show how, from entities which in their fundamental nature are non-extended acts or units of thinking it is possible to derive other entities of so entirely different a nature as that of geometrical extension. He did so by showing, first, that all the characters of body and matter, and crucially that of extension, can be demonstrated to be characters which pertain strictly to a plurality of entities, i.e., to a group or aggregate, as such, and not to one single entity. As he summarily stated his point with regard to extension in a letter to De Volder: "I do not think that substance is constituted by extension alone, since the concept of extension is incomplete. Nor do I think that extension can be conceived in itself, but I consider it an analyzable and relative concept, for it can be resolved into plurality, continuity, and the coexistence or the existence of parts at one and the same time."[14] Now clearly, plurality, continuity, and coexistence are abstractions. Concretely, plurality implies many entities; continuity implies something which is continuous; and coexistence implies many entities existing at one and the same time. Thus, as Leibniz put his argument to De Volder:

extension is an abstraction from the extended and can no more be considered substance than can number or multitude, for it expresses nothing but a certain non-successive (i.e. unlike duration) but simultaneous diffusion and repetition of some particular nature, or what amounts to the same thing, a multitude of things of this same nature which exist together with some order between them; and it is this nature, I say, which is extended or diffused. The notion of extension is thus relative, or extension is the extension of something. . . . But this nature which is said to be diffused, repeated, and continued is that which constitutes a physical body.[15]

He is saying here, (1) that a physical body is constituted by a "multitude of things" (monads), (2) that this multitude exhibits a "simultaneous diffusion and repetition of some particular nature," (3) that this "diffusion and repetition" is effected by an "ordering" whereby the units are "related," (4) that the "particular nature," which is constituted by this ordered relatedness, is thereby "diffused, repeated, and

13. Cf. e.g., "A New System of Nature and the Communication of Substances," Gerhardt, 4:479; Loemker, 454.
14. Gerhardt, 2:169; Loemker, 516.
15. Loemker, 536; Gerhardt, 2:269.

continued," and (5) that thereby this "particular nature" is the nature pertaining to a multiplicity, qua multiplicity; it cannot be the nature of any single constituent monad or substance. That is why, as he said in the last sentence of the passage quoted, "this nature which is said to be diffused, repeated, and continued, is that which constitutes a physical body."

We have seen that according to the physical theory of the elements which so profoundly determined the thought of the time, body is conceived as a compound and not as one single ultimate entity as in the Aristotelian scheme. This means that what really exists are the elementary constituents or atoms; a body is not really one single entity, but only appears to be so. Now, Leibniz points out, body appears to be one single entity by virtue of its features such as extension, impenetrability, etc., as Newton had indeed made very clear. This means that these features must be admitted to be appearances and not the features of what really exists, analogously to the way in which thinkers had already widely admitted the sensory features as appearances. In other words, body must be seen to be phenomenal, and matter must be seen to be phenomenal. Thus, Leibniz was the one seventeenth-century thinker who consistently developed and accepted the philosophical implications of the physical theory of the elements according to which body is a compound.

6
LEIBNIZ AND THE ANALYSIS OF MATTER AND MOTION

I

The advances in physical science in the twentieth century have necessitated some important changes in concepts which were fundamental to the post-Newtonian cosmology, concepts such as space, time, and matter. Because these concepts were fundamental, they were accepted as ultimate, not only by scientists, but also by a great many philosophers. It is not surprising, therefore, that the changes in these concepts introduced in this century have been felt to be revolutionary and that their acceptance has not been entirely thoroughgoing—in fact, the changes necessitated are even more far-reaching than is realized by all but a few.

There is another concept—motion—which is equally fundamental to the post-Newtonian cosmology; but this concept, it is almost universally supposed, has not been affected by the recent advances. The meaning of *motion*, it is assumed, is clear and evident; motion is something ultimate, and there is just no way to conceive of it other than as it has been thought of during the past few centuries. This assumption, I shall argue, is an error; twentieth-century developments have affected the concept of motion no less than they have affected the others. The reason, in part, is that the concept of motion is intimately bound up with the modern concept of matter; consequently, the change in the latter inevitably involves the former also.

The thought of Leibniz on the topic of motion is of special relevance to us today. That motion is not an ultimate, irreducible notion was clear to Leibniz in the seventeenth century, but his insight was virtually ignored in his day, and it has continued to be so down to the present. There is particular value in the fact that Leibniz's analysis and criticism came at a time when the modern concept of motion had come into dominant acceptance after a long period of development.

Leibniz's awareness of that development was a significant factor in his recognition of what the concept entailed. Indeed, there is no better way to come to this recognition than to see the concept in its development.

II

This development of the modern concept of motion is so much a concomitant of the development of the modern concept of matter that it cannot be understood in its full implications without a consideration of the development of the concept of matter: this is where we must start. It is a long and complicated account;[1] here we cannot do more than indicate some of the salient points.

A main feature of this development was a gradual transformation of the Aristotelian concept of *hyle*, a process which began in the late Middle Ages and reached its crucial stage in the seventeenth century. For Aristotle, *hyle* (which had been rendered as *materia* in Latin) is the principle which is correlative to *eidos*, "form"; *hyle* is that which receives form or definiteness, that which is formed. It is not to be understood as a "stuff"—there is, for example, an intellectual *hyle*, as well as the sensible *hyle* found in body. Also, *hyle*, per se, is not to be thought of as a self-subsistent entity, one which is capable of a separate existence, distinct from form. It cannot so exist since, in itself, it is devoid of all the determinations necessary to being; in Aristotle's words, "By *hyle* I mean that which in itself is neither a particular thing nor of a certain quantity nor assigned to any other of the categories by which being is determined."[2] Thus, for Aristotle, *hyle* was a relative and analogical concept; it is relative to the particular *ousia* or existent in question and its form, and it is arrived at by analogy and always understood analogically: as the wood out of which the bed is made stands to the fully formed bed, so generally stands *hyle*, that which is formed, to the entity, whatever it is, which exists as formed.

This Aristotelian conception of *hyle*, or matter, as a principle correlative to form was maintained all the way down to the sixteenth century, but in the Scholastic period some important changes occurred which tended to weaken the essentially analogical nature which the concept had for Aristotle. Averroës, in the twelfth century, accepting Aristotle's designation of *prote hyle* ("prime matter") as pure poten-

---

1. I have gone into this at some length in *NPE*, chaps. 8–11.
2. Aristotle, *Metaphysics*, 1029a19–21 (Ross trans., with substitution of *hyle* for *matter*).

tiality, interpreted this doctrine as entailing that the forms must be contained in matter, to be educed therefrom by God. But this tended to imply that there is matter with a distinct status of its own, which is a departure from the Aristotelian analogical conception. This tendency to conceive of matter as an entity per se went much further in the next century. Richard of Middleton conceived of matter as having a minimum of actuality, since it is in the power of God to create matter without form, had he willed to do so. Henry of Ghent and John Duns Scotus both maintained that there is an "essence" of matter not derivable from form, e.g., the form of corporeity as held by Avicenna. Before them, Roger Bacon too had conceived of matter with its own essence different from form. The potentiality of matter, he maintained, is not a mere passive capacity to receive form; the potentiality of matter is constituted by a positive craving in matter for its perfection. This he explained in terms of the Augustinian doctrine of "seminal reasons"; a seminal reason, according to Bacon, "is the very essence of matter which, being incomplete, can be brought to completion, as a seed can become a tree."[3]

Thomas Aquinas continued this tendency away from the Aristotelian conception, his divergence indeed being of a kind which was to have very considerable consequences for the future. In his scheme, matter ceased being a general correlative to form but was confined to the realm of sensible existence. Further, in this realm Aquinas conceived of matter as the principle of extensive quantity. For Aristotle, the categories of quantity and quality were analyzed in terms of form, and subsequent thinkers followed him in this. Aquinas now took the category of quantity out of form and ascribed it to matter as such. Thereby, matter became extensive stuff. It remained for him, however, a correlative of form; matter was not conceived of by Thomas as an independent existent, as substance.

III

Aquinas had continued the Neoplatonic emphasis on the ontological primacy of form over matter. But the tendencies we have pointed to resulted in a sixteenth-century reversal of emphasis: it was matter which came to be thought of as primary, though still remaining the correlative of form. Form came to be conceived of in its relation to matter as the soul of matter, and soul was the principle of activity of

---

3. *Opera hactenus inedita fratris Rogeri Baconis* (Oxford: Oxford University Press, 1905), 2:84; cf. E. Gilson, *History of Christian Philosophy in the Middle Ages* (London: Sheed & Ward, 1955), 298.

matter. Thus, physical substance was conceived of as material substance, but it was ensouled matter. The next and crucial stage in the development of the modern conception of matter came in the next century, initially in response to scientific rather than to explicitly philosophical inquiries.

A number of medical men, among whom were Paracelsus, Fracastoro, Cardano, Scaliger, and William Gilbert, were concerned with the problem of chemical change. They came to the conclusion that the elements do not alter as maintained in the Aristotelian analysis, but remain constant in chemical change, and that accordingly this change must be constituted by a proportional variation of quantity of the elements. This position was plainly akin to that of the Greek atomists, the explanatory possibilities of whose doctrine was seized upon. This position was also consonant with the tendencies to conceive of matter as substance. The elements of physics and chemistry thus came to be identified with the philosopher's matter, and therewith another change was introduced in the concept of matter. The medical thinkers conceived of the elements as in themselves unalterable *ongkoi*, "bulks"—this Greek word being rendered *corpuscula* by Daniel Sennert. Thus the term *matter* acquired the connotation of bulky stuff.

In the early seventeenth century, Daniel Sennert, David Gorlaeus, and Sebastian Basso in particular began to see some of the philosophical implications of the new theory. If the corpuscles are in themselves unchanging, then in chemical combination the only change which can occur is the change of these corpuscles from one place or locus to another, e.g., when numbers of them are brought together, or when they group together, in different patterns. According to this theory, the only motion allowable is locomotion.

IV

In addition to the concept of motion, however, this theory affects the basic understanding of being or actuality. Since Greek times, the close correlation between motion and being or actuality had been recognized, and the Greek insight was epitomized by Aristotle's doctrine of motion (*kinesis*) as fundamental to nature (*physis*), the concept of *physis* being closely related to *ousia*, "being." As Aristotle put it, in his famous definition: "Nature [*physis*] in the primary and proper sense is the being [*ousia*] of things which have in themselves as such a source of motion [*kinesis*]."[4] This Greek conception was determinative through

---

4. Aristotle, *Metaphysics*, 1015a14–16 (my translation).

the Middle Ages into the Renaissance; and from the twelfth century on, it was specifically the doctrine of Aristotle which was influential. In the Aristotelian analysis, the *kinesis* of natural things (i.e., those things whose nature intrinsically involves *genesis*, "becoming") is fundamentally constituted by each thing's achieving its actuality (*energeia*). That is to say, every natural existent or *ousia*, since it is in becoming (*genesis*), involves a transition from its potentiality (*dynamis*) to its actuality (*energeia*). It is this transition from *dynamis* to its achieved *energeia*, "actuality," which is its *kinesis*, "motion."[5] This *kinesis* may involve *phora, translatio*, i.e., a going from here to there, locomotion, but this locomotion does not constitute the fundamental sense of *kinesis*. Thus, for Aristotle, *kinesis* is far from being reducible to change of place; basically, *kinesis*, "motion," is the transition from potentiality to actuality.

This Aristotelian doctrine was seen by Gorlaeus to be inconsistent with the new theory of the elements as changeless corpuscles, and he attacked the Aristotelian contrast of *dynamis-energeia*, "potentiality-actuality," maintaining that actuality is not to be educed from potentiality. Actuality is the sheer *existence* of the thing, distinguishing that thing from nothing, nonexistence. The corpuscles or atoms of the new theory simply *are*: they do not *become*, that is, they have no internal process of change, that which Aristotle had conceived as *kinesis*.

It was Sebastian Basso—who undoubtedly had an influence on later thinkers like Pierre Gassendi—who specifically tackled the problem of motion. Prior to Basso, the concept of motion was still very largely under the influence of medieval Aristotelianism. For example, Basso's contemporary, Francis Bacon—whose contribution to the development of the corpuscular or atomistic theory was by no means negligible—enumerated nineteen different kinds or species of motion.[6] Basso maintained that all kinds of motion are ultimately reducible to change of place, that is, of locomotion. This came increasingly to be the accepted idea—indeed, it was not long before the essential meaning of the term *motion* came to be "change of place," a meaning which has been retained to the present day as the fundamental meaning; this is why we today have such difficulty in grasping the earlier meaning of the term.

This new concept of motion, therefore, is the outcome of a new idea of actuality, one which does not involve becoming. In this connection,

---

5. Cf. Aristotle, *Physics*, 3.201a27–29: ἡ δὲ τοῦ δυνάμει ὄντος [ἐντελέχεια], ὅταν ἐντελεχείᾳ ὂν ἐνεργῇ οὐχ ᾗ αὐτὸ ἀλλ' ᾗ κινητόν, κίνησίς ἐστιν.
6. Cf. *Novum Organum*, ed. T. Fowler, 2nd ed. (Oxford: Oxford University Press, 1889), 2:48.

Bernardino Telesio in the sixteenth century had already gone back to Parmenides. Gorlaeus and Basso appealed to Plato and Democritus. These two thinkers also, like their predecessors Telesio and others (who had thought in terms of matter as ensouled), insisted that the corpuscles or atoms have an inherent power or force. But this force has nothing to do with becoming; the atom *is*, fully, with its power. That is, this power or force is not one of internal change; rather, it is that whereby there is external change, namely, change of place. It is the force whereby there is locomotion. Thus, in the new theory the only *kinesis*, motion in the original sense, which is possible is locomotion.

In the new doctrine, therefore, motion is as fundamental to the concept of "nature" as it is in the doctrine of Aristotle. Indeed, the Aristotelian definition of "nature" is simply carried over—but with a very different concept of "motion." Physics, the science of nature, now becomes the science of locomotion. The subjects of motion are pieces of matter which themselves fully *are*, involving in themselves no internal process of becoming but only change of places. This is the essential mechanical conception of nature upon which was based the epoch-making advance from J. Kepler and Galileo through Descartes to Christiaan Huygens and Newton. On this basis, physics could be conceived as a kinetics or kinematics, or, indeed, as phoronomy, as it was by Descartes. The most concerted attempt to achieve a pure kinetics—that is, to understand all nature in terms solely of material particles and their locomotion—was made by Huygens.

V

During this period of scientific advance there occurred a parallel philosophical advance involving clarification of the concept of "matter." This philosophical development was largely a carrying through to conclusion of implications which had begun to reveal themselves even in the preceding Renaissance thought. Descartes and Gassendi represented two divergent outcomes of this development.

Ever since the rise of the concept of matter as an independent existent or substance—in contrast with the previously held Aristotelian concept of matter as a principle correlative to form—it was seen that the pertinence of some of Aristotle's arguments could nevertheless not be ignored. One relevant consideration which came to the fore in Renaissance thought was that, if matter constitutes body, then matter is per se bulky and extended. This means that whatever exists as a physical existent is bulky, "full." Now this entailed, as Aristotle had pointed out, that, since all that which exists is "full," there could accordingly be no void; i.e., a nonfull means nonexistence, and since what does not exist cannot be extended, a "void" would mean an extended nonexistent, which is exactly "nothing." Thus, thinkers had previously accepted Aristotle's view that "void" strictly could only mean a place where a macroscopic body is not but might be. This unoccupied extent must in actuality be occupied by a fine, subtle matter—usually called "aether"—which is not evident to the senses. By some, the aether was thought of as a continuous fluid; by more strict adherents of the corpuscular theory, however, such as Giordano Bruno and, later, Huygens, the aether was conceived of as itself corpuscular.

Descartes's conception of matter was the outcome of this entire line of consideration. The fundamental feature of matter is that it extensively fills every place: matter is the "full," and there cannot be anything else physically existing. Thus, the defining characteristic or essence of this existent is "extension": it is a *res extensa*. It is not that matter "has" extension, among other attributes; extension, for Descartes, is the sole attribute necessary to *constitute* matter. Extension is as such geometrical, and therewith we have the fundamental basis of the new quantitative physics, according to Descartes.

But this physics involves not only the quantitative, measurability; it also involves motion, i.e., locomotion. Here Descartes ran into difficulty, for if matter be constituted solely by extension, this excludes "power" or "force"—which the Renaissance thinkers had conceived of as an inherent feature of matter. But there can be no locomotion—change of place—unless there be some kind of force or power. Since for Descartes this could in no way be inherent in matter—"extension" in no respect entails "force"—he had no alternative but to bring "force" or "power" in from outside the physical: God's is the force or power which brings motion into a wholly inert matter.

Starting with the Renaissance thinkers, another line of consideration led to Gassendi. This consideration was involved in the increasingly accepted corpuscular theory. This theory had to face the Aristotelian arguments concerning the divisibility of the continuum. Aristotle had maintained that, since continuity necessarily implies infinite divisibility, it follows that the atomic theory is false. The concept of an "atom" is that of a not-further-divisible particle (it is *a-tomos*, "uncuttable"), but since this supposed atom is extended, it is continuous, and thereby divisible, ad infinitum. Bruno, Eilhard Lubin, and Basso had struggled hard to find a way round the Aristotelian objection to atomism, but they did not validly manage to extricate themselves from what Leibniz was fond of referring to as the "labyrinth of the composition of the continuum"; they had sought to reduce the mathematical point to a physical entity, insisting on its necessary extensiveness. Gassendi considered himself to have found a way out of the difficulty by insisting on the fundamental difference between the mathematical and the physical. The mathematical continuum is certainly infinitely divisible, but it does not follow that therefore the physical existent is also infinitely divisible. Physical or material atoms are those bodies which are ultimately simple, i.e., noncomposite. They are, it is true, mathematically divisible, but that pertains to thought; in physical actuality, they are not divided nor divisible.

Gassendi, like Descartes, accepted, with his predecessors, that the fundamental characteristic of matter or physical existence is that it is "full." But adhering to a strict atomistic theory, he could not, like Descartes, conceive of the primary feature or meaning of "fullness" to be extensiveness; a strict atomism must admit an extensive nonfull, i.e., a void. Gassendi maintained that the *full* means the "solid"—sheer dense "stuff." So the ultimate character of matter for Gassendi is "solidity," and by virtue of this, he held, the atoms of matter have size (*magnitudo*) and shape (*figura*). This theory is certainly open to the Cartesian objection that extensiveness is not entailed in solidity, conceived as the ultimate feature of physical *existence*, as indeed the theory tacitly admits, since according to it, *non*existence, i.e., the void, also is extensive. Further, on the idea of solidity as ultimate, the relation of the mathematical to the physical or matter is left completely inexplicable. However, despite the weight of these arguments, the Gassendist conception of matter as solidity finally gained the majority adherence, many Cartesians also deserting their master in this respect. Many thinkers, like John Locke, sought a compromise, conceiving of "solidity *and* extension" as the ultimate character of matter.[7]

But Gassendi's idea of matter—and certainly also no less the compromise one—runs into difficulty regarding motion analogous to that involved in the Cartesian conception: for "locomotion" is no less entailed in "solidity" than it is in "extensiveness." Gassendi was indeed quite clear about this, and, like Descartes, he had to resort to God for the "force" to put the atoms into motion.

What occurred in this entire development through Descartes and Gassendi and beyond them is that, with the clarification of the concept of "matter," there was lost to matter that feature of "power" or "activity" whereby it moved. It was far from being the case that this fea-

---

7. Cf. John Locke, *An Essay Concerning Human Understanding*, bk. 2, chap. 8.

ture of "power" was regarded as undesirable, unwanted, or unnecessary; it is that "power," "activity," was seen to be inconsistent with what had come to be analyzed as constituting the essence of matter—extension or solid stuff, or solidity and extension. Extension just simply is *not* "active," nor does it in any respect entail "activity"; and the same holds for solidity; rather, both extension and solidity are the very converse: passive and inertial.

VI

Now, this theory makes acute a fundamental philosophical problem, that of the explanation of motion. Two thinkers in particular came to see clearly that this problem had to be faced, and that this was necessary indeed for the sake of physical science—which consideration made the recourse to a *deus ex machina* additionally unacceptable. These thinkers were Newton and Leibniz.

Newton adhered to the conception of matter as it was then most widely accepted. He expressed this view clearly in his *Opticks*:

It seems probable to me, that God in the Beginning form'd Matter in solid, massy, hard, impenetrable, movable Particles, of such Sizes and Figures, and with such other Properties, and in such Proportion to Space, as most conduced to the End for which he form'd them; and that these primitive Particles being Solids, are incomparably harder than any porous Bodies compounded of them; even so very hard, as never to wear or break to pieces; no ordinary Power being able to divide what God himself made one in the first Creation.[8]

Matter is purely passive—as Newton says, "*movable*," i.e., capable of being put into motion. In itself, matter possesses only a *vis inertiae*. But, Newton insists: "The *Vis inertiae* is a passive Principle by which Bodies persist in their Motion or Rest, receive Motion in proportion to the Force impressing it, and resist as much as they are resisted. *By this Principle alone there never could have been any Motion in the World. Some other Principle was necessary for putting Bodies into Motion*; and now they are in Motion, some other Principle is necessary for conserving the Motion."[9] The concept of matter does not permit the required "active principle" being found in matter as such, as an inherent attribute or feature of matter, and Newton, like Descartes and Gassendi, maintained that it must therefore come from outside matter. Newton, following Henry More, held the "active principle" to be God. But in his conception, unlike those of Descartes and Gassendi, this was not an

---

8. Newton, *Opticks*, 400.
9. Ibid., 397 (italics added).

appeal beyond the scheme of the world. For Newton, God is "a powerful ever-living Agent, who being in all Places, is more able by his Will to move the Bodies within his boundless uniform Sensorium, and thereby to form and reform the Parts of the Universe, than we are by our Will to move the Parts of our own Bodies."[10]

Leibniz was not at all impressed with this doctrine; he saw it as involving the fallacy of a *deus ex machina* no less than did the doctrines of Descartes and Gassendi. Nor indeed did this particular doctrine of Newton's have any wide appeal to his contemporaries and successors. Leibniz was in accord with Newton in insisting on the insufficiency for physics of a purely passive matter, that some "active force" had to be acknowledged as necessary. But, he insisted, this "active force" must be found *within* matter and not be something brought in from the outside. He adduced a variety of physical considerations to "prove that the body contains something dynamic by virtue of which the laws of power are observed. It therefore contains something besides extension and antitypy, for no such thing can be proved from these two alone."[11]

The insistence by Newton and Leibniz on an "active force" became widely accepted in the eighteenth century, and physics developed into a "dynamics" instead of the pure kinetics of Huygens, the term *dynamics* having been accepted from Leibniz. Little more was accepted from Leibniz, however, than that the active force must be something "in" matter. But what this amounted to was a recurrence during the eighteenth century to one aspect of the Renaissance conception of matter. This is, of course, not quite true of the later Kantian development, but this had relatively little effect on scientific thought. What I want mainly to point out is, first, that this eighteenth-century recurrence to the Renaissance concept of matter involved an ignoring of the philosophical issues; and second, that this eighteenth-century concept, after the important seventeenth-century philosophical developments, was thoroughly unsatisfactory. This condition continued through the nineteenth century, and twentieth-century physical theory is paying the price in a great deal of confusion.

VII

It was the singular genius of Leibniz to have seen with remarkable clarity where the trouble really lies, and his analysis is still of the great-

---

10. Ibid., 403.
11. Leibniz to De Volder, Gerhardt, 2:184; Loemker, 520.

est significance—indeed, it is highly pertinent to the twentieth-century situation. The difficulty, Leibniz saw, lies in the concept of matter and the correlative concept of motion as these had developed and unquestioningly had been accepted by his time, as they have been since. What was then—and still is—requisite is to subject these two concepts to the closest scrutiny and analysis, and this is what Leibniz did.

Two of the most fundamental features of matter in the seventeenth-century development of the concept, as we have seen, were extension and solidity. This implies that these features are ultimate and primitive, that the concept of them is not capable of being analyzed. Leibniz challenged that implication. As he put it in a letter to de Volder: "The Cartesians think that some substance can be constituted by extension alone because they conceive of extension as something primitive. But if they undertook to analyze the concept, they would see that extension alone cannot suffice for an extended being, any more than number suffices for the things that are enumerated."[12] His own analysis is summarily expressed in this passage, also in a letter to de Volder:

> I do not think that substance is constituted by extension alone, since the concept of extension is incomplete. Nor do I think that extension can be conceived in itself, but I consider it an analysable and relative concept, for it can be resolved into plurality, continuity, and coexistence or the existence of parts at one and the same time. Plurality is also contained in number, and continuity also in time and motion; coexistence really applies to extension only. But it would appear from this that something must always be assumed which is continuous or diffused, such as the white in milk, the color, ductility, and weight in gold, and resistance in matter. For by itself, continuity (for extension is nothing but simultaneous continuity) no more constitutes substance than does multitude or number, where something is necessary to be numbered, repeated, and continued.[13]

Extension was being accepted—as indeed it still is by most—as a quality inherent in a thing. Leibniz's basic argument is that extension is erroneously conceived of as a quality or as inhering analogously to a quality: *extension is a relation*. I would mention here that in this century the analysis made by Alfred North Whitehead, quite independently of Leibniz, comes to the same conclusion, namely, that extension is a relation.

Now if extension be a relation, it cannot pertain to just one single entity, as can a quality. This means that extension, as a relation, is a feature of a plurality, and not of a single entity. Thus, when there is extension, there must be a plurality of entities in relation. Further, the

12. Gerhardt, 2:240–41; Loemker, 527.
13. Gerhardt, 2:169–70; Loemker, 516.

relation between the plurality which constitutes extension is a relation between a contemporary plurality only, in which the relation features, as Leibniz put it in the above passage, as something "continuous and diffused" between the contemporary plurality.

It will not be necessary for our present purposes to pursue this analysis further; suffice it to say that extension is not an ultimate primitive quality, but a relation, and it is accordingly a feature pertaining to a plurality. What is the significance for the concept of matter?

Leibniz does not conclude that therefore matter is not extensive. Matter *is* extensive, and indeed as a fundamental feature, as the entire seventeenth-century development had made abundantly clear. Moreover, it is these extensive material bodies and their locomotion which constitute the subject matter of the science of physics.[14] Leibniz agrees that this must be accepted. The error of the prevalent doctrine, he maintained, lies in the ontological analysis of matter, the analysis of the kind of being which is to be accorded to matter. Starting with the late medieval departure from Aristotle and continuing through the Renaissance to Leibniz's own day, matter had come to be accepted as an ultimate existent, as a substance. The corpuscular and atomistic doctrine produced a refinement: not a macroscopic body, but each corpuscle or atom constituting a macroscopic body is a substance, and each is an instance of "matter," which is to say, each has the ultimate features of extension and solidity.

But if Leibniz's analysis of extension as a relation be correct, then the final constituents of bodies, i.e., the substantial existents, cannot be extensive, for, if they were, they would themselves be composite, and thus could not be substances or ultimate physical existents at all. In other words, it is impossible that the ultimate existents be "material." Leibniz maintained accordingly that it is necessary to distinguish two kinds of entity, which are distinct and different in ontological status. There are, on the one hand, the ontologically ultimate or primitive existents—which he termed "monads," and which in themselves are nonextensive; and, on the other hand, there are the material bodies, which are extensive. The latter, the material bodies, have monads as their constituents. But *matter* is not merely a collective name for a group of monads. *Matter* is the name of a distinct kind of entity, having features different from those of the constituents. The distinctive features of matter—extension, solidity, inertia, etc.—are constituted by relations between the constituent monads. I have given Leibniz's analysis of extension as a relational feature; in this paper I cannot

---

14. Cf. e.g., "Specimen Dynamicum," Gerhardt M, 6:504–16; Loemker, 498–508.

undertake an exposition of Leibniz's analogous analyses of solidity—which he shows to be reducible to antitypy or impenetrability—and inertia; nor can I go into much detail here as to how these relational features are derivative from the ontologically different features of the individual monads. It is sufficient for the moment to have brought out, first, that matter is an entity with a nature distinct and different from that of the ontologically primary existents; and second, that matter is a derivative entity, the distinguishing features of this entity, matter, being constituted by the *relations* between the primary existents.

VIII

We must now consider the concept of motion, which will be seriously affected by Leibniz's analysis of matter. In the concept of matter which Leibniz rejected, matter was taken to be ontologically ultimate, and along with this went a particular conception of motion: motion means change of place, i.e., motion is locomotion, and this was thought of as something ontologically primitive. Leibniz insisted, however, that this concept of motion (locomotion) is far from being ultimate and primitive: analogously to extension, locomotion can be analyzed into constituents, and what is more, it too is relational.

When we subject the concept of locomotion—change of place—to analysis, it is evident that there is, first, the factor of "change," and second, there is "place"—not only one place, but at least two, for the concept involves a change from one place to another place. So, manifestly the concept of locomotion is complex, and clearly it involves a plurality. Moreover, the concept of locomotion must pertain to a plurality, since the concept of locomotion, change of place, can have no significance for an entity considered purely in itself, without respect to anything else. For this concept to have any meaning, there is necessitated a complex of relations: first, between the entity in question and "its place"; second, between that place and another place where the entity is not but will be as a result of the change which constitutes locomotion. This situation is far from being metaphysically simple. Motion is not to be conceived analogously to an inhering quality. Also, there is involved the very important problem of the meaning and ontological status of "place." But I shall leave aside this problem and deal with the other factor relevant here: that of the "change" involved in locomotion.

First, we have to note that this factor of change too is relational, for it means the "*transition* between one place and another." The factor of "change" refers to the "transition" in distinction from the "places," but it is a transition *between* the places. Thus, this transition has no meaning except in relation to a plurality—of places, at least. That is to say, this transition can have no significance in respect of an entity considered purely in itself; the concept of "transition" pertains not to a single entity in itself, but to a relationship between a plurality. The concept of locomotion, therefore, is definitely a relational concept.

The analysis has to be pushed further, however. As with "place," so with the "transition" involved in locomotion: there is the problem of its ontological status and meaning. Leibniz was clear that it is philosophically superficial to take it to be some ultimate kind of occurrence or datum about which nothing further can be said. It was evident to Newton and Leibniz—as indeed it was to Descartes and Gassendi and other philosophically acute thinkers—that the transition of locomotion is impossible without some "act" or "active force."

Implicit in this is that there is a very important distinction between the "act," on the one hand, and the "transition," on the other, and this was recognized by those theories which ascribed the act to God and the transition to matter. But after Newton, this distinction came to be blurred or indeed not to be recognized; the act and the transition were implicitly identified—so that, today, when "activity" is spoken of, it usually means quantity of locomotion. It was the great merit of Leibniz clearly to have seen that the distinction between what I have called the "act" and the "transition" is one of first importance, and further so fully to have appreciated the implications of this distinction. One of the most important implications is that the transition of locomotion is the outcome of, and is thus derivative from, the quite different "transition" involved in the act. In other words, Leibniz saw that there is a transition involved in act, but that this is ontologically a different and distinct transition from that involved in locomotion. The former is ontologically primary, whereas the latter is derivative. Moreover, this ontological difference means that the transition of act is not, and does not involve, locomotion or change of place; it is a transition quite different from that of locomotion, and must necessarily be so. Leibniz was very clear about this, and he was also clear that in maintaining this he was returning to Aristotle. As he put it:

It was thus necessary to restore and as it were, to rehabilitate the *substantial forms* which are in such disrepute today, but in a way which makes them intelligible and separates their proper use from their previous abuse. I found then that their nature consists of force and that there follows from this something analogous to sense and appetite. . . . Aristotle calls them *first entelechies*. I call them, more intelligibly perhaps, *primitive forces*, which contain not only the *actuality* or the *completion* of possibility but an original *activity* as well.[15]

In my previous brief analysis of the Aristotelian doctrine, I showed that the fundamental *kinesis* for Aristotle is the transition from potentiality to actuality, this being basic to the very *einai*, "to be," of an *ousia* or individual existent. That is to say, *kinesis* is the ultimate transition involved in the act of becoming. This is the more readily appreciated when we remember that the prototype of an Aristotelian *ousia* is a living being; the "act," *energeia*, of a living being is the actualization of its potentiality (the acorn becomes an oak, the boy becomes a man), and *kinesis* is the transition involved in that act of becoming. Leibniz's position is fundamentally in accord with this. His ultimate existents, the monads, are *active* beings; their "act" is that of *perceptio*. As Leibniz put it in the *Monadology*, "This is the only thing—namely, perceptions and their changes—that can be found in simple substance. It is in this alone that the *internal actions* of simple substances can consist."[16]

The important advance which Leibniz made on Aristotle was to distinguish this internal *kinesis* very clearly from the transition of locomotion. In Aristotle, the latter is subordinate, but he seems often to conceive of it as nevertheless sometimes *involved in* the fundamental *kinesis*. Leibniz has shown that this cannot be the case. Locomotion is wholly derivative, and only confusion can result from conceiving the fundamental act as itself locomotive. Locomotion is not only not fundamental, but it is of a different order and kind from the transition involved in the ultimate act of the existent. In Leibniz's doctrine, the monads act—they perceive; and this act is intelligible in the case of each monad considered purely by itself, without regard to any other—insofar as perception involves a relation, it is for Leibniz "phenomenal." The concept of locomotion, on the other hand, necessarily involves relations; it is derivative and does not pertain to the monads as such. Locomotion pertains exclusively to a plurality; it is a feature of a plurality, the plurality which constitutes "matter" or "body."

This analysis by Leibniz makes clear the nature and status of locomotion and its essential connection with the modern concept of matter. Leibniz displays too how the "active force" upon which locomotion is dependent can be "in" matter, without that "active force" itself being a feature of matter per se. For Leibniz, locomotion is derivative

---

15. "A New System of the nature and communication of Substances," Gerhardt, 4:478–79; Loemker, 454.
16. *Monadology*, sect. 17, Gerhardt, 4:609; Loemker, 644.

from this "active force" of the monads, locomotion being the resultant change of locus of monads relatively to each other. I refrain here from discussing the details of Leibniz's analysis so as not to obscure the basic position—this obscuring, it seems to me, has all too frequently occurred, the wood not being seen for the trees.

Further, it is important not to be sidetracked and prevented from recognizing the fundamental distinctions which Leibniz made on account of finding his doctrine of the phenomenality of relations unacceptable, as has frequently happened from his own time onward, for the validity of these distinctions is not dependent upon that doctrine of the nature of relations.

Leibniz's distinction between the monads or fundamental existents and their acting, on the one hand, and the derivative matter or bodies and their locomotion, on the other, is one of the greatest significance at the present time. Research in physical science in this century has entered a new stage with the discovery of "micro-entities." But they continue to be called and treated as "particles." That is, thought about them proceeds on the presupposition that they are not different in kind but only smaller than the particles of matter, the atoms, which were the subject matter of the physics of the previous centuries. But these entities are different in basic respects: the laws of motion of the so-called classical physics do not hold for them; they exhibit "quantum" characteristics, and a new mechanics has had to be developed. However, they continue to be thought of as "material bodies" in motion. But might it not be that these categories are inappropriate in this realm? Might it not be that in this realm we are concerned with a different order of entities, a primary order, and their "acts," and not with a derivative order of entities and their locomotion? A significantly different interpretation of data becomes possible if the presupposition be abandoned that the only "activity" of elementary entities is "locomotion."

It may well be crucial for the future to recover an understanding of the fundamental distinctions which it was the tremendous achievement of Leibniz to have made, distinctions which were blurred again by Kant—or at least by the way in which Kant was understood—and which subsequently were lost sight of almost completely. Now that the inadequacy of the foundations of the physics of the last few centuries to the twentieth-century developments is more fully coming to be appreciated,[17] there is a great deal to be learned from Leibniz in our effort to reconstruct our foundations.

17. This point has been very well brought out by Milič Čapek in *The Philosophical Impact of Contemporary Physics* (Princeton, N.J.: D. Van Nostrand, 1961).

7

CONCEPTS OF SPACE

By the nineteenth century the phrase "a spatial extent" came to make sense; it would not have done so prior to about the mid-eighteenth century. In fact, the adjective *spatial*, according to the *OED*, was of mid-nineteenth-century origin.[1] Previously, the phrase "spatial extent" would have been a pleonasm; it would have meant "extensive extent." The introduction of this adjective, meaning "of or pertaining to space," signifies a new meaning of the word "space," one which has now very much come to be taken for granted, indeed by most as the basic meaning of the word.

Until the seventeenth century the word "space" had the general meaning of "extent," and in English, back to the fourteenth century, it was used in two main specific senses, one in regard to time, an extent or lapse or interval of time, and the other in respect of linear distance, an extent or interval between two or more points, and consequently also a superficial extent or area. This general meaning with these specific uses was also that of the Latin *spatium*, the word deriving from the Indo-European stem giving *spaein* in Greek, "to draw, stretch out," from which specifically "a certain stretch, extent, area of ground, an expanse," especially such an extent used for running races—whence *spadion* in Doric Greek and *stadion* in Attic Greek. From this general meaning of *spatium* as an "extent, stretch, interval" various derivative meanings arose, in Latin and later other languages, such as *de loco, in quo ambulatur,* "a place or extent in which to walk," whence the verb *to space*, meaning "to walk"—Latin *spatiari*, Italian *spaziari*, Spanish *espaciar*, French *espacer*, German *spazieren*. The older general meaning of *space* as "extent, stretch, expanse, interval" still continues; this has not been superseded or rendered obsolete by the new meaning developed in the eighteenth century. It is a meaning distinct from and not derivative from the new meaning, as is too often supposed.

The new meaning emerged as the outcome of a long development,

---

1. By W. Whewell in *Philosophy of the Inductive Sciences* (London, 1840).

from the sixteenth to eighteenth centuries, and some appreciation of this development is important for a proper comprehension of the new meaning.

A new conception of nature emerged in the early seventeenth century, the conception of nature as "matter." Contrary to the antecedent view of nature, the conception of nature as "matter" entailed that nature was entirely without qualitative features such as colors, sounds, etc.; its features were purely quantitative, shape, size, etc. And further, matter qua matter was in itself changeless, always remaining just what it was, "matter," without any internal process of change or becoming. The only change possible for matter was change in respect of place, i.e., locomotion. The new physical science, i.e., knowledge of nature, of the seventeenth century was a mechanics, culminating in Newton's *Philosophiae Naturalis Principia Mathematica* in 1686. In this science it was not matter per se which was the object of study, but the *motion*, more strictly *locomotion*, of matter. Nature was investigated and understood in terms of a mathematical analysis of the locomotion of matter. The fundamental laws of nature were laws of motion, and these were expressed in mathematical formulae.

The scientific measurement of motion meant the measurement of the change or transference of a body from one *place* to another. This necessitated clarification of what was meant by *place*. "Place," Aristotle had argued, is evidently dimensional, and it could be neither larger nor smaller than the dimension of the body in it. That is, the dimension of the place of the body had to be coincident with the dimension of the body. However, the dimension of the place could not be identified with the dimension of the body, for if it were this would entail that the body takes its place along with it when it moves, in which case measurement from one place to another would be impossible. Aristotle resolved this issue by defining place as "the innermost limit of the enclosing body," the definition of place which was accepted until the sixteenth century.[2] Then it came under attack for its identifying place with superficies, boundaries, whereas it was the entire *inner volume*, it was argued, which was to be identified with place. It was to express this conception that the word *spatium* was brought into use: place was to be conceived as *spatium vel locus internus*, "space or internal place." That is to say, what we are concerned with in "place" is the "extent" (*spatium*) constituting the "internal place" (*locus internus*).

The problem then arose as to the ontological status of this *spatium vel locus internus*, i.e., what kind of being or existent it is. It was gener-

---

2. Aristotle, *Physics*, 212a20–21.

ally argued that this *spatium* (extent) of place had to be distinguished from the extent of the body occupying it, and that it had to be left behind when the body moved. But when the body moved, did this imply that the *spatium* (extent) of the place remained vacant? Gassendi, who had resuscitated the ancient atomist doctrine in the 1620s, maintained that it did, in other words, that we had to accept the validity of the conception of "void extents." The overwhelming majority of thinkers, however, rejected this on the ground that a "void extent" (or "empty space") strictly meant an "extent of nothing," which was a contradiction, for "nothing" could not be extended. That is to say, the space or extent constituting the internal place had to be filled with something, for extent had to be the extent of something. This led to Descartes's solution that the physical universe had necessarily to be a plenum, and that extension was the very essence of the physical *res* or existent. This entailed that there could be no "void place." What we think of as *spatium vel locus internus* was a distinction of reason: "space or internal place and the corporeal substance contained in it, are not different otherwise than in the mode in which they are conceived by us."[3]

This doctrine entailed that when motion occurred, place had to be conceived relatively. For in Descartes's theory motion "is the transference of one part of matter or body from the vicinity of those bodies that are in immediate contact with it, and which we regard as in repose, into the vicinity of others."[4] The difficulty is that the respective "vicinities" had to be regarded "as in repose," for if they were themselves moving there would be no way to measure the motion from one place to another; but there could be no assurance whatever that the "vicinities" would not themselves be in motion.

Newton came to see very clearly that accurate measurement could not be possible if the places moved. It was therefore indispensably necessary to physical science, which was fundamentally the measurement of the motion of bodies, that place be not "relative," but on the contrary that it be "absolute," for "that the primary places of things should be movable, is absurd."[5] It was indispensable therefore to admit ultimate, absolute places, and these absolute, immovable places, Newton said in the first *Scholium* of his *Principia*, "constitute, what I call, immovable space (*spatiumque constituant quod immobile appello*)."[6]

3. Descartes, *Principles of Philosophy*, pt. 2, princ. 10.
4. Ibid., princ. 25.
5. Newton, *Philosophiae Naturalis Principia Mathematica*, trans. Andrew Motte, rev. F. Cajori (Berkeley and Los Angeles: University of California Press, 1962), 8.
6. Ibid., 9.

This again made acute the problem of the ontological status of these "places" or "space"—Newton now using the term *space* for the "totality of places," a usage which thereafter became common, for example, being accepted too by Leibniz and by Kant.[7] Newton was a far more penetrating philosophical thinker than most of his contemporaries, including Leibniz, acknowledged him to be. He saw very clearly that the supposition that space or the totality of immovable places be ascribed the status of a self-subsistent being or existent was quite untenable. Accordingly, the supposition of space as a physical something had to be entirely rejected and an entirely different analysis and conception of space produced. Newton had a highly ingenious solution to the problem. In common with all thinkers of the period, Newton accepted the doctrine of God as agent creator of the universe. This entailed, Newton held, that God, as creating agent, was active, acting, i.e., creating beings, *everywhere*, and *everywhen*. "Where" God acts, creating a body, is the "place" of that body. That is, "where" or "place" neither pertains to nor is derivative from the body; on the contrary, the "where," the "place," pertains to God's acting as being "there" and "then."

It is interesting to see that Newton's philosophical doctrine was mostly not taken account of or simply discounted by his contemporaries, with the consequence that he was understood to be holding a conception of space as some kind of actual existent as a "container" in which everything is, including God's acting. Even Leibniz was guilty of this misconception of Newton. Samuel Clarke, Newton's follower and protagonist, in his famous correspondence with Leibniz, tried hard to disabuse Leibniz of this error: "God does not exist In Space, and In Time; but His Existence causes Space and Time. And when, according to the Analogy of vulgar Speech we say that he exists in All Space and in All Time; the words mean only that he is Omnipresent and Eternal, that is, that Boundless Space and Time are necessary Consequences of his Existence; and not, that Space and Time are Beings distinct from Him, and IN which he exists."[8]

Almost universally from the early eighteenth century onward, the doctrine of space and time as some kind of absolute, self-subsistent beings or existents was ascribed to Newton, and has continued till today to be regarded as the "Newtonian doctrine." Not only that, but the doctrine came increasingly to be accepted, more particularly by scientists, as true. Some philosophers in the eighteenth century, notably

7. See chap. 8, below.
8. Gerhardt, 7:427.

Berkeley and Hume in Britain, rejected it as fallacious—though still erroneously ascribing it to Newton.

In Germany, and elsewhere on the Continent, Leibniz's conception of space as essentially a relation was the accepted doctrine, including by Kant in his pre-critical period. By 1768, however, Kant came to see fundamental difficulties in the relationist conception. On this view, place and the totality of places, i.e., space, was the result, the outcome, of acts of relating. Kant came to see that, contrary to this, place was *presupposed by* the act of relating; for example, to perceive a thing meant relating to the thing, but this presupposed that the thing was "there"; its "being there" was not dependent upon the act of perceiving, and thus a result of the perceiving. This meant that the "thereness," i.e., places, of things had to be absolute and not relative. But what was entailed in holding that space, or the place of things, was absolute? Kant faced this issue in his dissertation *De Mundi Sensibilis* (1780) inaugurating not only his occupancy of the Chair of Logic and Metaphysics in the University of Königsberg, but also his new "critical" philosophy. The currently accepted views of space he found quite unsatisfactory:

> Those who defend the reality of space, either conceive it as an absolute and boundless receptacle of possible things (the view commends itself to most geometers, following the English), or hold that it is itself a relation of existent things, vanishing therefore if things be annihilated, and not thinkable except in actual things (as, following Leibniz, most of our countrymen maintain). The former is an empty figment of reason [*illud inane rationis*], since it imagines an infinity of possible relations without any things which are so related, pertains to the world of fable.[9]

In his *Critique of Pure Reason* (1781) he dismissed this doctrine as the conception of a "non-entity" (*Unding*).[10] Contrary to these two views he maintained a momentously new position, explicitly stated in *De Mundi Sensibilis*: "*Space is not something objective and real*, neither substance nor accident, nor relation, *but subjective and ideal*; and, as it were, a schema, issuing by a constant law from the nature of the mind, for the co-ordinating of all outer sensa whatsoever."[11] In his *Metaphysical Foundations of Natural Science* (1786) Kant formulated his doctrine alternatively as follows: "space in general does not belong to the properties or relations of things in themselves, which would necessarily have to admit of reduction to objective concepts, but belongs

---

9. *Kant's Inaugural Dissertation*, trans. J. Handyside (Chicago: Open Court, 1928), 61–62.
10. Kant, *Critique of Pure Reason*, A39, B56.
11. Kant, *Inaugural Dissertation*, 61.

merely to the subjective form of our sensible intuition of things or relations, which must remain wholly unknown to us as regards what they may be in themselves."[12]

This new Kantian conception of space came into some appreciable acceptance only in the next century—except by avowed Kantians, of course. What continued to be accepted was the conception of space mistakenly attributed to Newton; this persisted, despite the criticism of Leibniz and of Kant, throughout the eighteenth and nineteenth centuries. This doctrine gained widespread adherence particularly by scientists, among whom a philosophical interest had sharply dwindled in the post-Newtonian epoch. It was found easy to accept the statement "there is space" without troubling to face the difficult question as to the meaning óf *is* in that statement, i.e., to ask what kind of "being" space was supposed to have. In other words, it was easy to reify "extension" without facing the fact that, as Kant said, we thereby have an *Unding*, a "non-entity."

On the plus side this doctrine had the definite advantage that it freed the concept of "place," required by mathematical physics, of the relativity which was inevitable if extension were fundamentally the extension of matter, as Descartes had maintained.

Further, this so-called Newtonian conception of space as an actual existent had another important advantage. If extension pertained fundamentally to the physical or matter, and this material extension were essentially mathematical, it meant, as Descartes had correctly maintained, that the *object* of mathematics, and of geometry in particular, was matter, and thus that pure mathematics was the study of the essence of the physical. This raised a serious difficulty, however, as to the difference between mathematics and physics. In the course of the seventeenth century it came to be increasingly clearly recognized that the two sciences of physics and mathematics were not identical. The so-called Newtonian conception of space as an actual existent enabled the "objects," and thus the subject matters, of physics and mathematics to be separated. The object of physics was the physical, i.e., matter, whereas the object of mathematics, and of geometry in particular, was space. This was why this conception of space, as Kant said, "commends itself to most geometers." I might add that the discovery of non-Euclidean geometry in the early nineteenth century constituted the first chapter in the destruction of this conception of space. To pursue this topic, however, is beyond the scope of our present concern.

12. Kant, *Metaphysical Foundations of Natural Science*, trans. James Ellington (New York: Bobbs-Merrill, 1970), 23–24.

8

THE MEANING OF "SPACE" IN KANT

My concern here will be the meaning of the word *space—spatium, der Raum*—in Kant's usage. This is not an attempt merely at another exposition of Kant's doctrine of space as transcendentally ideal and empirically real. I want to get at the meaning of the word as Kant understood it. This is worth doing, I suggest, since we tend to approach Kant's theory with a meaning which has become implicit as a result of the virtually complete dominance of the Newtonian inheritance from the early nineteenth century onward. In our time the noun *space* (*der Raum*), implicitly carries the connotation of some sort of entity. This was not so with the word *spatium—space* in English—in its original meaning, which persisted through the seventeenth century. In its original general and basic sense the word meant "an interval, a stretch or extent, between things"—which certainly did not connote an entity. That is, originally *spatium*, and *space* in English, was an abstract noun, whereas it later became a concrete noun.

This change in the meaning of the word was beginning to take place in the eighteenth century and became general in the nineteenth. The original abstract sense nevertheless persisted, though much subordinately, and has done so to the present time. Today the prevailing presupposition is that the term has one fundamental basic meaning, which is constant whenever the term is used in philosophical discourse; there is extraordinarily little appreciation of the shifts in sense in the various occurrences of its usage, even in the same writer, and often in the same sentence or paragraph. This variation in sense is further confounded by the use of *space* (and *der Raum* as the German equivalent) as synonymous with *place*.

It is clearly important for a correct understanding of Kant to avoid implicitly importing a sense of the word which is not that which Kant held. We need accordingly to attempt to be clear as to the meaning of the word in Kant—for example, whether and to what extent he thought in terms of the new concrete sense of the word. To achieve this clarification it is necessary to go into the background of thought, to see what was in controversy in the sixteenth and seventeenth centuries, in order to appreciate how the change in sense came about.

Now at that time what was in controversy was not "space," as is commonly supposed. This supposition rests upon the nineteenth-century sense of space as an entity, and constitutes a block to the inquiry before us. There was then indeed no concept of space at all in the modern sense. The relevant controversy in the sixteenth and seventeenth centuries was concerning "place."

In the sixteenth century the concept of motion, i.e., locomotion, had come to the fore, and thinkers like Scaliger and Telesio argued that the concept of motion as change of place was not properly intelligible in terms of the Aristotelian definition of place. Aristotle had defined place as the innermost bounding surface of the containing body—which of course coincided with the outer boundary of the contained body. The point of the sixteenth-century criticism was that in the Aristotelian doctrine place is tied too closely to body—place not only cannot be defined except in terms of body, but if there be no containing body (as there is not beyond the universe) then there is no place possible at all. The modern thinkers argued that the concept of motion implied a body's leaving a place behind when it moved, which entailed that place must be both logically and ontologically distinct and separate from body.

The solution to the problem, put forward by Scaliger and Telesio, which later became generally accepted, was to identify place, not as by the Aristotelians with the bounding surfaces, but with the whole inner extent occupied by the body. As Scaliger put it: "Thus place is not the encompassing surface of the exterior of the body: but it is what is contained within this surface."[1] It is this whole inner extent, which the body leaves behind in moving, this extent itself remaining constant, as Telesio said, "itself not receding or driven away, but remaining perpetually the same and most promptly taking up succeeding entities."[2]

Because at that time the term *place* was so predominantly understood with the Aristotelian meaning, i.e., as referring to bounding surfaces, the protagonists of the new conception took to using not simply the word *locus* but to speaking of *locus internus*.

To ensure the ontological distinction and separation of place from body, Scaliger identified place and void but redefined void as "an extent (*spatium*) in which there is body"[3]—as opposed to the Aristotelian

---

1. J. C. Scaliger, *Exotericarum exercitationum liber ad Hieronymum Cardanum* (1557), exer. 5.3.
2. B. Telesio, *De rerum natura* (1586), lib. 1, caput 25.
3. Scaliger, exer. 5.3.

and generally accepted meaning of void as place *without* any body in it.[4] The problem of the connection between void and place came to receive a great deal of attention from sixteenth- and seventeenth-century thinkers, almost all coming to the conclusion, in agreement with Aristotle, that void conceived as an extent with absolutely nothing in it, that is an extent of sheer nothingness, is a contradiction, for an extent of nothing is a nonexistent extent. If there is to be any extent at all there must be something which is extended; an extent cannot exist just by itself. This argument was extremely important for and was accepted by almost all sixteenth- and seventeenth-century thinkers down to and including Newton.

This does not mean that no thinkers accepted the conception of extents which are void of body. Many certainly did not, and maintained a plenum doctrine—including many of the first seventeenth-century atomists such as Sennert, Gorlaeus, and Basso, who held that the atoms are completely contiguous. Some thinkers, of whom Bruno was a notable instance, did maintain a doctrine of void extent (*vacuum spatium*). But for them all extents void of body had necessarily to be filled with some other existent, for otherwise such extents would not be possible at all. Bruno on the whole avoided the word *vacuum* because it tended to have the connotation of sheer nothingness. Instead, he spoke of the extents vacant of body as *aether*, *aer*, or *spiritus* (the world soul). And when he was referring to this extent purely as such, in an abstract sense, and not in respect of its content (in which case it would be called *aether*, etc.), he used the Latin word for extent or interval, namely, *spatium*.

In this Bruno exemplified a new technical sense of *spatium* which was beginning to come into use at the end of the sixteenth and early seventeenth century. These thinkers, as we have noted, were maintaining that place (*locus*) is to be identified, not as by the commonly accepted Aristotelian conception with exterior bounding surfaces, but with the entire extended area or room within those bounds. To put the emphasis on this internal extent or room as opposed to the boundary, the word *spatium*, i.e., extent or extended area, room, came gradually into use with the meaning, in this context, of "the extent or room in which body is or might be as the place of body." This was, for example, Bruno's use of the term. In general, because this use of the word *spatium* was new, it was common to explicate it by the phrase *spatium vel locus internus*.

What is particularly to be noted is that in the seventeenth century

---

4. Cf. Aristotle, *Physics*, 214a13, 19.

the term *spatium* meant *locus*, "place." This is quite clear in Descartes, for example, in his *Principles of Philosophy*, especially part 2, principles 10–15, where he explicitly discusses the concept of *spatium*. In principle 10, which is headed "*Quid sit spatium, sive locus internus*," the word *spatium*, "space," is quite definitely throughout the paragraph used with the meaning of *locus*, "place." In the succeeding principles he often speaks explicitly of "*spatium vel locus*," and in principle 14 he goes on to examine "Wherein space and place differ." The difference is that "place (*locus*) indicates situation (*situs*) more explicitly than magnitude or figure; while, on the contrary, we more often think of the latter when we speak of space (*spatium*)." Descartes constitutes most important evidence for the current usage of the word *spatium*; he was not only a very clear writer but also a particularly clear and penetrating thinker. Further, his influence was very considerable.

It was this meaning of the word *spatium* which was accepted by Leibniz and right through to the pre-critical Kant. This was also the meaning current in England, as is clearly evidenced in Joseph Raphson, a Cambridge mathematician and younger contemporary of Newton, who was not only an enthusiastic proponent of Newton's system but wrote a most important explication of the philosophical basis of Newton's work, in which *spatium* is explicitly defined and spoken of as *locus internus*.[5]

In the latter part of the seventeenth century, as the new special meaning of *spatium* came into currency, it was less and less necessary to add the words *locus internus*. But concomitant with this there occurred a further important development in the usage of the term, to which Newton's thought constituted a major contribution. In addition to the new general meaning of *spatium* as *locus internus* it came to be used also in a slightly more special sense, of "all places in their totality," or "the extent constituted by all places in their totality." This is Newton's use of the term in the General Scholium in his *Principia*. Newton's conception of *spatium* was not, as has subsequently come to be so widely misinterpreted, that of an "entity." It was that of "place," the *locus* of God's activity, i.e., *where* God is present and active. To substantiate this of course requires a much more extensive discussion; I here do no more than merely adumbrate Newton's conception.[6]

Further and most important evidence of this later usage of the term

---

5. J. Raphson, the appendix entitled "De Spatio Reali seu Ente Infinito conamen Mathematico Metaphysicum," to the 2nd edition of his *Analysis Aequationum Universalis*, def. 1. Cf. A. Koyré, *From the Closed World to the Infinite Universe* (Baltimore–London: The Johns Hopkins University Press, 1957), chap. 8.

6. I have dealt with this in detail in *NPE*.

spatium as the totality of places is presented by Leibniz in his controversy with Clarke. Having experienced much difficulty in getting his theory understood, Leibniz was driven, in his Fifth Letter, to an explication of the meaning of the term *space* (para. 47). He started this by explaining in some detail the meaning of "place," and then went on to show that "that which comprehends all those places is called *space*," or as he put it alternatively, "*space* is that which results from taking places together." Space is the sum total of places. It is clearly no entity, neither for Leibniz nor for Newton. What is of first importance to appreciate is that the concept of *place* was fundamental in the concept of "space," in both Leibniz and Newton. Basically what was at issue between them was the nature and ontological status of *place*.

Newton had maintained the conception of place as ontologically distinct from bodies and as immovable in order to have a clear and unambiguous meaning for the concept of motion as change of place. Newton's grounding of place ontologically in God was quite unacceptable to Leibniz. But Leibniz's own ontology involved difficulties in regard to the concept of place, difficulties which eventually led Kant to the position of the Inaugural Dissertation and the first *Critique*.

On the basis of his ontology Leibniz could not accept the widely current conception of place as ontologically distinct and separate from body. For Leibniz, the only actual existents or substances were the monads, and it was impossible that place be a monad. Hence the only possibility for him was to define place, basically as Aristotle had done, by reference to actual existents. Now, the notion of place can have no sense by reference to a single existent or monad, isolatedly and in itself. Place, therefore, Leibniz maintained, has to be defined and determined by reference to a plurality of monads. That is to say, the place occupied by any particular monad has to be defined by reference to its situation relatively to other monads. Thus Leibniz is in agreement with Descartes that place (*locus*) connotes situation (*situs*). Leibniz saw clearly that on his ontological basis place must be a relative concept; that is, place is "where" one entity is situated with reference to where other entities are. The entities concerned here must of course be coexistent. All coexistents must be mutually external to each other, i.e., each is situated elsewhere in reference to each other. Their situation in reference to each other is quite definite, and abstractly considered constitutes a certain order of places. The total abstract order of places, Leibniz explained, is what is meant by the term *space*.

This is the conception and meaning of "space" which was inherited by Kant, as is clear in his first published writing, *Thoughts on the True Estimation of Living Forces*, 1747. Kant held a theory of monads at that time, but his theory differed from that of Leibniz in that he maintained a dualism: for him there were bodily or physical monads as well as spiritual ones. This treatise was primarily concerned with the physical monads. He conceived them as units of force, and in the first paragraph he made explicit his agreement with Leibniz "that there inheres in body a force which is essential to it, and which indeed belongs to it prior to its extension." Kant's monads, however, were not windowless. The forces of the physical monads act on and affect each other. If the monads did not so act on each other there would be no connection, no relation, between them. They would exist in total isolation. Indeed, as Kant said: "Since every self-sufficient being contains within itself the complete source of all its determinations, it is not necessary for its existence that it stand in relation to other things."[7] This means that unless and until the monads act on each other, there will be no connection, no relation. Connection, and relation, are *brought into being* by their action on each other.

Now, as Kant goes on to point out a few lines later in this paragraph 7, "there can be no place without external connections, situations and relations." This is the Leibnizian doctrine: the concept of place cannot pertain to an entity in isolation; the concept can enter only with entities in relation. Place is where an entity is in relation to other entities. Since there can be no relation unless and until entities act on each other, thereby bringing about a connection and relation, place is dependent upon the acting of the monads. Consequently, the totality of order of situation in reference to each other, which is called "space," is dependent upon the acting of the monads. Indeed, there is no extension either without that activity's effecting relations and connections; extension for Kant, as for Leibniz, is not a concept which can pertain to a monad in itself. Thus, as he says in the heading of paragraph 9, "If the substances had no force whereby they could act outside themselves, there would be no extension, and also no space." The point is, he insists, that "without a force of this kind there is no connection, without this connection no order, and without this order no space." Here it is quite clear that Kant understood "space," *der Raum*, as meaning the totality of the order of places—the late-seventeenth-century meaning of the word, as it had been made clear by Leibniz.

That this was Kant's understanding of the concept of space comes out clearly again in his public disputation nine years later, the *Monadologiam Physicam* (1756), in which he elaborated his doctrine of the physical monads as units of activity. By their acting on each other they

---

7. Kant, *Thoughts on the True Estimation of Living Forces* (1747), para. 7.

bring about connections and relations, and therewith extension (which is constituted by their "sphere of activity"—*sphaera activitatis* [*Monadologiam*, prop. 6]) and also place or situation in reference to each other, and therewith the totality of order of situation which is space. Accordingly, he maintained, "the ground of filled space is not to be looked for in the mere position of substance, but it is to be sought in the external relations [of substances]." He makes the point repeatedly that space is brought about solely by external relations, e.g., in propositio 7 *passim*. This contention is only intelligible if "space" means the order of the respective relations of the entities, i.e. "where" they are in reference to each other.

This means that place, i.e., situation in reference to each other, and thus the total order of places or situations, is determinable only by reference to the active monads.

Twelve years after this essay Kant ran into a serious difficulty involved in this conception. If this order of relations of situation be determinable solely by reference to the physical substances, then the fact of incongruent counterparts becomes unintelligible. For example, considered thus purely relationally, the order of the parts of a left hand and a right hand are identical, but one cannot put a right hand into a left-handed glove. Kant concluded in his momentous short treatise "On the First Ground of the Distinction of Regions in Space" (1768) that the order of places relatively to each other cannot be dependent upon, and thus follow from, physical existents and their activity of relating to each other. That order must be somehow ontologically distinct and separate, and presupposed by the activities of the existents—presupposed because unless this be so the activities will be without a sense of direction, i.e., they would have no basis upon which to act, or move, in one direction rather than another. Kant here made a definite break with the Leibnizian doctrine. This break does not consist in the abandonment of the relational concept of space; on the contrary, Kant continues to conceive space as the totality of the order of places relatively to each other. The break consists in maintaining that order to be independent of physical existents, and not determinable by reference to them.

The problem which then arose was how that order could be independent of physical existents. Kant completely and emphatically rejected the supposition that this independence meant that that order could itself be some kind of substantial existent, some kind of entity. The solution came to him the following year, 1769, when a "great light" dawned on him. "Where" physical existents are in relation to each other is determinable not by reference to themselves and their activities, as he had formerly thought, but by reference to the perceiver and his activity of perception. This is the new doctrine of the *De mundi sensibilis*, his dissertation of the next year (1770), and of the *Critique of Pure Reason*. Kant's understanding of "space" remains as before, namely, the totality of the order of places or situations relatively to each other. But "where" things are relatively to each other is no longer determined by reference to things and their activities, but by reference to the perceiving activity of the observing mind.

PART III
ISSUES

9

THE PROBLEM OF THE PHYSICAL EXISTENT

I

My concern in this chapter is to inquire into some fundamental presuppositions which are involved in modern thought, philosophical and scientific, about the nature of physical existence.

When a theory, such as the seventeenth-century conception of material atomism, first appears it arises in the context of certain sets of problems brought into prominence by the particular intellectual situation obtaining at the time. The theory emerges into dominance in a competitive struggle in which not only is it subjected to searching scrutiny, but through the dialectical interchange between rival views the basic issues at stake become elucidated and are kept in the foreground of thought. Thereby a considerable detail of comprehension of the theory in question and of what it involves is achieved.

This detail of understanding tends subsequently to diminish and fade away as the theory gains dominant acceptance, for the conditions requisite to this understanding are gradually lost. With the victory of the theory not only does intellectual interest tend to move rapidly away from the fundamental issues to others, but also the falling away of rivals means the petering out of the dialectic and therewith the loss of the vital contrast essential to the clear perception of fundamentals. The result is that what had formerly stood out as one possibility among others, requiring justification, comes to retreat to the status of tacit presupposition, having the seeming obviousness of the self-evident, with no serious alternative.

When in the course of intellectual development this theory comes to be abandoned, the presuppositions which it engendered tend, because they have become tacit, to be carried over into the superseding thought, creating difficulties and hampering progress. This is exemplified in the sixteenth century when the advance of new theories was restricted and hindered by the implications of the theory of substantial form, which had by the end of the Middle Ages become such tacit presuppositions. In the course of the last couple of centuries certain fundamental ideas have analogously come to be accepted as tacit presuppositions which now in this century are restrictive of thought.

The most important factor contributing to the resolution of the sixteenth-century difficulties was the revival of ancient sources during the previous century. This not only restored attention to Plato and the Neoplatonists but also brought into currency the thought of thinkers such as Seneca and Cicero, Lucretius and Epicurus, Leucippus and Democritus, Empedocles and Anaxagoras, of medical men such as Asklepiades and Galen, and mathematicians such as Aristarchos, Archimedes, Euclid, Heron of Alexandria, and Ptolemy.

Much more important than the alternatives to the dominant Aristotelianism which these presented is that they provided that contrast which is indispensable to the distinguishing and elucidating of fundamental concepts. In our time, too, a recourse to historical materials is necessary for the same end.

II

For our present purposes we need to return to the context of thought of the sixteenth century, in which are rooted the presuppositions which are my concern here. Then, as in earlier times, medicine was prominent in stimulating an interest in the constitution of the physical world. For the treatment of illness it is important to understand the composition of the body, what its components are, particularly in terms of a theory of chemical constituents. The theory of the elements and the theory of chemical combination are thus of immediate concern to medicine, but during this period they also came to have enormous consequences for the whole of the scientific revolution, and the new philosophy then beginning. For it was these, and more particularly the theory of the elements, which were determinative of the new conception of the physical existent, which at that time came to supersede the medieval Aristotelian conception.

At the beginning of the century Agrippa of Nettesheim (1486–1535), under Pythagorean, Platonic, and Cabbalistic influence, had introduced some quantitative features into the traditional purely qualitative conception of the elements. His influential contemporary, the medical man Paracelsus (1473–1541), went further and rejected the ultimacy of the four Aristotelian elements, substituting sulphur, mercury, and salt. The fundamental significance of this was that the elements of Paracelsus, unlike those of Aristotle, were conceived as generically different from each other and not capable of change into one another.

This conception of the elements as changeless was beginning to take root in other thinkers, too, under the influence of a new conception of matter which was the sixteenth-century outcome of a gradual transformation of the concept (which had slowly begun in the thirteenth century) from the Aristotelian correlative of form into that of a self-subsistent actuality. In their challenge to the Aristotelian theory of the elements, the physical philosophers Fracastoro, Telesio, and Patrizzi, and the medical men Cardano, Scaliger, and William Gilbert, were gradually bringing into effect the conception of the elements in terms of the new theory of matter.

However, the Aristotelian theory of substantial form continued considerably to control the presuppositions of thought, and it was not until toward the end of the first quarter of the seventeenth century, with Gorlaeus, Jean d'Espagnet, Tommaso Campanella, and the influential French medical man Sebastian Basso, that the doctrine of the changeability of the elements into each other came to be firmly repudiated. This step went together with an equally definite acceptance of an atomistic theory, by these thinkers and others such as Bruno, Lubin, Jean Bodin, Francis Bacon, and another physician, Daniel Sennert. In the new theory, at that time being developed, the elements were conceived as material atoms or corpuscles, in themselves ultimate and changeless.

This conception of the elements had most important implications for medicine. On the old theory of changing elements, the elements as constituting food were conceived as undergoing change into the substance of the human or animal body which had ingested the food. Such a substantial change was not possible in the new theory of the elements. This in turn implied that the body could not be a single, integral substance as maintained in the Aristotelian doctrine; a human or animal body had to be conceived as a compound, an aggregate of many substances.

It was clear that the new theory of the elements had profound metaphysical implications, for it entailed important changes in the concept of substance as it had hitherto been maintained. For, following Aristotle, a living body (with its particular substantial form) had been accepted as the paradigm instance of a substance. The new theory of bodies as aggregate compounds implied that not they but their constituents were to be identified as metaphysical substances or the ultimate physical existents.

In this context the theory of chemical combination was seen by the thinkers of the early seventeenth century to be of special relevance, both from a scientific and a philosophical point of view. Scientifically this was important because the previously accepted Aristotelian theory of chemical combination definitely maintained that the constituents combined or blended with each other. Philosophically this theory was equally important because the Aristotelian theory held that chemical combination presented one clear case of substantial change.

Aristotle had argued that a definite distinction is to be made between, on the one hand, an aggregate juxtaposition (σύνθεσις) of, e.g., mixed grains of wheat and barley or a mixture of sand grains and water, and on the other a genuine chemical combination (μίξις), in which there is a κρᾶσις, "blending," of the constituents into a different substance,[1] as for example when an acid dissolves a metal. Aristotle maintained that there will not, however, be such a blending or μίξις if the constituents entirely disappear; in that case there will have occurred the γένεσις, "coming-into-being," of one substance and the φθορά, "destruction," of two or more constituents. So the Aristotelian theory accorded a special status to chemical combination (μίξις), distinguishing it from the condition of a mere aggregate compound (σύνθεσις) on the one hand and from coming-into-being (γένεσις) and passing-away (φθορά) on the other.

There is a special problem in the Aristotelian theory of chemical combination which must be mentioned here not only for its importance to the early seventeenth-century disputes but also because it will become relevant in the later portions of this paper. The problem is how it is possible for the constituents to continue to exist in a μίξις without this being a case of an aggregate juxtaposition (σύνθεσις), in which the combination is merely apparent, a *mistio ad sensum*, that is, only seeming so to our senses, though not to the keen eyesight of a Lynkeus.[2]

Aristotle held that this problem is solved if his distinction between potential and actual existence be acknowledged. His famous brief statement of his solution is: "Since, however, some things *are-potentially* while others *are-actually*, the constituents combined in a compound can 'be' in a sense and yet 'not-be'. The compound may *be-actually* other than the constituents from which it has resulted; nevertheless each of them may still *be-potentially* what it was before they were combined, and both of them may survive undestroyed."[3]

---

1. Aristotle, *De Gen. et Cor.*, 1.10, esp. 328a5–13.
2. Cf. ibid., 328a13–18.
3. Ibid., 327b23–27, trans. H. H. Joachim, in the Oxford translation of Aristotle: ἐπεὶ δ' ἐστὶ μὲν δυνάμει τὰ δ' ἐνεργείᾳ τῶν ὄντων, ἐνδέχεται τὰ μιχθέντα εἶναί πως καὶ

The Problem of the Physical Existent   111

This solution came into dominant acceptance, especially during the period from the tenth to the fifteenth centuries after the Persian medical man Avicenna had brought the whole theory of chemical mixture into prominence again. But Aristotle's doctrine involves a serious difficulty. This became clear with the criticism by Averroës of Avicenna's interpretation, and this set going a protracted controversy, to which the contributions of Albertus Magnus and Thomas Aquinas were of special importance.

The difficulty consisted in the problem of how precisely to conceive the "potential-being" of the constituents in a chemical combination. What exactly does "potential existence" mean here? How is the notion to be understood? Avicenna held it to mean that the substantial forms of the constituents remain undisturbed, with only the attributes changing. Averroës rejected this on the ground that if the substantial forms remain unchanged this means that the entities in question are *actually* existing, and so in that case there could be no genuine combination or mixing. We need not pursue the controversy here. It suffices for our purposes to indicate the crux of the difficulty and the way in which it was tackled. A satisfactory solution to the problem of "potential existence" was not found; this holds also for the doctrine of Aquinas according to which the substantial forms remain not *actu* but *virtute*, for "virtual existence" stands in as much need of elucidation as does "potential existence."

This whole issue as to "potential being" was radically affected by the new theory of the elements developed in the sixteenth and seventeenth centuries; on that basis it could be dismissed as irrelevant. For if the elements be changeless in themselves, it follows that they must remain and cannot be either altered or destroyed. This therefore implies, as Basso in particular insisted, that in chemical combination there could be no μίξις at all as Aristotle had maintained it; the compound could only be constituted by the aggregate juxtaposition of the constituent elements—i.e., it could only be the Aristotelian σύνθεσις. The "mixture" therefore could be a *mistio ad sensum* only.

The new theory of the elements as changeless matter was thus the basis upon which the Aristotelian theory of chemical combination was rejected. It was also the basis for the rejection of the Aristotelian theory of substance. The consequences were momentous. In the first place, as already shown, it implied that a body could not be a substance, that a body is an aggregation (an Aristotelian σύνθεσις) of

---

μὴ εἶναι, ἐνεργείᾳ μὲν ἑτέρου ὄντος τοῦ γεγονότος ἐξ αὐτῶν, δυνάμει δ' ἔτι ἑκατέρου ἅπερ ἦσταν πρὶν μυχθῆναι, καὶ οὐκ ἀπολωλότα.

constituents, and this meant that only the final atomic constituents of compounds could be regarded as genuine metaphysical substances. Secondly, and this was of the greatest import, since the atomic elements are changeless in their nature, this meant, as Gorlaeus forcefully pointed out, that the Aristotelian conception of substance as involving a transition from potentiality to actuality is ruled out; the atoms are just what they are, fully actual, devoid of any internal process of becoming. Basso saw that consequently the Aristotelian plurality of kinds of change, or κίνησις—qualitative change, change in shape and size, growth—are reduced to one: change of place. In the new philosophy there is only locomotion of changeless atoms. There is no γένεσις, "coming-into-being," other than the formation of groups of atoms, and no φθορά, "passing-away," other than the constituents of the group ceasing to be together, through their locomotion. Galileo discovered the laws of this motion, and on this basis the new science of physics advanced rapidly to its triumph in Newton's *Principia*. Therewith also the new philosophy came into dominant acceptance.

III

It is the metaphysical implications of this new philosophy which especially concern me here. The first point I wish to make is that this philosophy involves taking up a particular position in respect to a fundamental metaphysical issue; that is, it entails a particular answer to a basic metaphysical problem. This is the problem of the nature and identity of the ultimate physical existent or substance. What entity is to be taken to be an ultimate existent? What is a characteristic instance of such an existent?

To these questions Aristotle's reply had been: a human being, animal, or plant, as one integral whole. These are instances of primary physical existents, i.e., natural (φύσει) beings; these are οὐσίαι if anything is.[4]

The new philosophical theory of the modern era completely rejects this Aristotelian answer. Especially to those medical men who were prominent in the new advances of thought, the human or animal body was not a single, homogeneous whole but a compound reducible ultimately to certain elementary constituents. The body, in other words, is an aggregation, what Aristotle had called a σύνθεσις, of certain entities which are its elements, i.e., literally, primary constituents. These are elementary since they are not themselves analyzable into

---

4. Aristotle, *Metaphysics*, 1032a19–21.

The Problem of the Physical Existent   113

constituents; they are the ultimate entities entering into the constitution of all compounds.

Thus, the rejection of Aristotle was based on the scientific advances, beginning with the theory of the elements, which led to considerable scientific success in chemistry and physiology, when bodies were conceived as aggregations of certain elementary constituents. This conception then gained further strength as the basis for the new science of mechanics. For if a body be an aggregation of material atoms, all of the same kind, there can be a ready empirical and mathematical investigation of the laws of motion; since the body used in experiment will be no more than the sum of its constituents, its size, shape, mass, will be irrelevant to its motion, that is, the motion of the whole could not be different from that of its constituents, which means that ultimately the discovered laws of motion will be those of the atomic constituents.

But my primary concern here is the philosophical theory involved in the new science, and more particularly I am interested in the answers given by this philosophical theory to the basic metaphysical problem of the nature and identity of the ultimate physical existent. This answer is that the physical existents are to be identified with the elements, that is, with the simplest, irreducible constituent entities.

It is this answer to the metaphysical problem which in the end came into dominant acceptance in the modern era. But it did not do so without considerable opposition. It was not accepted by Descartes, for example, nor by Spinoza. The ultimate material (identified with the physical) existent for Descartes was one single total *res extensa* which is infinitely divisible into parts through motion. Distinct from the one ultimate physical existent, there are also, he maintained, a plurality of mental existents, and God. For Spinoza there was only one ultimate existent, God or Nature, infinitely pluralized in modes, which are not as such ultimate existents. But the success of the new physical science secured an overwhelming adherence to the basic metaphysical position that the ultimate existents must be identified with the smallest atomic constituents of compounds.

This position was accepted even by Leibniz,[5] the most profound

---

5. Leibniz's theory of monads is here interpreted as the metaphysical doctrine that the monads alone are ultimate existents or *res verae*. A characteristic statement of this doctrine is this passage in a letter to De Volder: "But since only simple things are true beings [*verae res*], and the rest are beings by aggregation and therefore phenomena, existing, as Democritus puts it, by convention and not by nature [νόμῳ not φύσει] . . . ." (ed. Gerhardt, 2:252; trans. Loemker, 531). Cf. also the opening paragraphs of the *Monadology*. In the correspondence with Des Bosses and also in *The Principles of Nature and of Grace*, he introduced the concept of "compound substance," but this, as I show below, involves him in inconsistency with his basic position.

seventeenth-century critic of the new materialistic philosophy, and this metaphysical conception has continued in dominant acceptance down into the present time. It has, significantly, also been adhered to by Whitehead in his attempt to provide a new philosophical basis for the science of the twentieth century. By the end of the nineteenth century this metaphysical position had long since come to acquire the status of a tacit presupposition for all philosophical thought which had retained any intimate contact with science, and it was, I think, largely as such accepted by Whitehead.

IV

This metaphysical conception of the ultimate existent has, however, some most important implications which require more critical scrutiny than they have thus far received.

If the atomic elements be the ultimate existents, then a body, which is a composite of these elementary constituents, is an aggregation, an Aristotelian σύνθεσις of them. Now this implies that, ontologically considered, body is different in kind from the atomic constituents; that is, body is an entity on an ontologically different level from that of the elementary constituents. Only the atomic elements are ultimate, or true, physical existents; a body can thus not be an ultimate existent but is an entity of a derivative kind.

Most of the leading seventeenth-century thinkers saw this, but their recognition of it wavered, especially in regard to its implications, different thinkers varying greatly in their apprehension of these. Of the thinkers accepting this metaphysical conception of the ultimate existent, it was Leibniz who comprehended its implications most clearly and explicitly and who most fully accepted its consequences.

Thus, Leibniz perceived what Newton and the majority did not, that in view of the difference in ontological status between body and its constituents, it is fallacious to ascribe to the ultimate existents as their basic character attributes which pertain manifestly, and properly, to body. This fallacy was being committed by all thinkers who maintained the theory of materialistic atomism, for the primary characteristics of matter—e.g., extension, solidity—are precisely the observed characteristics of body. But since body is an aggregate, these observed characters are the characters of an aggregate and accordingly cannot be the characters of an atom, which by definition is not an aggregate. So an atom cannot be a corpuscle, i.e., small body.[6]

6. The third of Newton's "Rules of Reasoning" in his preface to book 3 of his *Phi-*

The physics of the twentieth century has come to abandon the conception of *materialistic* atomism—not, of course, on philosophical grounds—so there ought now to be less resistance to the philosophical recognition of a difference in ontological status between body and its constituents. For the importance of this distinction extends much beyond the question, fundamental as it is, of whether the atomic constituents are to be conceived as material, that is, as small bodies, corpuscles. In present-day thought the ultimate entities are predominantly conceived as units of energy, but this does not alter the position that there is an ontological difference between them and the bodies which they constitute.

This ontological difference was clear to Basso when he maintained that the conception of changeless atomic elements implies that in chemical combination there is no Aristotelian $\mu\acute{\iota}\xi\iota\varsigma$ but only an aggregation of the constituents, so that the "mixture" is but apparent, a *mistio ad sensum* only. The compound *appears* to be one homogeneous whole, but in fact it is an aggregate of disparate entities. It *appears* to be one single continuous thing, but in fact it is discontinuous, a collection of many discrete things. Which of the characteristics of macroscopic bodies can escape this attribution of the merely apparent? Certainly none of the qualitative ones, as was becoming widely recognized at the time. A strong attempt was made by Gassendi and Huygens to exempt solidity, but Descartes, Newton, and Leibniz all insisted on the sensory basis of this concept.

It was Leibniz who finally clearly saw that if all these features, and especially that of the continuous extension of a body, be but apparent, then body as such is an appearance, a phenomenon, and not a *Ding an sich*, a conclusion which later Kant also came to accept. This conception of body as phenomenal is the final, and inevitable, implication of the philosophical theory which emerged in the early seventeenth century from the sixteenth-century struggles with the theory of the elements and that of chemical combination.

V

This implication of the philosophical theory which identifies the physical existent with the ultimate constituents of compounds needs to be inquired into in much further detail. It will be especially valuable to examine the significance of this implication's being basically the

---

losophiae Naturalis Principia Mathematica is a classic instance of this fallacy; he clearly stated the reasoning typically and most widely accepted, then and subsequently.

same for metaphysical positions as divergent as the spiritual monadism of Leibniz, on the one hand, and the materialistic atomism of Basso, Gassendi, Newton, and the subsequent scientific tradition, on the other. The one feature common to these doctrines, it is to be observed, is that only the ultimate irreducible constituents of compounds can be true physical existents; no compound can be a substance, which means that all compounds are entities having the ontological status of derivatives.

The theory of materialistic atomism has the ineluctable consequence—as Galileo and Hobbes particularly saw—that the characteristics which a compound, any compound, presents to us in sensory perception must be not only apparent, but wholly subjective to the observer. This is because, since the materialistic atoms are in their own nature changeless, their aggregation cannot result in the coming into being of any characteristics other than the numerical sum of their individual features. Which is to say that a compound can have no character qua compound which is different from that of the constituent individuals. Hence, the characters of compounds as we perceive them, especially with their qualitative features, must be subjective appearances.

Leibniz's position is much more complex than that of materialistic atomism. For Leibniz, the ultimate atomic existents are not in their nature changeless; his monads are units of activity, each undergoing an internal process of transition in perception and from one perception to another. But to maintain his fundamental metaphysical position that "only simple things are true beings [*verae res*]," he had to prevent this internal change from being of a kind which would permit of a number of monads combining to constitute a compound substance with a character of its own. This was secured by his doctrine that the internal process of change or transition is confined strictly and exclusively to the subjectivity of each monad. Thereby all compounds are necessarily "beings by aggregation" and thus incapable of having an independent character of their own; their character could accordingly not be other than phenomenal.

But there is an important difference between Leibniz and materialistic atomism with regard to this outcome that the character of an aggregate must be apparent, phenomenal. For Leibniz, it is an appearance, not exclusively to external observers as it is for materialistic atomism, but to the constituent monads themselves.

Now, this involves a weighty consequence for the problem of the nature and status of body. On the basis of materialistic atomism body can have the status only of a subjective appearance entertained by an outside observer, the reality corresponding to that appearance being an aggregation which is merely a disjunctive multiplicity of atoms. But for Leibniz the body can be something more. By virtue of the preestablished harmony, the aggregation of monads into a particular compound or group is not something which is purely accidental to the monads; the essential nature of each has necessarily to be affected, through its perceptions, by that particular compresence. This means that each member of the compound or body perceives the whole as in a particular perspectival relationship to itself; this perception is therefore how the whole appears to it. Accordingly, Leibniz could justifiably claim that the appearance is a *phenomenon bene fundatum*, and further that this makes it a very different thing from the merely subjective appearance of the materialistic theory. For when a group of monads constitutes a body, by virtue of their perceptual relationship there is something more than a merely numerical aggregate.

It was this "something more" which justified Leibniz, in view of the issues he was driven to face in his correspondence with Bartholemeus Des Bosses, in resuscitating the late Scholastic theory of a *vinculum substantiale* and also in speaking there of a "compound substance." But the notion of a substantial chain inevitably presents a grave difficulty to Leibniz. Since the constituent monads alone are real existents, what could be the ontological status of the *vinculum*? It cannot itself be a real existent distinct from the monads; in the end it must be admitted that it is not able to be anything other than an item within each of the monads severally. Closely linked with this theory of a *vinculum* is Leibniz's endeavor to maintain a conception of a "compound substance," of which organic bodies are mentioned as instances. This conception would imply that there is a character, or substantial form, of the compound substance which is something more than and not reducible to the constituent simple substances. But again, on his fundamental metaphysical basis this is not possible, as toward the end of the Des Bosses correspondence he had to concede; the character of the compound can exist only as a feature within each monad. It, and any relationship linking the monads, such as a *vinculum*, can in the end only be phenomenal.

The fundamental point I wish to bring out is that, although in one respect a body or compound is for Leibniz something more than the bare aggregate which it is for the theory of materialistic atomism, since for him this "something more" must be phenomenal, the reality corresponding to that appearance cannot be other than an aggregate. That is to say, in Leibniz's theory a body or compound cannot have a character of its own, qua body, since a body, not being an *ens reale*, cannot sustain a character. Nor is there a unity of a body or compound qua compound (such as a *vinculum substantiale* might be supposed to furnish); the "unity" of the compound can for Leibniz be no more than an experiential feature within the constituent monads severally.

VI

Now, it has been maintained that since this outcome for Leibniz is manifestly the consequence of the "windowlessness" of his monads, the rejection of the latter doctrine will secure the denial of the phenomenality of relations. With the reality of relations admitted, body can accordingly definitely be something more than the aggregate which in the end it has to be for Leibniz.

Let us turn to a leading twentieth-century proponent of this view, namely, Whitehead. An examination of Whitehead's doctrine will be of particular significance to our inquiry because here we have a philosophical conception which, it can be maintained, has a valid theory of real relations, and therewith has not only laid the specter of phenomenalism but has also been able to overcome the Leibnizian difficulties about the nature and status of body. Whitehead has secured the reality of relations by having them constitutive of the actual entities themselves, through their fundamental act of prehension which, in complete contrast to the exclusive subjectivity of the perceptual acts of the Leibnizian monads, is conceived as a real connection with entities transcending the individual prehenders.

With this doctrine, it is to be noted, Whitehead, like Leibniz, completely repudiates the conception basic to materialistic atomism that the ultimate existents are changeless in their nature. Like Leibniz, he reverts to the Aristotelian doctrine that the being of the ultimate existents is their activity.[7] But Whitehead, with Leibniz, agrees with the doctrine of materialistic atomism, against Aristotle, that the ultimate existents are to be identified with the primary and irreducible constituents of compounds. Whitehead's actual entities are, as he explicitly says, "the final real things of which the world is made up."[8] They are simple in the sense in which Leibniz's monads are simple, namely, that they are not themselves compounds but are the final real constituents of all compounds.

---

7. Leibniz was well aware that this was a return to Aristotle (cf. his paper on "A New System of the Nature and Communication of Substances," *Journal des Savants*, June 27, 1695), but Whitehead was less so.
8. Whitehead, *PR* (C), 24; (M), 27.

In Whitehead's philosophical theory as he developed it in *Process and Reality* no compound can be an actual entity; only the final simples can be "actual," in the strict sense of acting, of being true agents. This is the true basis of Whitehead's polemic against antecedent philosophy, that it had committed the "fallacy of misplaced concreteness," that is, that it had mistakenly regarded as concrete or actual various entities, such as bodies, which are compounds and thus could not be true actual entities. Indeed, according to Whitehead, even Leibniz had not succeeded in avoiding this fallacy, for his monads, which he conceived as enduring entities, are strictly compound, since they are, in respect to their duration, analyzable into a supersession of epochal existences—as Leibniz himself was aware when he agreed with Descartes about the perpetual re-creation of the world by God.[9] Whitehead, in his own conception of the nature of the ultimate existents, went to an extreme atomism, spatially and temporally; his minute actual entities exist but briefly, coming into being and perishing in continuous supersession.

Bodies, along with all compounds, are for Whitehead quite explicitly on a different ontological level from *actual* entities. Bodies, and all compounds, are "societies" of actual entities. A "society" is a derivative entity constituted by a plurality of actual entities which are in a genetic interrelatedness, by virtue of which they have some particular feature or form in common, this common form being the "defining characteristic" of the relevant society.[10] In this theory the determinative factor constitutive of a society is the common form which the actual entities share and which they each derive by their prehensive relatedness to each other.

By virtue of this real relatedness Whitehead maintains that he can have what Leibniz strictly could not, namely, a compound or body with a character of its own, qua that compound. For with that relatedness a Whiteheadian society is more than a mere aggregate. In an aggregate the character common to the members can signify nothing more than a mere class characteristic; in Whitehead's theory, however, "a society is more than a set of entities to which the same class-name applies."[11] This is because the character in question is the character of an interrelationship.

9. Cf., e.g., *Monadology*, 47 (Gerhardt, 6:614), and Leibniz's letter of Oct. 11, 1705, to De Volder (Gerhardt, 2:278–79). On this point see Werner Gent, *Die Philosophie des Raumes und der Zeit*, 2nd ed. (Hildesheim: Georg Olms, 1962), 189–95, and the essay by Milič Čapek, "Leibniz on Matter Memory" in *The Philosophy of Leibniz and the Modern World*, ed. Ivor Leclerc (Nashville: Vanderbilt University Press, 1973), 78–113.
10. Whitehead, *PR*, pt. 1, chap. 3, sect. 2.
11. *PR* (C), 124; (M), 137.

But there is a problem here. It comes to light when we explicitly inquire about the ontological status of a society. What sort of being is the being of a society? The problem is that a society is claimed to be an entity having a character of its own, without its being an actual entity, and in Whitehead's philosophy only an actual entity is able to sustain a character—this is explicit in his "ontological principle."[12] As he has said, "by the ontological principle whatever things there are in any sense of 'existence,' are derived by abstraction from actual occasions."[13] A society is thus explicitly an existent derivative from the component actual entities, and therefore the character of the society exists strictly only as a feature of the individual entities. That is, it is not the society as such but the constituent actual entities which sustain the social character in question.

The difficulty I am seeking to bring out is that Whitehead wants a society to be more than an aggregate—to which only a class name can apply. Accordingly, he maintains: "The point of a 'society,' as the term is here used, is that it is self-sustaining; in other words, that it is its own reason."[14] But when he explicitly pays attention to the issue of ontological status, he states: "This ontological principle means that actual entities are the only *reasons*; so that to search for a *reason* is to search for one or more actual entities."[15] This means that a society cannot be its own "reason"; for the "reason" of a society we have to go to its constituent actual entities. Accordingly, this implies that the society is not "self-sustaining" except in a derivative sense; it is the constituent actual entities which individually "sustain" the defining character of the society.

VII

Now, the outcome of this investigation is that in one most important respect Whitehead's position is not different from that of Leibniz. For both of them the character of a body or society, whereby it is body or society, exists strictly as a feature within each of the component monads or actual entities.

The implication accepted by Leibniz, as we have seen, is that there is not one single, unitary substance which is body; body is but an aggregate—an "aggregate" because the members do not constitute one unitary entity, the "unity" being but a feature within each member

12. *PR* (C), 33; (M), 37.
13. *PR* (C), 101; (M), 113.
14. *PR* (C), 124; (M), 137.
15. *PR* (C), 33; (M), 37.

monad individually. For Leibniz this meant that the "unity" was phenomenal.

We must now examine whether Whitehead's position is any different from this. For Whitehead a society is not a unitary entity of the kind which is a substance or actual entity; it is "unitary" only in a derivative sense, namely, that its unity is an experiential feature within each constituent actual entity. The situation is not different from that of a number of human beings uniting by common interest to form, say, a philosophical society; the defining characteristic of this society is the particular philosophical interest which the members have in common, i.e., which defines their prehensive relationships with each other. The relevant point is that the society strictly exists as a feature within each individual member, that feature being his philosophical interest—that is, the society does not exist as "independently real." This accords strictly with Whitehead, for whom only an actual entity and not a society is a *res vera*. In other words, a society is not a "real being"—in the strict meaning of *real* in its derivation from the medieval usage of *realis*, "belonging to the thing itself"; the "being" of the society does not "belong to itself" but is derivative from the being of its constituent actual entities, in that it exists as a feature within each of the constituent actual entities.

In this respect therefore Whitehead's position is not different from that of Leibniz. Does this mean that Whitehead is committed, as is Leibniz, to a phenomenalism? It is clear, I think, that this is not so, since it can validly be accepted that relations for Whitehead, in contrast to Leibniz, are not mere *entia mentalia* but are "real." However, the relations are "real," not in themselves—for they are not as such actual entities or substances—but by reference to the actual entities of which they are features. It is to be noted that the relations are not "real" by reference to the *societies* which are constituted by those relations.

This last point is of particular significance, for it makes clear that though Whitehead avoids Leibniz's phenomenalism, nevertheless for him society or body must be an aggregate in the same fundamental sense as it is for Leibniz, namely, that it does not constitute a real unitary entity, the "unity" of the society being a feature within each of the component actual entities individually.

What emerges from this is that the true basic difficulty in Leibniz's philosophy is not, as has usually been supposed, his phenomenalism, but the metaphysical conception as to the ultimate existent which he shares with materialistic atomism. And it is also this conception that is the basic difficulty in Whitehead's philosophy. The point is that though both Leibniz and Whitehead clearly see the necessity that body or society be something more than an aggregate, on the basis of their metaphysical conception of the ultimate existent they cannot succeed in having it so.

This point becomes clearer if we discuss the issue in the terms which Aristotle introduced for the handling of this problem. For this is indeed fundamentally the same problem which Aristotle and the medieval thinkers grappled with in their concern over the question of the nature of chemical combination. The problem is how a compound can have a character which is not reducible to that of the component individuals. Aristotle had seen clearly that there cannot be such a character if the compound be an aggregate, a σύνθεσις. If a compound does have such a character of its own, then this is an instance of what he called a μίξις. Further, Aristotle saw that two conditions are necessary to secure this. The first is that the compound must itself be an οὐσία, a substance, an actual entity, for only an actual entity, i.e., a real being, is able to sustain a character. The second is that the constituents of the compound must remain in the compound and not disappear or cease to exist.

Now, what both Leibniz and Whitehead sought in wanting "something more" than an aggregate is the condition which Aristotle had in his μίξις, namely, an entity able to sustain a character qua compound. But for them this is impossible, for such an entity would necessarily have to be a substance, and on their metaphysical basis no compound can be a substance.

VIII

The problem we have here is of much more than purely philosophical interest; it is also of considerable importance for science. For right after the inception of the atomistic theory in the early seventeenth century it was found necessary from a scientific point of view to introduce the concept of a "molecule," that is, the concept of an independent group of atoms which stay together and behave as a group and have a particular group structure and character—the concept was earliest arrived at by Basso, somewhat later by Lubin, Sennert, and Magnenus, the term *molecule* having been introduced for this concept by Gassendi. The point is that for scientific purposes the conception solely of atoms and their bare aggregation was not sufficient; it was found indispensable to have also the conception of structured groups of atoms, which have a group character and behavior essentially related to the particular structure of the group. The molecular conception came rapidly to be of the highest importance in scientific theory, and has continued so down to the present day.

Now, the significance of this is that scientific theory has been employing the concept of an entity which has features, qua molecule, which are not merely the sum of the characters of the constituent atoms. That is to say, the concept of a molecule entails that the entity have a group character dependent upon a group structure, and that this group structure—and concomitant character—is something over and above, and not reducible to, the individual characters of the constituents. For there is nothing in the individual natures of the atoms whereby a togetherness with others in a particular pattern or structure should result in a particular character of the group—for example, that one particular patterned togetherness should have the character of water, another of salt, and so on. It is important to note that the very concept of a geometrical pattern or structure of the group involves going beyond what is entailed in the characters of the atoms individually—i.e., the geometrical structure of the *group* is not reducible to the individual extendedness of the atoms.

Not only has scientific theory indispensably employed the concept of the molecule, but in twentieth-century physics what had formerly been supposed to be an atom (i.e., an indivisible entity) has been discovered to be composite, and a range of different "atoms" is distinguished by the divergent patterned structural relations of their constituents. In biology and biochemistry the "cell" is an analogous entity which is a complex structured whole, having a character and behavior as a cell directly related to the structure of the whole. That is to say, science employs concepts of compound entities which have characters and behavior qua those compounds and which are not reducible to those of their constituents. If they were so reducible, concepts such as the modern "atom," molecule, the chemical "organic compound," the biological cell and organ, could play no more significant a role in scientific theory than as convenient collective terms, which is manifestly not the case.

The special philosophical import of this irreducibility of the characters of the molecule and the modern compound atom to those of their constituents is that in these we have a case of a group which *sustains its character qua that group*. Now, this is obviously inconsistent with the fundamental metaphysical conception according to which only the constituents, as the sole substances, are able to sustain character. It is manifest that an analogous inconsistency is implied, too, in the cell theory, and indeed in the entire theory of the "organic," the concept of which entails that the whole is determinative of the functioning of the parts.

Although it is now evident that on the theory of materialistic atomism concepts such as molecules, cells, and so forth are without any philosophical basis at all, we must inquire whether this is the case too for theories such as those of Leibniz and Whitehead, which have indeed explicitly endeavored to provide such a philosophical foundation. It must be acknowledged that both these theories, and Whitehead's especially, go a long way toward furnishing the requisite basis. The question is whether they go far enough, whether in the end they are adequate.

Both these theories account for compound entities (such as molecules, cells) as having an independence and a structure as a group, by their conception that the behavior of each constituent is determined by reference to the rest of the group. Thereby the constituents act in concert, and the fact of the group's having a structure and character qua group is accounted for by this action in concert.

The question is whether this does indeed adequately account for these compound entities. Are compound "atoms," molecules, and cells in fact analogous to human societies, which might be adequately analyzable in terms of the action of each individual being in reference to the other members of the society? In this analysis, be it noted, human societies are not in the proper sense "organic," i.e., they are not organisms, for the concept of an organism entails that the concrete whole determines the character and functioning of the parts. The foregoing analysis provides only that the parts each function by reference to the several others; in this the "whole" is no concrete or real entity in itself, thereby able to determine the parts—the parts, in this conception, determine themselves (Whitehead) or are determined (Leibniz) with reference to the others of the collection.

In *Science and the Modern World*, when Whitehead was explicitly concerned with the inadequacy of the concept of mechanism—which is the inevitable corollary of the doctrine of materialistic atomism—he saw very clearly the implications of the opposed conception of organism. He wrote: "The concrete enduring entities are organisms, so that the plan of the *whole* influences the very characters of the various subordinate organisms which enter into it. In the case of an animal, the mental states enter into the plan of the total organism and thus modify the plans of the successive subordinate organisms until the ultimate smallest organisms, such as electrons, are reached. Thus an electron within a living body is different from an electron outside it,

The Problem of the Physical Existent 125

by reason of the plan of the body . . . and this plan includes the mental state."[16] That is to say, the compound entities with which science is concerned have in the end to be understood as organic. It is not the case that Whitehead later departed from this insight; but on the metaphysical position adopted in *Process and Reality*, that only the constituent actual entities are *res verae*, this full and proper organic conception was no longer strictly possible. For on this position the "enduring entities" cannot be "concrete," i.e., actual, but are societies, so there is not a concrete or actual whole to "influence the characters of the various subordinate organisms which enter into it." There is no "plan of the body including the mental state" which is over and above the "plan" and the "mental state" which are features within each individual constituent.

My conclusion is therefore that in the end Whitehead's theory is not able adequately to account for the organic and to provide a basis for the conception of compounds which have a unity and sustain a character qua compound. The only way, philosophically, for compounds to have a unity and a character of their own qua those compounds is for compounds to be admitted to the status of actual entities or real beings. And this entails the abandonment of the fundamental metaphysical theory which was adopted in the seventeenth century and which since then has come to be accepted as a tacit presupposition, that the real or actual entities, the ultimate physical existents, must be conceived as restricted to the final constituents of compounds.

IX

We are thus faced with the necessity of finding an alternative metaphysical theory of the nature of the ultimate existent. The first step toward this must be the recognition of the untenability of the conception which was the basis in the seventeenth century for the metaphysical theory as to the ultimate existents, which we have seen must be rejected. This basic conception was that the ultimate existents are in their nature changeless. We have noted that Leibniz rejected this doctrine on philosophical grounds. It must be acknowledged, I think, that the conception of changeless substance has been essentially abandoned by twentieth-century physics, in which the concepts of energy and fields have replaced the notion of inertial matter, which means that thought is now in terms of active entities in interrelationship and not of changeless entities which merely move from one location to an-

---

16. Whitehead, *SMW* (C), 89–99; (M), 116; italics in original.

other. Moreover, in recent physics it is maintained on definite empirical evidence that there occurs a transmutation of the so-called elementary particles into each other. This, if anything, constitutes a complete controversion of the seventeenth-century concept of changeless entities—a concept which had been explicitly developed in rejection of the Aristotelian theory of the elements as changing into each other.

However, presuppositions are not easily got rid of, and this one continues in a significant respect, namely, that scientists continue to suppose that there is no change in the nature or mode of existence of entities when coming to be constituents of a compound. Thus, an electron is not thought to be different outside an atom from what it is as part of the atomic complex; there is no difference between a free atom and that atom when it becomes part of a molecular structure; a molecule remains the same whether it is a constituent of a cell or not; and so on. Whitehead scandalized scientists when, in *Science and the Modern World*, he proclaimed a difference.[17] This difference is indeed of the greatest relevance to the present enquiry.

The particular respect in which it is relevant becomes clear when we examine the implications of the rejection of the conception of changeless existence. When the seventeenth-century thinkers put forward the theory of substance as in itself changeless, they saw, as we have noted, that this entailed that substance is as such fully actual, and accordingly that the Aristotelian distinction between potentiality (δύναμις) and actuality (ἐνέργεια) had to be dismissed as invalid. But if this doctrine of changeless actuality be rejected, the validity of the Aristotelian potentiality-actuality distinction must once again be recognized. Indeed, contemporary scientists could not make statements such as the following by Heisenberg unless that distinction were valid: "All the elementary particles can, at sufficiently high energies, be transmuted into other particles, or they can simply be created from kinetic energy and can be annihilated into energy, for instance to radiation."[18] For antecedent to such a transmutation that transmutation must have been a potentiality, which then subsequently was actualized. Some physicists like Heisenberg have attained an appreciable realization that recent physics has significantly brought back the concept of potentiality after its long banishment since the seventeenth century; the following is one of Heisenberg's explicit statements of this: "One perceives from this that in modern physics the concept of potentiality,

---

17. As, for example, in the passage quoted above.
18. Werner Heisenberg, *Physics and Philosophy* (New York: Harper & Row, 1958), 160.

which had played such a decisive role in the philosophy of Aristotle, has again been forced into a central position. One can interpret the mathematical laws of quantum theory as a quantitative formulation of this Aristotelian concept of 'dynamis' or 'potentia'."[19]

The special point I wish to make here is that in the case of compounds of the kind of the modern "atom," of molecules, cells, and the like, which must be regarded as having a unity qua compound, the distinction between actuality and potentiality is fundamental to the analysis of the relations of the constituents to the compound they constitute.

If the constituents be themselves completely independent actuals, then there can be no question but that the compound must necessarily be a mere aggregate and can have no unity qua compound. If, on the other hand, the compound does have a unity qua compound, then by virtue of this unity the compound as such must be an actuality—for only an actuality can be a unity. In that case the constituents must necessarily stand in the relation of potentialities to a supervening actuality. Alternatively stated, my argument is that the constituents individually do not actualize the unity of the compound—as in the case of Leibniz's monads—but that the actualization of the unity must necessarily transcend them, so that from the standpoint of the actual unity the constituents are potential.

The problem is how there can be such a unity qua compound. Essential to this unity, distinguishing it from the kind of unity of an aggregate, is that it is an integral unity, i.e., the unity of a whole. This means that the unity of the compound is a unity effected by an integration of the constituents. That is, there can be a unity of a compound only by the unifying of the constituents, by their integration into a new whole. Now this unifying is an act, and this implies an agent acting, i.e., an agent effecting this unity. This unifying agent cannot be itself one of the constituents unified, for it could not then be a constituent. If there is to be an integral unity qua compound, the unifying agent must transcend the constituents. This implies that the actuality of the unifying agent must itself be emergent in the unifying. This is hardly a novel theory; Aristotle had maintained as much in holding that actuality is the outcome of a transition from potentiality.

But if an emergent actuality be granted, there is the problem of how the integrating agency is to be understood. For it cannot be antecedent to the integration. Where then is it to come from? My proposal

---

19. Werner Heisenberg, *Zwei Vorträge* (Bad Godesberg: Alexander von Humboldt Stiftung, 1967), 30 (my translation). Cf. also his *Physics and Philosophy*, esp. chaps. 3 and 10.

is that it arises from the agency of the constituents, by each of the constituents contributing its agency to constitute an integral combined agency. That is, the agency of each is taken up into, as constitutive of, an integrated agency. Each is thereby part of a new whole which, as an integrated agency, is more than the mere sum of the parts.

Antecedently to the integrative relationship the constituents must each be independently actual, which implies that each is a substantive agent. But when they are in the integrative relationship, the potency of each constituent is not directed to itself as actual, but instead is directed to a supervening actuality. This means that as in that relationship the constituents are not independent actuals but are severally potentials for an actuality transcending them individually. Thus the "potentiality" of the constituents means: (1) that their potency and thus activity is directed not to their own being and actuality but as contributions to the being and actuality of a supervening agent; (2) that as so contributing they cease to be independently actual; (3) that but for that integration of which they are part they would be independently actual; and (4) that they are capable of such independent actuality should that participative relationship cease.

This theory is thus in full accord with Aristotle in his statement, quoted above, that "the compound may *be-actually* other than its constituents from which it has resulted," and that "nevertheless each of them may still *be-potentially* what it was before they were combined." It is essential to make clear that the "potential existence" of the constituents does not mean that as potential they cease entirely to be actual, for then there would be no compound. What is requisite is that we must recognize, with Aristotle, that an entity must be actual in order to be potential. To be "actual" implies to be "in-act," and here this means contributing its agency to the constitution of a supervening integral agent. Thus, with reference to itself as an agent the constituent is "actual," i.e., in-act as an agent, but its agency or acting is "potential" with reference to the supervening agent toward which it is contributing.

Now, every act necessarily has a character or form whereby it is determinately that act and not another. This form or character is thus the form of that agent. So the individual contributory agents have each their individual characters, and there is the character of the compound agent. For example, there are the individual electronic, protonic, neutronic, and other characters of the constituents of the modern compound "atom," and there is the integral atomic character or form of the atomic whole. This character of the compound "atom" is thus a true integral character of the compound actuality, and is thus something quite different from the kind of character ascribable to a mere aggregate. Further, this character of the compound exists not as a feature within each of its constituents in the way in which the "defining characteristic" of a Whiteheadian society or the explicitly phenomenal character of body in the Leibnizian theory does, but as belonging to the compound as such by virtue of its status as a fully actual or real being.

It is evident that there is no reason to restrict the conception of compound actual or real beings to compounds of the first order. There can be compound real beings whose constituents are other compound beings, to considerable complexity. When seen in these terms, this is, I suggest, precisely what the scientific evidence presents us, in the so-called modern "atoms," in molecules, and especially in the complex molecules of biochemistry, in cells, and in biological organisms. Only on such a theory of compound actual or real beings is the concept of organism properly intelligible. And this theory, I suggest, is also able to give a more adequate and coherent conception of the human person than is possible in terms of the current presupposition of actual beings as restricted to ultimate simples.

10

THE PHYSICAL EXISTENT AS A COMPOUND ACTUALITY

I

The scientific developments which in the sixteenth century had begun to force an abandonment of the Aristotelian philosophy of nature and thereby necessitated a new concept of the physical existent, in the seventeenth century brought the atomistic theory into the ascendent. Fundamentally involved in this theory is that the atoms are the ultimate physical existents, and that they alone are. In other words, only the atoms are in the proper sense substances. Contrary to Aristotle, bodies are not substances but compounds, mere aggregates, and thus ontologically have the status of derivatives. This was the case whether the atoms were conceived as material stuff or, with Leibniz, as analogous to minds or souls. This modern theory therefore identifies the physical existents or substances with the *constituents* of compounds, the corollary being that no compound can be a substance.

This metaphysical conception has ruled as a tacit presupposition in science down to the present day, and has also done so in philosophical thought which has been in close contact with science. A notable example of the latter in this century is the philosophy of A. N. Whitehead. In his doctrine the ultimate existents or actual entities are simples of this kind, i.e., themselves not compounds but the final constituents of compounds; in his theory all compounds are "societies" of actual entities.

The fundamental consequence of this metaphysical conception of the ultimate existents is that compounds or bodies, since they are mere aggregates, cannot have any features qua aggregate which are not reducible to the characters of the individual constituents. On the theory of the physical existents as material atoms it was clear already in the early seventeenth century that all qualitative features of bodies could accordingly have no other status than that of the apparent. Leibniz, fully accepting the implications of the new metaphysical conception, saw that it entailed that all the characters of body, in terms of which we think of and identify it as "body," must be phenomenal. In general this metaphysical conception that the sole realities or actualities are the individual constituents, each with its own individual character, implies that since only a substance can sustain a character, no aggregate qua aggregate is able to do so. That is, no aggregate can have a character of its own transcending the individual characters of its constituents.

However, right at the inception of the atomistic theory in the early seventeenth century it was found necessary to introduce the concept of a "molecule." That is to say, for scientific purposes the conception solely of atoms and their mere aggregation was not sufficient; it was found indispensible to have also *the conception of structured groups of atoms, which have group character and behavior essentially related to the particular structure of the group.*

The significant point, usually ignored, is that this structure is something over and above, and not reducible to, the individual characters of the constituents; there is nothing in the individual natures of the atoms whereby a togetherness with others in a particular pattern or structure should result in a particular character of the group—for example, that one particular patterned togetherness should have the character of mercury, another of sulphur, and so on. Further, from a philosophical point of view, the molecular theory implies that such a group must *sustain its character qua that group*, since the group character in question is not reducible to the individual characters of the constituents. But this is fundamentally inconsistent with the metaphysical conception according to which only the constituents, as the sole substances, are able to sustain character. An analogous inconsistency is implied too in the cell theory, and in the entire theory of the "organic," the concept of which entails that the whole is determinative of the functioning of the parts.

I have shown earlier that the alternatives to materialistic atomism of the kind produced by Leibniz and Whitehead do not succeed in overcoming the fundamental difficulty of the metaphysical conception that constituents of compounds are the sole physical existents or substances.[1] This difficulty is that on the basis of this conception it is impossible for a group, qua group, to sustain a character. All which is possible is that the substantial constituents act in concert—through a harmony preestablished by God in Leibniz's theory, and in Whitehead's through a prehensive interrelatedness determined by a subjec-

---

1. See chap. 9, above.

tive aim, also derivative from God. But this concerted action is individual action, and it is each constituent alone which individually sustains a character. In that respect in which the characters of the constituents are the same or similar, this can be spoken of as the group or "social" character. It is manifest, however, and in Whitehead's theory quite explicit, that the group or society can be said to have this character only in a derivative sense, for to speak of the group or society is merely to speak of the *individuals*, collectively. To put this fundamental point which I am urging in another way, the group or society remains a plurality and has no *unity* qua group; the "unity" of the group, in Whitehead's doctrine as in Leibniz's, is solely an experiential feature within each component.

I wish to submit that from a philosophical point of view it is the outcome of the science of the modern period that both the traditionally accepted metaphysical conceptions of the physical existent, viz., the Aristotelian conception (as it was commonly understood) and that which superseded it in the seventeenth century, are inadequate. In the Aristotelian theory the physical existent is a single, unitary, homogeneous entity, with its individual, and homogeneous, substantial form. Thus, for example, according to this theory a human being or animal is such a single, homogeneous substance. It was this conception, more particularly of bodies as single homogeneous substances, which the sixteenth-century and early seventeenth-century scientists, especially medical men, rejected, proclaiming human and animal bodies to be aggregate compounds of more elementary constituents.

Now, in some most important respects the new view has been amply confirmed by all subsequent empirical science, down to and including the twentieth-century discovery of a large number of subatomic entities. Modern science has demonstrated that we have indispensably to think in terms of compounds and their constituents. But this does not imply, I am maintaining, that the constituents are to be identified as the ultimate physical existents or substances, with compounds purely derivative entities. In the present time we stand in urgent need of a new theory of the physical existent.

II

As a first step toward such a new theory, it is requisite to be clear about the metaphysical grounds upon which the modern theory, which identified the physical existent with the primary constituents of compounds, was adopted. Inquiry into this reveals that these grounds do not constitute a fundamental divergence from Aristotle except on one point. Thus, for example, it is Aristotle's explicit doctrine that "no substance is composed of substances,"[2] and the basis of this is the conception that a substance must necessarily be a single, unitary entity, with a single, unitary essence or nature. Now, if for valid reasons it can be maintained that, for example, a human or animal body is not a single entity but an aggregation of many entities, then the conclusion is evident that such a body cannot be a substance. So where the seventeenth-century thinkers diverged from Aristotle was not in respect of the fundamental concept of substance as a unitary entity, but only as regards what is to be identified as being instances of such unitary entities.

Next, we must look at the conception they have in common, namely, that of substance as necessarily a single, unitary entity. This conception is grounded in the great line of Greek ontological inquiry, initiating in Parmenides' struggles with the implications of ἔστιν, "it is," which led him to the insight that "it is one," through Plato's critical examination of the relations of being and unity in the second part of his *Parmenides* and in the *Sophistes*, to Aristotle's masterly analysis of the being of unity in chapter 2 of book 10 of his *Metaphysics*. The outcome, enunciated by Aristotle, and reaffirmed by subsequent ontological thought, through the Scholastics and down to the present day, was the conception that what is, οὐσία, substance, *ens reale*, monad, primary existent, actual entity, call it what you will, is necessarily a single, unitary entity.

Where thinkers have disagreed is concerning how precisely the "unity" of that entity is to be understood. And it was this which was basically at issue in the seventeenth-century divergence from Aristotle. The modern thinkers rejected the Aristotelian doctrine that body is a substance, for the reason that body is an aggregate and an aggregate cannot be a substance since it can have no unity other than the phenomenal. Now, the ground for the conception of body as an aggregate was the theory of substance developed in the late sixteenth and the early seventeenth century, according to which substance is in itself changeless, devoid of any internal process of becoming—in opposition to the Aristotelian theory in which substance was necessarily in process from potentiality to actuality. This constitutes the fundamental divergence from Aristotle. In this new theory the unity of substance consisted in the sheer homogeneousness of quantitative stuff.

This seventeenth-century theory had a most important corollary,

---

2. Aristotle, *Metaphysics*, Z, 1041a5 (Ross translation): οὔτ' ἐστὶν οὐσία οὐδεμὶ ἐξ οὐσιῶν.

namely, that every compound is necessarily an aggregate and thus unable to be a substance. This corollary had been explicitly developed in the early seventeenth century by thinkers such as Sebastian Basso, in controversion of the Aristotelian theory of chemical combination. For according to Aristotle we have in chemical combination ($μίξις$) an instance of a compound which is not constituted by a mere aggregate juxtaposition ($σύνθεσις$) of entities and which therefore has a substantial unity.[3] Aristotle affirmed that in a mere aggregation ($σύνθεσις$)—as in a compound of mixed grains of wheat and barley—the constituents remain fully actual and unaltered by their juxtaposition, but maintained that in a $μίξις$ there is involved some change in the constituents whereby they constitute a new whole. But this change is not a change into a new substance involving that the constituents entirely cease to exist—for if that were to happen there would not result a compound and so this would not be an instance of chemical combination ($μίξις$) but it would be a case of the $γένεσις$, "coming-into-being," of one substance and the $φθορά$, "destruction," of the constituent substances. To the question how the constituents can remain in the $μίξις$ without this being an instance of mere aggregate juxtaposition, Aristotle's theory was that they exist in the $μίξις$ not as themselves actual, $ἐνέργεια$, but as potential, $δύναμις$.[4] The basic reason why the Aristotelian theory was unacceptable to the seventeenth-century thinkers was that it involved entities undergoing a change when becoming constituents of a compound. Since in their theory substance is changeless, all compounds are necessarily aggregates, and accordingly in chemical combination there is *mistio ad sensum* only. Thus, the essential ground and basis for the conception of the constituents as alone real and compounds necessarily aggregates is the theory of substance as wholly devoid of internal change.

III

Now it must be acknowledged, I think, that the conception of changeless substance has been essentially abandoned by twentieth-century physics, in which the concepts of energy and fields have replaced the notion of inert matter, which means that thought is now in terms of active entities in interrelationship and not of changeless entities which merely move from one location to another. Moreover, in recent physics it is maintained on definite empirical evidence that

3. For Aristotle's theory, see *De Gen. et Cor.*, 1.10.
4. Cf. ibid., 327b24–27.

there occurs a transmutation of the so-called "elementary particles" into each other. This, if anything, constitutes a complete controversion of the seventeenth-century concept of changeless primary entities—a concept which had been explicitly developed in rejection of the Aristotelian theory of the elements as changing into each other.

Despite this fundamental twentieth-century divergence from the thought of the immediate past, the presupposition inherited from the seventeenth century nevertheless persists that there is no change in the nature or mode of existence of entities when coming into a compound. An electron is not different outside an atom from what it is as part of the atomic complex; there is no difference between a free atom and that atom when it becomes part of a molecular structure; a molecule remains the same whether it is a constituent of a cell or not; and so on.

Now, when the seventeenth-century thinkers put forward their theory of changeless substance, they were clear this entailed that substance as such is fully actual, and therefore that the Aristotelian distinction between potentiality and actuality had to be dismissed as invalid. But if we do not maintain the conception of changeless actuality—and we have seen that contemporary physics lends scant support to such a conception—then, I submit, Aristotle's potentiality-actuality distinction retains a fundamental validity. For example, this distinction is implied in characteristic statements by contemporary physicists, such as this by Heisenberg: "All the elementary particles can, at sufficiently high energies, be transmuted into other particles, or they can simply be created from kinetic energy and can be annihilated into energy, for instance into radiation."[5] For antecedently to such a transmutation that transmutation must have been a potentiality, which then subsequently was actualized.

This is an instance of what I would maintain generally, namely, that recent physics has significantly brought back the concept of potentiality after its long banishment since the seventeenth century. Among physicists, Heisenberg in particular has had a realization of this: "One perceives from this that in modern physics the concept of potentiality, which had played such a decisive role in the philosophy of Aristotle, has again been forced into a central position. One can interpret the mathematical laws of quantum theory as a quantitative formulation of this Aristotelian concept of 'dynamis' or 'potentiality'."[6]

---

5. Werner Heisenberg, *Physics and Philosophy* (New York: Harper & Row, 1958), 160.
6. Werner Heisenberg, *Zwei Vorträge* (Bad Godesberg: Alexander von Humboldt Stiftung, 1967), 30 (my translation). Cf. also his *Physics and Philosophy*, esp. chaps. 3 and 10.

My special contention here is that in the case of compounds of the kind of atoms, molecules, cells, etc., which must be regarded as having a unity qua compound, the distinction between actuality and potentiality is fundamental in the analysis of the relations of the constituents to the compound they constitute.

If the constituents be themselves completely independent actuals, then there can be no question but that the compound must necessarily be a mere aggregate and can have no unity qua compound. If, on the other hand, the compound does have a unity qua compound, then by virtue of this unity the compound as such will be an actuality. In that case the constituents must necessarily stand in the relation of potentialities to a supervening actuality. Alternatively stated, my argument is that the constituents individually do not actualize the unity of the compound—as in the case of Leibniz's monads—but that the actualization of the unity must necessarily transcend them, so that from the standpoint of the actual unity the constituents are potential.

IV

The problem is how there can be such a unity qua compound. Essential to this unity, distinguishing it from the kind of unity of an aggregate, is that it is an integral unity, i.e., the unity of a whole. This means that the unity of the compound is a unity effected by an integration of the constituents. That is, there can be a unity of a compound qua compound only by the unifying of the constituents, by their integration into a new whole. Now, unifying is an act, and this implies an agent acting, i.e., an agent effecting this unity. This unifying agent cannot be itself one of the constituents unified, for it could then not be a constituent. If there is to be an integral unity qua compound, the unifying must transcend the constituents. This implies that the actuality of the unifying agent must itself be emergent in the unifying. This is hardly a novel theory; Aristotle had maintained as much in holding that actuality is the outcome of a transition from potentiality.

But even if we grant an emergent actuality, how is the integrating agency to be understood? For it cannot be antecedent to the integration. Where, then, is it to come from? My proposal is that it arises from the agency of the constituents, by each of the constituents contributing its agency to constitute an integral combined agency. That is, the agency of each is taken up into, as constitutive of, an integrated agency. Each is thereby part of a new whole which, as an integrated agency, is more than the mere sum of the parts.

Antecedently to the integrative relationship the constituents must each be independently actual, which implies that each is a substantive agent. But when they are in the integrative relationship, the potency of each constituent is not directed to itself as actual, but instead is directed to a supervening actuality. This means that as in that relationship the constituents are not independent actuals but are severally potentials for an actuality transcending them individually. Thus the "potentiality" of the constituents means: (1) that their potency and thus activity is directed not to their own being and actuality but as contributions to the being and actuality of a supervening agent; (2) that as so contributing they cease to be independently actual; (3) that but for that integration of which they are part they would be independently actual; and (4) that they are capable of such independent actuality should that participative relationship cease.

This theory is thus in full accord with Aristotle when he maintains that "the compound may *be-actually* other than its constituents from which it has resulted," and that "nevertheless each of them may still *be-potentially* what they were before they were combined."[7] It is essential to be clear that the "potential existence" of the constituents does not mean that as potential they cease entirely to be actual, for then there would be no compound. Modern science, I have argued, has made clear the need for having both the constituents as actual and the compound as actual. What is requisite is the recognition, which was clear to Aristotle, that an entity must be actual in order to be potential. To be "actual" implies to be "in-act," and here this means contributing its agency to the constitution of a supervening integral agent. Thus, with reference to itself as an agent, the constituent is "actual," i.e., in act as an agent; but its agency or acting is "potential" with reference to the supervening agent toward which it is contributing.

Now, every act necessarily has a character or form whereby it is determinately that act and not another. This form or character is thus the form of that agent. So the individual contributory agents have each their individual forms, and there is a form or character of the compound agent. For example, there are the individual electronic, protonic, neutronic, etc., forms of the constituents, and there is the integral atomic form of the compound. This form or character of the compound is thus a true integral substantial form of that compound actuality, and is manifestly something quite different from the kind of character ascribable to a mere aggregate.

It is, I submit, only such a conception of compound actuality consti-

---

7. Aristotle, *De Gen. et Cor.*, 325b25–28 (trans. H. H. Joachim).

tuted by other actualities which can make adequately intelligible the notion of the organic, which has become increasingly fundamental in the science of the last hundred years. Not only in cells is this the case; in the entire realm of the biochemical it is evident that there is a structure (i.e., form) of the molecular whole which is determinative of the role and function of the constituents—that is, there pertains a situation quite other than what would follow if the whole were a mere aggregate. And the same is true of the molecules of chemistry in general and of the "atomic" wholes of micro-physics. Moreover, this organic concept also requires that the constituents of the whole be actualities, for otherwise they could not *function* in reference to the whole.

11

THE PROBLEM OF RELATIONS

I

The issue of relations constitutes an ancient and persistent problem in philosophy, one which in certain epochs of thought has come into particular prominence. For example, it did so in the high Scholastic period, and then again in the seventeenth century with the rise of modern science and philosophy. Now in this century it is once more being brought to the fore by the twentieth-century developments in science, though so far the issue has been receiving far less attention than its importance in the present-day context merits. It seems to me that the issue of relations is today of greater significance for thought than it has ever been. It is fundamentally important, I shall argue, for contemporary scientific thought, and also for philosophical thought as a whole.

Let us consider briefly how twentieth-century science brought this issue into prominence and into need of philosophical examination. This came very arrestingly with the development by Einstein of the relativity theory in the first decade of the century. This theory brought space and time into a close and intrinsic relation with each other, in this sharply contrasting with the antecedent conception of space and time in which they were seen as completely independent of each other, which means that they were not conceived as in relation with each other. The Einsteinian theory received empirical verification in 1915, but long before that it had begun to be clear that this theory, together with developments in electromagnetic theory which had occurred in the later nineteenth century, had rendered untenable the scheme of fundamental ideas in terms of which modern physical science had so fruitfully advanced during the two preceding centuries.

We need to be clear about this scheme of fundamental ideas as it was conceived in the nineteenth century before the recent revolutionary advances. Central to the scheme was the conception of the physical as "matter." Matter was conceived as fully actual being, in itself changeless. Above all, this meant that there was no process of acting involved in matter, and thus no process of becoming—every particle of matter was and remained just what it was, unchangingly identical. This conception of the physical as matter had been introduced in the seventeenth century in explicit antithesis to the medieval Aristotelian conception of the physical as essentially in a process of becoming, of growth and development, as thus involving internal change, and as having the source of that change in itself by virtue of its own acting, its own agency. Now the physics of the modern period was not an inquiry into this in-itself-changeless matter per se, but an investigation of the motion of matter from one place to another, the mode of understanding this locomotion of matter being by mathematical calculation. But since matter was wholly inert, i.e., without any acting or agency, it followed that matter was only capable of being moved, not of moving itself. This meant that "motion" was in no respect derivable from "matter," and accordingly "motion" had to be acknowledged as a second, quite distinct, ultimate datum.

Further, since this motion, or more strictly locomotion, is, as the latter word literally means, a translation from one *place* to another, the issue is raised as to the nature and status of "places." "Place" is not a concept derivable from "motion," since clearly "place" is *presupposed by* locomotion or motion from one place to another. Also, the concept of place is not derivable from matter, for matter does not require to be in any place to be matter. Moreover, highly relevant to the concept of place, as Newton insisted, is that for true mathematical calculation of motion to be possible, place also had to be absolute, in itself changeless, because "that the primary places of things should be movable, is absurd."[1] These ultimate, immovable places, Newton had said, "constitute, what I call, immovable space,"[2] and so, following him, "space," i.e., the totality of immovable places, was recognized as a third independent ultimate necessitated by the new physics.

The mathematical investigation of motion also necessitated the concept of "time." But this, too, was not derivable from matter, nor from space or place, and further was presupposed in the concept of locomotion. It had therefore to be acknowledged as a fourth ultimate necessitated by the new physics.

---

1. Newton, *Philosophiae Naturalis Principia Mathematica*, 8.
2. Ibid., 9.

II

These four, matter, motion, space or place, and time, were not only the ultimates at the base of traditional, so-called classical modern physical science, but as such ultimates they were entirely independent of each other, and thus essentially unrelated to each other. It is in respect of this unrelatedness that the twentieth-century developments in physical science have particularly disrupted that scheme. Not only has the Einsteinian theory, as mentioned earlier, brought space and time into intrinsic relation to each other, but the subsequent work of Einstein and others has brought matter and motion into intrinsic relation to space-time. The result is that in contemporary physical theory matter is not to be conceived apart from motion, and equally not from space and time. Moreover, these four are no longer to be conceived as absolute; they are all conceived relatively to each other.

However, the biggest and most fundamental change in the scheme effected by contemporary developments has been in respect of the central concept, that of the physical as "matter." In present-day physics the physical existents are no longer conceived as inert, with no internal change; on the contrary, they are conceived as "active," as centers of "energy," producing effects on other entities. Now, this means that the conception of the physical as matter—as matter had been conceived since the seventeenth century, as Newton expressed it, as "solid, massy, hard, impenetrable, movable Particles"[3] completely without any inherent activity—this conception of the physical has been entirely abandoned. The new conception of the physical entities as essentially active, acting, entails further that these entities are necessarily by their acting in relation with one another. What we have today is a conception of the physical fundamentally different from the conception of the physical as matter, so much so that the appropriateness of the continued use of the term *matter* in present-day science is highly questionable. This continued use of the term has had the effect, I would suggest, of obscuring and hindering the full recognition of the fundamental change which has occurred in the conception of the physical. Most importantly, it has tended to obscure the importance in contemporary physical science of the concept of "relation" and what it entails.

So far I have been speaking about the "physical science"—today more usually called "physics"—which had developed with thinkers

---

3. Newton, *Opticks*, 400.

such as Galileo, Descartes, Huygens, and Newton, as a mechanics. But it had preempted the title "physical science," i.e., science of nature, because that with which it dealt, the subjects of its inquiry, were the atoms of matter, and these, in the general theory, i.e., philosophy, of the physical as matter, were to be regarded as the ultimate physical or natural existents. Physicists, it is true, in their experiments used macroscopic lumps of matter and not individual microscopic atoms, but since all such lumps strictly constituted an arithmetical sum of the constituent atoms, the discovered laws of motion pertained not only to the macroscopic aggregates but equally to each constituent material atom. Further, since these material atoms were the ultimate physical existents, it followed that all sciences such as chemistry and biology, which dealt specifically with larger bodies, were theoretically reducible to physics, because chemical molecules and biological cells could, in the final analysis, be conceived as nothing but aggregates of constituent material atoms. Thus, these sciences were to be regarded as in the end subdivisions of the fundamental science of physics.

That chemists, for example, on the whole accept this doctrine is evidenced by their continuing still to conceive the constituent entities of chemical compounds as aggregates of inert physical matter. But some chemists at least are today coming to see the inadequacy of the traditional materialist theory to the data of their science. For example, D. W. Theobald of Manchester University writes:

> I do not think that substances can be said to be heaps, aggregates, or collections of molecules, nor yet that molecules can be said to be heaps, aggregates, or collections of atoms. I would argue that the formula "H_2O" refers to that class of molecules every member of which is composed of H and O atoms *related in a certain way*, whereas the term "water" refers to that class of substances each member of which has "H_2O" molecules as members *related in a certain way*. So whereas molecules are properly said to be parts of water, and atoms properly parts of molecules, atoms are not properly speaking parts of water. I would be prepared to contend therefore that there are certain levels of organization to be recognized in the study of matter, and that these cannot be short-circuited without talking nonsense.[4]

Two points in this are to be specially noted. The first is the rejection of the conception of chemical entities as mere aggregates of constituent atoms. The second is that chemical substances and molecules are, contrary to the rejected conception of them as aggregates, to be conceived as the constituents "related in a certain way." Thus we see that here in

---

4. D. W. Theobald, "Some Considerations on the Philosophy of Chemistry," *Quarterly Reviews of the Chemical Society of London* (1976): 212 (my italics).

chemistry, too, the concept of "relation" is coming to the fore in a particularly fundamental way.

When we consider the other basic natural science, biology, it becomes clear that here also the concept of "relation" must be admitted as fundamental, for this science investigates living entities which have the characteristic of being "organisms." An organism in the biological sense is a kind of whole in which the parts are "organs," each functioning in relation to the whole. The relation of the parts of an organism to each other and to the organic whole is quite different from the relation of the parts of a mechanism to each other and to the whole mechanism. In the latter, for example in a clock, the parts, the wheels, are in a particular geometrical relationship to each other, this relationship however being in no respect intrinsic to the individual wheels; each would be exactly what it is, a metallic wheel, without that particular relationship to other wheels, whether they be in rotation or not, and indeed it would be just what it is without any relationship at all. That is, the relationships involved are wholly external to the nature of the parts per se. But in an organism there is a wholly other situation with respect to relations. The parts of an organism are intrinsically related to each other. That is, their nature as "organs" essentially involves functioning, each in its particular way, in relation to each other, so that if the functioning of any organ be disrupted, its nature as that organ is affected, and thereby also is every other organ which is dependent upon that functioning. In the extreme case, if a main organ, such as a heart, ceases functioning, the functioning of every other organ ceases, and the organs themselves quickly drastically change their nature (usually referred to as deterioration and disintegration), so that the organic whole ceases to exist.

The main point which I am concerned to bring out here is that the concept of relation is as fundamental to the sciences of chemistry and biology as to physics. That this has taken so long to be recognized is an interesting example of the determining importance in scientific thought of the fundamental underlying conceptions of the nature of the physical, whether this be held explicitly or only as a tacit presupposition.

III

Let us turn now to the explicit consideration of "relation" in general, that is, to a philosophical consideration. How is *relation* to be conceived? What does the term strictly mean? How do we think about relations? It was Aristotle who first made a systematic inquiry into how we think about existing things. When we think about a thing to know it, Aristotle held, we specify determinate or definite characters or features possessed by the thing. That is to say, we attribute, i.e., assign, certain characters or features to the thing. From a logical point of view this means that we predicate, i.e., assert certain characters as attributes of the thing. The word Aristotle used for this "predication," i.e., assertion of attributes, was *kategoria*, a word which in its original sense meant an accusation or charge in an assembly, a law court, for example. Aristotle distinguished several different kinds of attributes or predicates in chapter 4 of his book entitled *Categories*, in the following order: (1) how large, (2) of what kind or sort, (3) with reference to what, (4) where, (5) when, (6) in what position or attitude, (7) in what state, (8) how active, (9) how acted on. The Latin word for the first of these predicates, "how large," is *quantus*, whence our "quantity," and the Latin for the second, viz., "of what kind or sort," is *qualis*, whence our "quality." For the third, "in reference to," Latin used *relatio*, the word literally meaning "a carrying or bringing back." For our purposes it will be sufficient to consider only these three categories. It is worth noting, incidentally, that the commonly accepted meaning of *category* in English today is not "predicate," but a division or mode of grouping according to relevant characteristics, that is, according to "kinds or sorts." Thus, the modern meaning conforms to the second of Aristotle's categories, i.e., of attributes specifying "of what kind or sort." The reason for this we shall see presently.

In the centuries after Aristotle there was much controversy about how the Aristotelian categories are to be understood. It will, however, not be necessary to go into this here. What interests us is the outcome of these deliberations in Neoplatonic philosophy in the third century A.D., for this doctrine very considerably dominated Western thought for a millennium. Aristotle had not ascribed any priority to any particular category, and moreover, in his analysis, the categories, especially those of quantity, quality, and relation, which he most frequently considered, were not reducible to or derivable from each other. Neoplatonism introduced a most important change, grounded in the new metaphysical doctrine of this school. This doctrine was that everything whatever derives from a single, transcendent, divine source—this doctrine standing in contrast to the philosophies of Plato and Aristotle, which held the necessity of three ultimate sources for actual existence. Fundamental in the Neoplatonic doctrine was that "being" is complete and in itself changeless. As Augustine, the most influential of the Church Fathers and through whom this came to be the most widely accepted doctrine in the Christian West, said: "For it is only that which remains in being without change that truly is."[5] Augustine accordingly identified "being" with God. It followed that created being, since it came from God who is perfect, had to be, in the most fundamental respect, complete, perfect in its kind, and changeless in its essence. This meant that every creature has certain attributes inherent in it constituting its essence.

Now this necessitates, in respect of the categories, a divergence from Aristotle, for those attributes constituting the essence of a creature were obviously those in Aristotle's second group, namely, those specifying "of what kind or sort" the creature is. This entailed that this category or predicate, that of "quality," had to be accorded a status superior to that of the other categories, for it specified the very essence of the thing, what it *is*. The other categories had to be regarded as ancillary to the category of quality, some even having the status of "accidents." A further consequence of great importance followed. Since qualities "inhere" in the created thing, and since this thing is complete in its being, the other categories, more especially quantity and relation, must also inhere in the thing. That is, the attributes of quantity and relation must be conceived on the paradigm of the category of quality. Because the category of quality was the primary category and the others were conceived as inhering in the thing almost as quasi-qualities, the term *quality* came to be used as synonymous with *attribute*, and it became common to speak of a thing or substance and its "qualities," which included quantities, etc. John Locke in the seventeenth century, for example, developed a theory of the primary and secondary qualities of matter, maintaining that the "primary and real qualities" of matter or body are "bulk, figure, number,"[6] that is, "quantities."

It would be an error to see this as merely a case of linguistic usage. On the contrary, the Neoplatonic doctrine that the other categories have to be treated on the paradigm of the category of quality is clearly exemplified in seventeenth-century thought, which represented a return to Neoplatonism after a few centuries of Aristotelian-Thomistic dominance. Descartes for example, who accepted the new doctrine of the physical as "matter" and of that matter as purely quantitative, devoid of all qualities, held that the essential attribute of matter is extension alone, and, fully in the Neoplatonic tradition, quite evidently conceived of extension, a quantity, as inhering in matter on the paradigm

---

5. St. Augustine, *Confessions*, bk. 7, chap. 11.
6. John Locke, *Essay Concerning Human Understanding*, 2.8.20.

of an inhering quality, like a color inhering as spread out in a surface. This way of conceiving the category of quantity, as an inhering quality, was not a peculiarity of Descartes; on the contrary, it was quite general in the seventeenth century—as evidenced by Locke, as we have just seen—and has persisted down to the present day.

IV

There was one highly important exception to this in the seventeenth century, that of Leibniz, which needs to be taken into account here because of its relevance to the present-day situation. Leibniz submitted to penetrating scrutiny the conception of extension as a single inhering attribute. I cannot here enter into details of his analysis;[7] I can give only its outcome, which was that "extension" could not be an attribute pertaining to a single thing or subject, and that it could be consistently and coherently conceived only as pertaining to a plurality of entities, more precisely to that plurality *in relation*. This held, Leibniz argued, not only for extension; all the other quantities characterizing body had to be analyzed as pertaining to a plurality *in relation*. Also, "motion" had to be understood in terms of a relation between a plurality of entities, and not as an attribute inhering in a single entity. Thus, the outcome of Leibniz's work on the problem of the nature of the physical was to bring the category of "relation" to the fore, and indeed to make it the primary category, with the category of quantity conceived as subordinate to it and involved in the category of relation. Briefly put, the relations, for Leibniz, were specifically mathematical. That is, the fundamental feature of the relations between physical entities was their mathematical character. It is interesting that it has taken physical science, which had followed Newton rather than Leibniz in the subsequent period, some two hundred years to reach a position similar to that of Leibniz, of relations as fundamental to the physical.

It is relevant to consider the reason why Leibniz's thought and analyses had failed to carry conviction. This was that Leibniz himself remained, in some crucial respects, in the Neoplatonic tradition. When he came to the analysis of "relations," he rejected the supposition that they could be some kind of real connection *between* entities. He could conceive them only, in accordance with the Neoplatonic doctrine, on the paradigm of inhering qualities. That is, a relation is strictly a feature in or "qualification of" a subject; a "relation" meant

---

7. For details, see *NPE*, chap. 20.

"this subject with reference to that entity," which entailed that the "reference" was made *by* the subject and was thus an attribute pertaining to, and thus *in*, the subject. The object entity was in no way affected. Leibniz argued that the act of "referring" was of the general nature of a "perceiving," so that relations were necessarily "phenomenal," i.e., how the object appeared to the perceiving subject. Relations as "real," Leibniz held, were impossible. Leibniz had to resort to God for an explanation of how purely subjective "appearances" could nevertheless coordinate with objective happenings; this was his famous doctrine of "pre-established harmony," which then and subsequently most thinkers have found difficult to accept. However, it should be noted that adherence to the basic Neoplatonic position was not abandoned. In the next century the Leibnizian quandary about relations as phenomenal was resolved by Kant's "critical" philosophy through bringing the object too into the fold of "phenomena."

Now, I wish to contend that the Neoplatonic conception of relation as a private qualification within a subject is completely unable to satisfy what is demanded of the kind of relations which we saw earlier to be necessitated in contemporary physical, chemical, and biological theory. Consider biological theory: the relation between the parts or organs of a biological entity is constituted by their functioning in a certain way with respect to each other, it being entailed that such functioning is a producing of an effect in others. That is, by their functioning there is a real connection between the organs. There does not seem to be much difficulty about acknowledging this.

There might, however, be some difficulty about recognizing relations between the parts or constituents of chemical substances as real connections. This is so because the parts (molecules, atoms) continue implicitly to be conceived as inert matter, and thus as not essentially related to each other. But if this Neoplatonic theory be abandoned, which I suggest is required by the scientific evidence, then the parts can be conceived as essentially related to each other. To be essentially related means that the relation makes a difference to the respective "essence" of the entities, i.e., to what each *is*, in itself. It is indeed such an essential relatedness which is involved when Dr. Theobald says that "the formula 'H_2O' refers to that class of molecules every member of which is composed of H and O atoms *related in a certain way*." That is, a water molecule is not a mere aggregate constituted by the arithmetical sum of two H atoms and one O atom. To constitute a water molecule those atoms have to be "related in a certain way." That relation includes their being situated with respect to each other in a certain geometrical pattern—we are all familiar with the intriguing diagrams chemists produce of molecular structure. But does a geometrical pattern or structure per se suffice to explain the character of the molecule as "water"? Also, what is the explanation of how the atoms come to be in that pattern, and then *maintain* that pattern? That pattern is a "relationship," and it is one which can be constituted only by some real *connection* between the atoms, a connection in which they are reciprocally *affected by* each other. Now this "affection" can come only from each of the respective entities themselves; it must be something in them whereby they affect, and produce a change in, each other.

V

It has been common to conceive this something as some "power" or "force." But this only raises the question as to what such a "power" or "force" conceivably could be. Is it something "physical"? But if the physical be "matter," as maintained in the early modern doctrine, then the "power" or "force" would be "material"; but this would be a contradiction, since the power or force was supposed to be something other than the material atoms. Maintaining it to be something other therefore entailed the introduction of an occult factor for which there could be no coherent explanation. Let me be clear that I am not rejecting the introduction of the concept of "force" or "power." What I am insisting on is the necessity of *explaining* it, and this can be coherently achieved only by grounding the power or force in the entities themselves. This means that the nature of these entities must be such that they are able, by their "nature," to exercise a power whereby others are affected.

Now, this is possible only if the entities in question be conceived as being the very contrary of "inert matter." That is to say, they must be essentially "active" entities, entities which "act on" each other. It is by its acting that an entity produces an effect on another, this other being "acted on," i.e., recipient of that effect. I wish to maintain that only such a conception of physical entities can be consistent with the scientific evidence.

This acting, it is clear, is an acting by entities in relation to each other. In other words, the acting is relational acting; relations are essentially entailed in acting. This holds equally for relations between biological entities, chemical entities, and physical entities. This is the philosophical conception of relations necessitated by twentieth-century scientific developments.

What we have here in this conception of relations is not merely an emphasis on relations much greater than was given them before; it goes much further, by according to relations a primary status among the categories, in this respect coming to a position similar to that to which Leibniz had been led. Seventeenth-century philosophy, having relegated the category of quality to the other side of the metaphysical dichotomy, as pertaining solely to mind, had made the category of quantity fundamental in the physical, and conceived this as inhering on the paradigm of the inherence of a quality. In Leibniz's analysis the category of relation emerged as fundamental, with the category of quantity subordinate to it, as involved in relation.

Now, this is the position to which contemporary physical science drives us, as Whitehead most clearly saw. Accordingly, he has maintained that what Descartes had "described as primary *attributes* of physical bodies [i.e., quantities, principally extension], are really the forms of internal relationships *between* actual occasions, and *within* actual occasions."[8] It must be emphasized that the "forms of relationships" are quantities such as extension. This means that there are no bare relations; relations necessarily each have a particular form, i.e., a particular definiteness, whereby they are characterized as *that* relation and not another. More specifically, the relations between physical entities have a mathematical definiteness; a relation is characterized as *from* this entity *here*, *to* that entity *there*, where "here" and "there" are geometrically exactly specifiable. That geometrical distance and perspective pertain to the relation as part of the essential character of the relation—and geometrical knowledge of that relation in scientific investigation is obtained by abstraction from the concreteness of the relation. Thus, in a molecule, for example, the specific geometrical structure, such as a specific crystalline pattern, displayed in the relatedness of the constituent atoms to each other concretely constitutes the form of definiteness of the relational acts of the atoms. I would myself want to go even further than this, and to argue that there is no reason to restrict the forms of definiteness of relations to the quantitative; the forms of definiteness can also be qualitative. With this, the vicious metaphysical dualism introduced in the seventeenth century is overcome.

There is one more point which seems to me very important to make. In the doctrine of material atomism, macroscopic bodies were regarded as mere aggregates of constituent atoms. But from early in the seventeenth century it was found necessary to acknowledge intermediate groupings, which Gassendi called "molecules," little masses. But on the theory of material atomism there is no explanation pos-

---

8. Whitehead, *PR* (C), 437; (M), 471.

sible for molecules, that is, why atoms should come together into molecular groups, and why the molecular groups should have definite patterned structures; this was accepted as a bare empirical datum. A philosophical explanation is, however, necessary. I would submit that on the basis of the conception of relational acting, the requisite explanation is coherently possible.

As we have seen earlier, wholes, such as biological ones, constituted by relational acting are not the mere arithmetical sum of the constituent parts. On the contrary, it is the relatedness involved in the wholes which constitutes them as entities which are something more than the arithmetical sum of the parts. The same is the case with the wholes constituting chemical molecules, and thus of the different chemical substances. And because it has been demonstrated since the beginning of this century that the so-called atoms are not at all atoms, i.e., *atomos*, that cannot be cut, that are indivisible, but are themselves compound wholes, they too, as wholes constituted by the relational acting of their parts, must be something more than the arithmetical sum of their parts. What we have in present-day so-called subatomic theory is patterned relationships of the subatomic constituents, each such pattern, which includes the quantity of the constituents, resulting in a whole with different characteristics. The vast complexity of nature is not constituted, as conceived in the theory of material atomism, by ever larger aggregations of atoms, but by the structural interrelationship first of comparatively simple wholes constituting larger and more complex wholes, which as such wholes enter into structural interrelationship with wholes of a like kind to constitute still more complex wholes, and so on to a great deal of complexity and variety.

Philosophically, I would want to argue that, in contrast to the theory of material atomism, in which the material atoms alone are actual existents, the various wholes (atoms, molecules, cells, and so forth) in ascending complexity of kinds, have each to be accorded the status of actual existents, each with its determinate character as that entity, its character being constituted by the definiteness of the conjoint acting of its constituents. Further, when such wholes (e.g., atoms) become constituents of a larger whole (e.g., a molecule), the determinate character of the larger whole (the molecule) is constituted by the acting of the atomic whole, and not by separate actings of the subatomic entities composing it. Likewise, each molecular whole is an agent, an acting subject; the acting of the molecular whole is not the mere arithmetical sum of its component actings.

This conception of interacting wholes is important not only for philosophy, that is, for a coherent general understanding of the nature of things. It seems to me no less important for science, because if a scientist investigates a whole such as a molecule in chemistry, on the presupposition of the whole as constituted by the relational actings of its constituents, a different theory will be necessitated from that entailed in the presupposition of the whole as simply the arithmetical sum of its parts. It will then be a case of deciding which theory most adequately satisfies the empirical evidence.

12
PHYSICAL EXISTENCE, MATTER, ACTIVITY

I

There is an interesting analogy between the situation in this century respecting the philosophical problems involved in scientific thought and that of the seventeenth century, the full significance of which has not received the attention its importance merits. This is that in both of these there has occurred a profound, indeed radical, change in the conception of the physical existent.

In the seventeenth century there had arisen a radically new conception of the physical, in opposition to the conception of the physical in medieval thought. In the twentieth century a new conception of the physical, no less radically different from its predecessor, has developed. But in this century far less clarity pertains respecting that difference than there was among seventeenth-century thinkers, because at that time science and philosophy were not as deeply separated as they have been since, with the consequence that then the crucial philosophical issues raised by the new conception of the physical were much appreciated and tackled. The contrary situation pertains today. The new seventeenth-century conception was of the physical as "matter" or "material substance," in contrast to the antecedent doctrine of medieval Aristotelianism of the physical as composite of form and matter. The tremendous philosophical significance of that contrast was especially clear to Descartes, who was the first to develop its implications, but it was clear also to the other great thinkers of that time.

In this century the full philosophical implications of the changed conception of the physical which has now arisen have not been appreciated with analogous clarity, except by a few, and because at the present time, especially in scientific thought, the physical existent continues to be thought of as "matter," the contrast with the conception in the preceding three centuries is therefore not so evident. Properly to appreciate it, the contemporary conception needs to be seen in contrast to the doctrine of these preceding centuries.

This means that it is important to be clear as to what exactly was the conception of the physical as "matter" which was introduced in the seventeenth century. In antecedent, medieval, thought the term *matter* connoted passive potentiality, the mere capacity to receive form, whereas the term *substance* denoted the natural or physical existent. The great philosophical innovation of the seventeenth century had been to conceive "matter" per se as the physical substance or existent. In this view the physical substance as "matter" connoted that the physical existent has the primary and essential feature of "passive potentiality." That is, a material substance is in itself completely devoid of "activity," "agency"—it is strictly "inert," as Kepler was the first to characterize it; it is "mov*able*," but cannot move itself. Moreover, as in itself having only the "capacity" or "passive potentiality" to receive motion, it is in itself entirely homogeneous, and undifferentiated—except in being quantitative. This entailed further that the physical existent is in itself fully "actual," not involving any internal process of "becoming." It simply "is"—in this we see the full victory of the return to Neoplatonism in the sixteenth and seventeenth centuries over the dominant Aristotelianism of the antecedent few centuries. This new conception of the physical existent was clearly and explicitly accepted by all the important seventeenth-century thinkers, from Kepler, Galileo, and Descartes to Huygens and Newton—with the notable exception of Leibniz.

The situation in this century is that the development of science, especially in the last hundred years, has resulted in a de facto abandonment of that early modern conception of the physical existent. It is now on the whole implicitly or explicitly accepted in the sciences that physical existents must be regarded as somehow and in some respect "active." This means that we are in our time urgently faced with the philosophical issue of the nature of the physical existent, with the problem of how the physical existent is to be conceived as "active." This problem is urgent because, in the absence of philosophical clarification, thought in the sciences can readily be prey to—and, I would suggest, is—proceeding in terms of incoherent philosophical presuppositions and implications.

This danger is inherent in the very terminology employed, for it is not the case that we can in every instance establish meanings by conventional decision; and where philosophical concepts are involved (whether explicitly or implicitly), this supposition about language is a very misleading one. A pertinent example is that although, as indicated above, the seventeenth-century conception of the physical existent has been abandoned, physical entities continue to be spoken of as "matter" and "material." Does this simply and only involve using an old term with a new meaning, as tends to be supposed? This supposition is very much open to question. It seems to me that there has occurred a carryover, in various respects and in varying degrees, of the features of the former connotation of the term, and that these cannot be accepted without scrutiny. Moreover, I would argue that the connotations thus carried over are being definitely a hindrance and obstruction to thought in present-day science.

One important carryover involved in the use of the term *matter* is the presupposition that the fundamental "change" involved in the physical is change of place, locomotion. For since matter is in itself fully actual, the only change possible for it is locomotion. A material entity remains self-identically the substrate of that locomotive change. This conception of the physical existent as basically the "substrate" of change is another implication involved in the term *matter*. There is a further frequent carryover relevant here, also involved in the connotation of matter as "passive potentiality." This is the presupposition of the physical existent as "extensive," its extensiveness being a quality passively inhering in the existent as subject.

The question has to be raised as a most importantly relevant philosophical problem, whether these or any other of the presuppositions involved in the connotation of "matter" are consistently and coherently tenable with a conception of the physical existent as "active." This is the issue which Whitehead faced and which led to his complete rejection of the physical existent as "material substance." If physical existents be "active," this entails that they cannot merely "be," that they are not simply "fully actual." To be "active" is not to *undergo* something; it is to be in an internal "process," a "becoming"—in contrast to merely "being." In maintaining this, Whitehead returned to the basic position of Aristotle respecting the physical existent (although Whitehead himself did not fully appreciate that this was the case), for what Whitehead termed *process* is what for Aristotle was *kinesis*—in his concept of *kinesis* as the inner process involved in the becoming of natural *ousiai*—is the process of the actualizing of potentiality. The main point here is Whitehead's insistence that the physical existent must be seen as "in process," in an internal process of "becoming"—as he put it: "its 'being' is constituted by its 'becoming.'"[1]

1. *PR*, Category of Explanation 9: (C), 26; (M), 29.

II

In the course of the foregoing exposition I have sought to explicate some of the issues involved in the philosophical problem of the nature of the physical existent, for this, viz., the problem of the nature of the physical existent, is the quite fundamental philosophical problem in the set of philosophical issues involved in science. We have so far proceeded only some way in clarifying that problem. Thus far, I have spoken of "the physical existent," or in the plural of "physical existents." I have done so intentionally so as not to beg philosophical questions, and in particular the question (a most important one which has explicitly to be tackled) of what we are to *identify* as a "physical existent."

In scientific thought today we are faced with a large number of different "entities": in physics for example, atoms, electrons, protons, neutrons, positrons, mesons, quarks, etc.; in chemistry, atoms and molecules; in molecular biology, highly complex molecular structures of simpler molecules, and cells; in biology, again molecular structures, cells, structures of cells into organs, a vast variety of different organisms. In some sense of the term these all "exist," and they are all "physical"—in the general meaning of the term *physical* as synonymous with *natural*—so that in some sense they could all indifferently be called "physical existents." But there is a most important philosophical issue involved here which would be obscured by thus indifferently applying this term to all these entities. For the philosophical problem is concerning the status respectively of the various entities.

We could approach the philosophical problem in the following way. In each of the different sciences the "entities" involved are not all on the same level; there are differences of status. In physics for example, electrons, protons, and other microentities have a significantly different status from atoms, for atoms are composite entities with electrons, protons, etc., as their constituents. There is an analogous difference in status in chemistry between atoms and molecules, and in biology between molecules and cells; and so on.

The *scientific problem* is the clarification of the relations of the constituent entities in constituting a composite entity, e.g., the number of constituents, and the pattern or structure displayed by them relatively to each other. The *philosophical problem* is respecting that difference of status per se, to understand wherein exactly it consists, to understand the nature of the relations involved such that they result in just those composites with just those features exhibited by the composites—an understanding which must be grounded in the nature of the constituents, which means that the philosophical problem basically concerns the nature of those constituents. But since from another perspective what we have here is wholes and parts, the philosophical problem is not only to elucidate the nature of the parts but also that of the wholes.

In the seventeenth century, with the philosophy of material substance, this philosophical problem was regarded as easy of solution. Scientific thought in the first quarter of that century had resulted in a rejection of the medieval Aristotelian conception of organic entities as constituting integral unitary wholes which as such were identifiable as the physical existents or natural substances. In the seventeenth century the conviction had grown that these wholes, of which the living organisms were the paradigm instances, were not integral wholes but were, rather, composites which were strictly aggregates. Thus, it was the ultimate constituents which were to be identified as the physical existents, for they were the ultimate units, not divisible into or reducible to anything more ultimate. The term *atom* then had its proper etymological meaning. The composites were seen to have the status of mere aggregate collections, their features as composites being no more than the arithmetical sum of the features of the constituents. This was incontestably demonstrable, it was thought, in experiments in mechanics, in which it made no difference what number or mass of matter were used, for the laws of motion were indifferently exhibited by all composites of whatever size; clearly, therefore, these laws must hold too for the invisible atomic constituents of those composite bodies.

Because the philosophical theory of the physical existent as material substance continued, explicitly or implicitly, in dominant acceptance, indeed down to this century, the *philosophical* problem constituted by, for example, the chemical theory of molecules as exhibiting definite structural relationships of the constituents, has not been faced up to. The philosophical issue is that since the particular features of the molecules (as gaseous, liquid, solid, as acid or alkaline, and so forth) were directly correlative to the structural relationships, the composite wholes could not be the mere arithmetical sum of the constituents: "structural relationship" implies something more than arithmetical sum. The philosophical problem is how "structural relationships" and the features dependent upon them are to be accounted for.

One aspect of this problem is, what is the nature and status of the entities respectively involved—for example, in chemistry the nature and status of the constituent atoms and the molecules? Another aspect of the problem is that of the nature and status of the constituent entities such that they can have the structural relationships which are empirically found; not only, e.g., that the molecule of water consists of one oxygen atom and two hydrogen atoms, but also that they are at a particular distance from each other and in a particular three-dimensional pattern? If this philosophical problem be posed, it is evident that the constituent entities cannot be "matter" as conceived in seventeenth-century thought. For that conception of "matter" contains nothing whatever whereby such structural relationships could result. The locomotion of material entities might fortuitously eventuate briefly in such a geometrical pattern, but there is no reason whatever in their nature as "matter" why they should continue in that pattern—on the contrary, their *not* so continuing is what would follow from the concept of "matter." Also, the conception of the constituent entities as "matter" provides nothing whatever whereby there could be what are termed "valency bonds" between the atoms. It is evident that a completely different conception of the nature of the constituent entities is requisite if those relationships are to be explicable.

It seems to me most important to appreciate that when there is structural relationship, we have to do with something which is more than mere arithmetical sum. We have then to raise the question of the ground of the structural relationship, whether, for example, it is to be grounded wholly in the constituents, and how it is to be so grounded; or whether it is in some way grounded in the whole which they constitute, and how this could be possible, or whether in both the constituents and the whole; and, again, how this could be possible.

III

The fundamental philosophical problem here is, what is the nature of the entities involved such that they can have these structural relationships, and what is the nature of these relationships? We can perhaps most fruitfully approach the issue by considering the problem of the nature of the "relationships" which we have here, for example, those involved between the constituent atoms in molecular structures. What must be the nature of those relationships such that there can be the maintenance of that structure? To deal with this question in terms of "forces" does not provide a philosophical answer, for it is precisely the concept of "force" which requires philosophical elucidation. The philosophical problem would be, what is the nature and ontological status of "force"? That is, what sort of "being" does it have? For example, is it something over and above the constituent entities as a kind of *tertium quid*, and if so, what could it be? If not, if it be grounded in the constituent entities, it must be explained in terms of the nature of the entities themselves.

Entities such as the "matter" of the thought of the seventeenth through nineteenth centuries had a nature which affords no possible basis for the explanation of relations, and more particularly of ones conceived as "forces." It has long been recognized in the philosophical tradition that the only possible basis for the explanation of relationships is in terms of "acting." That is to say, the entities in question must be "acting" entities, and the relationships must be a function of their acting. It comes down therefore to a question of the nature of the "acting" of the entities. How is it to be conceived? The acting must account for the particular structure of the relationships between the entities involved; it must account for the character of the relationships, for the character of the constituent entities, and for the character of the whole which is constituted by that structured relationship. One aspect of that character of the relationship is geometrical pattern. Another aspect of the character is that which is designated by such terms as *acid*, *alkaline*, and so forth, that is to say, its qualitative character, of what "kind" it is.

IV

In this context the concept of "emergence" has been introduced. But it should be clear that it does not constitute any solution; rather the term *emergence* signifies a problem requiring a solution. The term in this context entails a rejection of the conception of wholes as mere aggregates. But *emergence* also carries the connotation of features of the wholes "arising from" the constituents. Therefore, the constituents must be of such a nature that this is possible. It should be clear that it is not possible if the constituents be of the nature of "matter"—there has been much confusion of thought because this has not been sufficiently recognized. A quite different conception of the nature of the constituents is requisite if "emergence" is to be possible. Moreover, the "emergent character" of the whole is manifestly connected with the "relations" between the constituents, as is clear in chemistry, for example.

The one thinker in this century who has seen this entire issue most clearly is A. N. Whitehead, and he has explicitly tackled the problem in terms of a theory of the acting of the constituents. In his doctrine, the actings of the constituent entities effect relationships between them; indeed, for Whitehead the primary physical act *is* an act of relating. Each physical existent, or "actual entity" in his terminology, relates itself to others by its *act* of "prehending" them. A compound whole has what Whitehead calls its "defining characteristic," and it has this by virtue of the relational prehensive acting. That is, the constituents are in prehensive interrelation, and the defining characteristic of the whole is the definiteness of that relational acting. Each constituent is what it is in relation to all the others in that whole. Each, by its act of prehending, appropriates, from its perspective in the whole, that particular complex character of the whole. It is this complex defining characteristic, which each constituent individually manifests in its perspectival relatedness to the others, which determines the whole as exhibiting that particular defining characteristic. Thus, in Whitehead's theory, by reason of the acting being a relating, the whole determines the constituents, and the constituents, by their acting, determine the whole. In this theory, therefore, the character of the whole "arises from" or "emerges" from the constituents, and by virtue of the interrelatedness of their acting this character is not a mere sum of the characters of the constituents. Further, it is by virtue of this character's being mutually shared by the constituents in their acting that the particular character, and the character of the whole, is maintained. It is this which constitutes the "bond" between the constituents, the "force" which holds them together in that particular whole.

V

There is, however, another issue which must be brought into consideration here. In raising the problem of wholes and their constituents, above I did so in the context of chemistry, that is, of the molecular whole and its constituent atoms. The issue raised now is whether it is indeed these atoms which are to be taken as the "acting" entities, effecting by their acting the relationships whereby the molecular character comes into being. And in Whitehead's theory specifically, are the atoms the "prehending" entities? This issue is highly pertinent here because these so-called atoms are now recognized as not being "atomic" in the strict sense at all; they are themselves composites. Does this mean then that the relational acting is to be ascribed, not to these composite "atoms" per se, but to their constituents? Or perhaps to still more ultimate constituents? For the constituents of the "atoms" must themselves be either composites or ultimate simples, true atoms—i.e., not further divisible into constituent entities. If the former be the case then there must be ultimate simple constituents of those "subatomic" composites—for there cannot be a regressus ad infinitum.

Now, it seems to me that there are two possibilities as to the status respectively of the entities involved here. One is that the ultimate constituent entities are to be regarded as in the proper sense "acting" entities. In that case, all the composite entities are of a derivative kind, i.e., having an ontological status different from that of the ultimate constituents. This could be expressed by saying that only the ultimate constituents are per se self-subsistent; the composites are, in an unqualified sense, dependent upon the ultimate constituents for their being. The other possibility is that the composites are integral wholes which as such are acting entities, this acting of the whole not being reducible to the actings of the individual constituents. This second possibility entails a much greater complexity in regard to ontological status than that implied in the former possibility. In the former position—which was adopted by Whitehead in *Process and Reality* and which I briefly expounded above—only the ultimate constituents have the ontological status of physical existents in the proper sense of physically acting entities; all composites are without qualification of a derivative ontological status and could be regarded as "acting" only in a sense derivative from the individual actings of the constituents. The second position would permit of composites being integral wholes which per se are acting entities and as such therefore to be identifiable as physical existents. A question would arise whether such wholes which themselves function as constituents of larger integral wholes are to be regarded as physical existents, or whether this status is to be accorded only to the larger composites which are themselves not constituents of still larger wholes. This is a complicated problem which, however, we do not need to try to resolve now.

VI

The main issue, which primarily requires decision, is whether composites (e.g., either the so-called atoms or the molecules, or the larger composites) are to be regarded as per se *acting* entities. This issue has an empirical, scientific aspect, and a theoretical, philosophical aspect. I say "aspect" because it does not seem to me that the two questions, scientific and philosophical, are completely separable. The philosophical problem is whether the character and "activity" of the composite are adequately explicable in terms of the nature and acting of the ultimate constituents alone, or whether its "acting" is in some respect transcendent of, and not wholly derivative from, the actings of the constituents.

Let us elucidate this problem in terms of Whitehead's theory. In this, the constituents, by prehensive acting, mutually derive a common character which is the character of the compound whole. That is, this character of the whole is a dominant feature in the individual character of each of the constituents. This means that the ontological locus of the character of the whole is in each of the individual constituents; its locus is not the whole per se—that character pertains to the whole only derivatively. It is to be noted, however, that this derivative status is very different from that entailed in theories such as material atomism, in which the character of the whole can be no more than the arithmetical sum of that of the constituents—because the constituents in the latter kind of theory are fully what they are antecedent to entering into a compound as its constituents, so that their entry into the compound could make no difference to the constituents in respect of "what" they are. Whitehead's theory is the antithesis of this: for him "what" the constituents are, i.e., their character, is considerably dependent upon their participation in the respective compound wholes. The problem then arises as to what *determines* that participation. The final answer to this in Whitehead's doctrine is in terms of the "subjective aim" of each acting entity—for "acting" necessarily entails a teleological factor—and this in his system is ultimately determined by God as the "principle of concretion."[2]

The point I particularly wish to make in connection with Whitehead's theory could be brought out by an exemplification. It is not the atomic whole per se which determines by its acting its relation to the other atoms in the structured molecule, for the atom per se does not act. The determination is effected by the prehensive actings of each constituent of the compound "atom." By prehensive acting, each grasps prehensively the "atomic character" which it individually actualizes (in its perspective partiality) as a member of that compound. But, and this is important, it at the same time also prehends its relatedness to the other constituents of the atom as each also involving relatednesses to the individual constituents of the other atoms which together constitute the molecule. So by its prehensive acting each constituent exemplifies, and actualizes from its perspective in the whole, the molecular character of which it is an ultimate constituent. Further, it is also this individual prehension by each of the ultimate constituents which determines the relatedness of the molecule in con-

---

2. Cf. *SMW*, 216; *PR* (C), 488; (M), 523. Whitehead's theory, it should be added, avoids the serious objections to the "preestablished harmony" of Leibniz's system, but it must be recognized that in his doctrine a "principle of concretion" is a form of preestablished harmony—not that this can as such constitute any objection to his theory; some form of this conception is quite probably unavoidable for coherence in any system.

stituting more complex wholes such as cells, and so on to greater compounds such as organisms.

It is appropriate to raise the question why, in terms of this theory, with everything determined by the acting of the ultimate constituents, a hierarchy of compounds should be necessary at all. Why should there not be a single complex relatedness with all the other constituents of a larger compound such as a biological organism, as we find, e.g., in the system of Leibniz? Whitehead holds that the role of the various compounds such as atoms, molecules, upward, is to procure the requisite "intensity" of prehensive "experience" for the determination of the whole to have its particular character—without that "intensity" the prehensions would progressively lose their particular distinctiveness of difference of character. Theoretically considered, this answer is coherent. It serves to emphasize, however, that in Whitehead's system the entire ontological weight is borne by the ultimate individual constituents together with God as the "principle of concretion," with compounds, even biological organisms, having ontologically a very subordinate role. The question of the adequacy of this will be considered later.

Here I should like to bring out one further point of decisive importance in respect to Whitehead's theory. In this the prehensive acting is a "receiving" from others. In Whitehead's doctrine the generally accepted notion of causality is reversed. According to this generally accepted notion there is an "activity" in the *cause* "producing" an effect, the *effect* by contrast being a "passivity." For Whitehead it is the *effect*, i.e., the present prehending entity, which is active, whereas the *cause*, an entity in its past, has, as past, lost its activity. In this doctrine the "acting" of physical existents is only a prehensive "receiving." Cause, or determination in the sense of *actively* "producing" an effect, has been eliminated. Determination is partly by the "what" (the "form" or "definiteness") which is received, and partly by the "decision" of the prehensive, i.e., receptive, act.

VII

I have elaborated these points in Whitehead's theory because they bring to the fore some of the fundamental philosophical problems which are particularly pertinent to the philosophical interpretation of the scientific data. It is in respect of these problems that the adequacy of a philosophical theory must be tested. The immense complexity and difficulty of such a "testing" are not to be minimized. It is not a straightforward affair of "confronting" the theory with scientific data. For the data are themselves not accessible except in terms of theory—theory which is of course essentially scientific. But the crux of the situation is that scientific theory involves, if only as a tacit presupposition, some basic philosophical position (or positions). That is, the scientific theory will itself to some extent constitute an interpretation of the data in terms of some philosophical position, or indeed, what is more frequently the case, in terms of a mixture of philosophical positions (mostly implicitly entailed), which are finally inconsistent with each other.

We have arrived at a situation in which it is no longer satisfactory for scientific thought to proceed, as in the past two centuries, in terms of philosophical presuppositions inherited from the seventeenth century, supplemented by divergent new positions adopted ad hoc where the inherited ones have proved inadequate, without being clear about the full implications of either the inherited positions or of the new ones—because both remain largely implicit. One urgent need today is to be clear about the inherited philosophical presuppositions which continue to be operative in scientific thought. Equally, it is necessary to identify new philosophical presuppositions which have been introduced, and to work out what they philosophically imply. Only by being able to recognize these philosophical ingredients in scientific theory will the data be adequately available for alternative interpretation. Evidently there is a need for explicitly developed philosophical theories to constitute the bases for alternative interpretations of the data.

One philosophical presupposition which continues operative in contemporary scientific theory is that inherited from the seventeenth century, which was involved in material atomism, namely, that it is the ultimate constituents of compounds which are to be identified as the physical existents in the full ontological sense, and thus that all compounds are to be accorded a derivative ontological status. This, as we have seen, means that compounds are analyzable into, and to be understood in terms of, the natures of the constituents.

Further, to a very considerable extent, there also continues to be operative the philosophical presupposition of the ultimate physical constituents as "material." Insofar as the latter presupposition is even implicitly held, it means that chemistry, for example, is conceived as reducible to physics, i.e., that the data of chemistry are ultimately to be understood mechanistically, which is to say, in terms of the locomotion of the subatomic entities.

VIII

Now, the new philosophical position which has gradually and increasingly come into acceptance in this century is the conception of the physical existent as "active." An indication of the extent of the failure to appreciate the philosophical implications of this new position, and its antithesis to the seventeenth-century conception of the physical existent, is the fact that in contemporary scientific thought the physical existent is still mostly termed *matter* or *material*. It is one of the greatest and most urgent philosophical tasks of our time to work out the implications of this new philosophical conception of the physical existent, as it was the great task undertaken by the philosophers of the seventeenth century to work out the philosophical implications of the physical existent conceived as "matter." And now, as then, this is a task which will take generations.

Whitehead's is, I think, to be seen as the first great full-scale effort in this century to do so, as Descartes's was in the seventeenth century. But as Descartes's effort was much in the beginning of that undertaking at that time, so likewise, it seems to me, is Whitehead's now. Further, I would say that we are now at a juncture at which cooperation between the philosophical and the scientific endeavors is vital, both because of their being necessary to each other, and because of the enormous amount of specialization necessary in both fields, making it difficult for any one person adequately to encompass both—our situation in this respect being much in contrast to that of the seventeenth and the eighteenth centuries.

It seems to me that today perhaps the most fruitful areas of collaborative effort of philosophers and scientists, for their mutual advantage, are chemistry and biochemistry. Considering the inherited philosophical presuppositions mentioned above, is it not to be accepted today as clear that the data of chemistry, and more especially those of biochemistry (or molecular biology), are not adequately understandable in terms of the physical existents conceived as "matter"? If this be agreed to, then Whitehead's theory, as a major attempt consistently to conceive the physical existents as "active," merits careful consideration by scientists.[3] The problem is, to what extent it adequately explains the data.

---

3. The number of scientists having a good understanding of Whitehead is still very small. One who has achieved a very considerable knowledge of Whitehead is Joseph E. Earley: see his papers "On Applying Whitehead's First Category of Existence," *Process Studies* 11 (1981): 35–39; "Self-Organization and Agency: In Chemistry and Process Philosophy," *Process Studies* 12 (1981): 242–58; and a paper not yet published, "Evolutionary Biology, Physiological Psychology, Process Philosophy."

13

COMPOUNDS, BODY, CHANGE

I

In connection with the problem, raised at the end of the previous chapter, of the extent to which a philosophical theory such as Whitehead's explains the scientific data, it is necessary to take into account the other inherited presupposition mentioned above, namely, of the ultimate constituents of compounds as alone identifiable as the physical existents. In the previous chapter, I brought out that Whitehead, in his system as developed in *Process and Reality*, continued in adherence to this presupposition. We have to face the issue whether Whitehead's theory, or any other which identifies the physical existents as solely the ultimate constituents of compounds, is able adequately to explain composite entities such as, for example, molecules are revealed to be in contemporary scientific research.

We have seen that, philosophically considered, in Whitehead's theory, entities such as the composite "atoms," molecules, and so on have an ontologically derivative status, which means that their character and their acting are derivative and do not pertain to them per se. A question is whether the scientific data adequately confirm this, or whether they rather evidence the compounds as having a more enhanced status than that accorded to them in Whitehead's theory. That is to say, we need to consider whether the scientific evidence does not point to the need to abandon the philosophical presupposition inherited from the seventeenth century, that only the ultimate constituents of compounds are to be regarded as physical existents, i.e., as the only entities which are in the proper sense physically acting. The issue could be stated alternatively as the question whether scientific theory today does not implicitly involve the presupposition of compounds having a status different from that accorded them by the inherited presupposition.

If the latter be the case, there is then the need to develop philosophical theories of compound entities as themselves physical existents, i.e., entities capable per se of physical acting.

One possibility of achieving this is to modify Whitehead's theory so as to be able to identify *compounds* as "actual entities" ("actual occasions," as Whitehead alternatively terms the physical existents), as Lewis Ford has recently done, proposing that "we interpret such natural compounds as atoms, molecules, and cells as personally ordered strands of actual occasions rather than as structured societies as Whitehead does."[1] But this position still has to face the problem, which I raised above, whether such compounds are adequately accountable for in terms of the acting of the physical existents conceived as purely prehensive "receiving."

II

It is indeed the problem of the nature of physical acting which is the crucial issue. In *The Nature of Physical Existence* I proposed a theory of compound entities as physical existents based on a different view of physical acting.[2] In this I went back to the conception well known in philosophical thought since ancient times, and which in the modern period had been made use of particularly by Locke and Leibniz and by Kant in his pre-critical period, but which has subsequently been much ignored. Its earliest explicit formulation was by Plato in the *Theaetetus*, though it seems clear from the context that he had derived it from antecedent thought. According to this conception, Plato says, "there are two kinds of motion. Of each kind there are any number of instances, but they differ in that one kind is the power of acting, the other of being acted upon."[3] In medieval thought these two were distinguished as "active and passive power." Further, these two, the active and the passive, were recognized as being correlative and reciprocal. This means that the active power is an "acting on" and the passive power a "reacting to," "responding to," a "receiving of," that acting on. Moreover, as Leibniz and, even more clearly, Kant recognized, physical acting is both at once an "acting" and a "reacting," so that when, say, an entity A acts on entity B, B "reacts" to A both by receiving an effect from A and being affected by A in respect of what it becomes, of its definiteness or character. By this reciprocal transaction there is thus both an exertion of "force" by A's acting, and a

---

1. In a critical study of my *NPE* in *Process Studies* 3 (1973): 104–118.
2. See also above, chap. 11.
3. Plato, *Theaetetus*, 156A (trans. F. M. Cornford): τῆς δὲ κινήσεως δύο εἴδη, πλήθει μὲν ἄπειρον ἑκάστον, δύναμιν δὲ τὸ μὲν ποιεῖν ἔχον, τὸ δὲ πάσχειν.

"bond" between the two entities by virtue of the reciprocal acting and reacting. This means that physical acting effects a relation in the full sense of "connecting." This, I venture to suggest, is the philosophical explanation of the physical "bonds" (sometimes spoken of as "forces") which hold a number of entities together to constitute a composite whole.

By reason of the mutual actings and reactions, compound wholes are constituted which have a unity and thereby also a determinate character, which is definitely more than those of a mere aggregate. This means that the actings of the constituents combine to constitute the whole a new physical existent. Since the combined acting of the constituents effects a unity which transcends the constituents per se, the combined acting must have the *whole* entity as its subject—for the combined acting is not reducible to the constituents severally as its subject. Thus, from the combined acting and reacting of the constituents there emerges a new integral entity, a physical existent in the full sense of itself per se capable of acting. By such a compound entity's entering into interaction with other such entities, still more complex existents emerge.

Such emergent integral compound entities are in the proper sense "organisms." For the concept of an "organism" is that of an entity in which the parts function with reference to the whole; that is, the parts or constituents are "organs" (in the original Greek meaning of the term as "instruments") of the whole. An "organism," in other words, is an entity in which the whole determines the functioning, i.e., acting, of the parts or constituents. The whole teleologically determines the parts to constitute the whole—for the actings do not merely fortuitously result in the whole, since "acting" per se is no mere random "happening," but is necessarily, qua acting, "purposive"—and when constituted, the whole, as subject of its acting, exercises a determination on its constituent actings for the achievement of *its* "purposes."

This theory of physical acting, I submit, gives a more adequate understanding of compound wholes such as atomic nuclei, atoms, and of molecules of increasing grades of complexity, than is afforded by Whitehead's theory—achieving more adequately what he indeed sought in designating his "a philosophy of organism." The consequence of my theory of physical acting is that integral compound entities or "organisms" are accorded a different ontological status from that in Whitehead's theory. In his theory all compound entities are ontologically derivative entities, whereas in mine, integral compound entities are emergent entities, themselves, ontologically considered, being physical existents of greater complexity. In Whitehead's theory the physical existents, as ultimate constituents, are each individually accorded immense complexity. In my theory complexity is emergent, the product of the constitution of emergent organisms.

In Whitehead's doctrine all compound entities constitute "societies" of actual entities or physical existents. In my theory allowance is made for compound entities which are not "integral" wholes, but are wholes which much more adequately fit Whitehead's conception of "societies" of entities. Of special pertinence here, it seems to me, are the data of chemistry. Particularly significant in this is the work of Ilya Prigogine, which has necessitated a distinction between two kinds of "wholes": on the one hand, those such as the molecules which are "equilibrium structures" of constituent "atoms" and "elementary particles," and on the other, another kind of whole which Prigogine has termed "dissipative structures," found in "far from equilibrium conditions."[4] These dissipative structures are constituted, e.g., of systems of a variety of ordinary chemical molecules, which maintain their distinctive character and unity in a state of energy interchange with their environment. Joseph Earley has argued that "dissipative structures" are "compound individuals" to be accorded a status which is not ontologically different from that of the "integral compound entities" which I have conceived as physical existents in the full sense as themselves per se acting.[5] I would suggest that "dissipative structures" are more adequative analyzable as "societies," for it seems to me that those structures are wholes which are not per se agents. This is a philosophical issue of great moment and consequence; however, it cannot be entered into in detail here.

III

There is another aspect of the problem of the nature of physical existence which needs to be emphasized. From the beginnings of philosophical and scientific thinking among the Greeks, the physical was conceived as "bodily." It is not surprising that later the two concepts "physical" and "body" came so very frequently to be treated as synonymous or so close as to be virtually synonymous or equivalent. In the seventeenth century, when the physical was identified with mat-

---

4. Ilya Prigogine, *From Being to Becoming* (San Francisco: W. H. Freeman, 1980), and *Order out of Chaos* (New York: Bantam Books, 1984), 12 and 140–45.

5. See Joseph Earley, "Self-Organization and Agency: In Chemistry and Process Philosophy," *Process Studies* 12:242–58, esp. 253f.

ter, there arose the equivalence of the *three* concepts of "physical," "bodily," and "material." This was the conception dominant among scientists—the doctrines of Descartes and Leibniz, and also Hobbes, were rather more complex.

I have argued that the identification of the physical as matter is no longer tenable. This raises the problem regarding the question of the concepts of the "physical" and "body." This issue requires special consideration because of the continued inheritance in thought today, in the form of tacit presuppositions, of some of the consequences of the seventeenth-century philosophical situation.

The basic aspect of the seventeenth-century position relevant here is the ontological dualism which was the concomitant of the conception of the physical as matter. Therewith the "mental" was extruded from the physical and had to be accorded a quite independent ontological status. The question which has to be raised now is whether, with the rejection of the concept of the physical as "matter," the extrusion of the mental from the physical still has any validity at all. I submit that this ontological separation has entirely lost its foundation and merely persists in thought today as an inherited presupposition. Today the entire issue has to be very thoroughly rethought, and more particularly so for an adequate conception of the "physical."

Whitehead's has been the most significant attempt to overcome the inherited difficulties. From relatively early he engaged in a polemic against the inherited "bifurcation of nature," and in his later period he developed a philosophical theory which eliminated that bifurcation from nature. In this, however, it seems to me, he has still continued to be too much under the influence of the ontological status accorded to the mental by the Neoplatonic ontology which had been resuscitated in the seventeenth century and which had been dominant since. In Whitehead's own theory he conceived the acting of actual entities as essentially "mental," as is clear in the following quite characteristic statement: "With the purpose of obtaining a one-substance cosmology, 'prehensions' are a generalization from Descartes' mental 'cogitations', and from Locke's 'ideas', to express the most concrete mode of analysis applicable to every grade of individual actuality."[6] With good justification, therefore, Charles Hartshorne and others have characterized Whitehead's philosophy as a "panpsychism." It seems to me, however, that it was not Whitehead's intention to develop a panpsychism, that it only came to that because he had not sufficiently clearly rejected the seventeenth-century inheritance.

6. *PR* (C), 26; (M), 29.

IV

We need, I think, to take serious account of Whitehead's constructive theory, in which he distinguished the actual entity—all actual entities—as having both a "physical pole" and a "mental pole." These are characterized respectively by their prehensive acting, the former by "physical prehensions" and the latter by "conceptual prehensions." The basic distinction between these is that "physical prehension" is the acting of the entity which is directly in reference to other physical existents, i.e., it is the act of relating to other physical existents; while "conceptual prehension" is the acting in reference to what Plato had termed *eidos* or *idea*, which was rendered *forma* in Latin, and which Whitehead termed "eternal object," the factor of "definiteness"—that is, "conceptual prehension" is the acting which has the "forms of definiteness" as its object. In this theory we have a distinction of major importance; its chief weakness lies in the too restricted conception of "physical acting" it involves.

Let us examine first this analysis of "mental acting" or "conceptual acting or prehension." Mental acting has long in the philosophical tradition been characterized as "conceiving" (from *concipere*, "to take hold or lay hold of, to take to oneself, to take in, take, receive"), a "taking hold of" the form or factor of definiteness in abstraction from the physical entities exemplifying that definiteness. The noun *conception* means either the act of conceiving or the fact of conceiving, of taking hold of and holding something in the mind. Sometimes it is also used synonymously with *concept*, that which is so held, an "idea" or "thought." Whitehead's term *prehension* in its etymological meaning is close to this—deriving from *prehendere*, "to grasp, seize, catch." Since Whitehead uses the term *prehension* generally to cover both the physical and the mental "grasping" or "holding," his phrase *conceptual prehension* is equivalent to the usual meaning of *conception*.

That which is conceived or taken hold of is primarily the form or factor of definiteness, and this is per se necessarily "universal"—for, as Aristotle said, "that is called universal (*katholou*) which is such as to belong to more than one thing,"[7] since conceiving is an act of taking hold of, i.e., a mental "grasping" or "prehending," of a definiteness which thereby "belongs to" the conception, but a definiteness which also "belongs to" the physical entity from which it is abstracted. It is by virtue of this universality of its objects that mental acting or conception transcends the temporal—and pure concepts are atemporal—the temporal being grounded in the physical.

7. Aristotle, *Metaphysics*, 7.1038b11.

Now, it seems to me that an unsatisfactory theory results if we either oppose the mental to the physical, or reduce the physical to the mental—both these tendencies I find in Whitehead's theory. Rather, I think, we need to regard the mental as an "ingredient" in the total physical. Thus, for example, as Whitehead insisted, the mental is necessary to the teleological factor which is entailed in physical existents as "acting" and "becoming."

This brings us back to the problem of physical acting, the problem, that is, of its analysis. I have argued that this acting must be, in the first instance, a reciprocal relating. Of course, in thinking and speaking of this we necessarily do so in terms of abstractions, here particularly using the very abstract general term *relation*. It is important, however, to appreciate that what we are concerned with in the individual instances is very much concrete, and definite—that is, in any actual relation there is a specific individual definiteness. In other words, not only is the reciprocal action individual, but it is also necessarily of a precisely definite character. The acting is uniquely individual—it is only the concept "acting" which is general or universal—and its character, as determining that individual action, is likewise individual—although definiteness per se is universalizable (i.e., capable of being shared in). Action is uniquely individual because it is not per se repeatable; repetition is analyzable into a numerically other act with the same or similar character, it being the character or definiteness which is repeatable by virtue of its universality.

But there is no acting just as such; that is, acting per se is not an existent being. Rather, acting is the acting of an existent being, an agent, the subject which is acting. This does not entail, however, that the existent subject is separable from the acting; there is no agent if there be no acting. This entails that the existent entity cannot per se be a changeless substrate of the acting; as acting, the existent is necessarily in a process of change. Since it is not a changeless subject of change, the process of change it entails is a process of becoming.

Whitehead, in his scheme developed in *Process and Reality*, has interpreted this process as a radical generation of the individual existent, a coming-into-being without qualification. I would want to argue (which I cannot do at length here) that the process of becoming is not necessarily to be thought of as a radical coming-into-being or generation; it seems to me that Aristotle's conception of this process of becoming as a process of actualization of potentiality is a tenable theory, and one indeed more adequate to the conception of compound physical existents as organisms.

V

What I mainly want to bring out here are some of the principal philosophical issues involved in the problem of the nature of the physical existent conceived as *acting*. This conception entails that the "existence" of the physical entity is grounded in its acting, and its character or definiteness, i.e., "what" it is, is the definiteness of the acting. But this position must be seen as constituting a particular position in respect of the basic problem of the fundamentals involved in the analysis of physical existence. The problem of these fundamentals can perhaps be most readily appreciated by setting this position in contrast with the position—today still predominating as a presupposition—which it rejects.

This rejected position is a philosophical theory originating from Aquinas, although some of its central features are an inheritance from Neoplatonism and from some early misinterpretations of Aristotle—those which have resulted in the rendering of his term *ousia* as "substance." The fundamental analysis of the physical existent, according to this theory, is into a "matter" and a "form." The matter is (1) the substrate, in the double sense of that which receives form and that which underlies the changes of form, in this respect being identifiable with the physical existent as "subject"; and (2) a passive "stuff" which is per se extensive—this being the particular Thomist contribution to the position. Form determines the definiteness of the physical existent as an attribute qualifying the matter, inhering in it on the paradigm of a color inhering in something extended. In this theory the physical existent is "bodily" by reason of the passive, extended substrate, the matter. This position came into widespread acceptance, beyond the Thomist school, and acquired another feature from the Neoplatonic inheritance through Augustinianism, augmented by Averroism. This is that the principle of activity of the physical existent had to be ascribed to form, since matter is inherently passive and not able to be the principle of activity. The philosophical innovation of the seventeenth century had been to identify the passive extended substrate, matter, as the physical existent. Thus the physical existent as passively extended matter was bodily, but since it was shorn of all form (except the geometrical), it was therewith also shorn of any principle of activity. For the principle or source of the locomotion of matter most seventeenth-century thinkers had recourse to God, under the influence of the Thomist doctrine of God as *actus purus*.

The scientific developments of our time, having necessitated a return to the conception of the physical existent as per se "active," have thereby necessitated too, as Whitehead was the first most clearly to see, a thoroughgoing reassessment of the fundamentals involved in the philosophical analysis of the physical existent. The outcome was the development by Whitehead of what must be acknowledged as a very significant philosophical innovation. In his position Whitehead has retained, as fundamentally necessary in the analysis of the physical, the two principles which Greek thought had discovered as ultimate, namely, the factor of *eidos* ("form, definiteness"), and the factor of *hypokeimenon* ("substrate")—these being particularly clear in the late Plato and in Aristotle. Whitehead's position rejects the Neoplatonic conception of form as the principle of activity, returning instead to the Platonic insight of the forms per se as immutable, constituting the principles of definiteness. Whitehead agreed with Aristotle on the necessity of an ultimate substrate, and of this as the recipient of definiteness. He has, however, completely rejected the conception of the substrate as passive, extended "stuff"—the Thomist conception of it—maintaining instead that the substrate is to be conceived as the complete contrary of "passive," and also not as extended "stuff."

Whitehead conceives of an ultimate substrate "activity" (to which he has given the name "creativity"), per se indeterminate, and the recipient of determinateness, of the forms of definiteness (in his terminology, "eternal objects"). As "informed" by the principles of definiteness, the indeterminate substrate activity is individualized as a plurality of acting subjects, which are the physical existents ("actual entities"). In this position, therefore, the principle of the activity of physical existents is the ultimate substrate. This conception of the principle of activity is significantly new, especially as developed into an elaborate and coherent theory, although it could be regarded as having been anticipated by other thinkers, not least, it seems to me, by Aristotle when he identified his substrate *hyle* with *dynamis*, the latter term not connoting a *passive* "potentiality" (as it has commonly been interpreted under the influence of the Neoplatonic tradition), but "potency," "power," and "force," the factor which is fundamental to "acting," as Leibniz had insisted,[8] and which Plato had also recognized.[9]

But these anticipations do not detract from the greatness of Whitehead's achievement. This position which he has developed in respect of the fundamental analysis of physical existence is, moreover, one most consonant with contemporary scientific inquiry.

8. E.g., in "Systeme nouveau pour expliquer la nature . . . ," Gerhardt, 4:479; Loemker, 454.
9. Cf. Plato, *Sophist*, 247 C, E.

There remains for consideration the problem of what this position, having rejected completely the notion of passive "stuff," entails respecting the "bodiliness" of the physical existent. The concept of "body," as the clearest thinkers of the seventeenth century saw, entails above all "extensiveness" (especially bounded extensiveness) and "impenetrability" or "antitypy," as Leibniz spoke of it; some thinkers added "mass." In terms of the foregoing analysis of the fundamental principles, these features must be grounded either in "acting" or in "form," or in both together. In Whitehead's theory the "extensiveness" of the physical is analyzed as a form determining the definiteness of the acting.

In my analysis of "acting" as a reciprocal relating, as an "acting on" by one subject on another and a "reacting," the other being necessarily being elsewhere/when in relation to the subject, it is evident that physical acting per se involves "extensiveness." This is perhaps not so clear in Whitehead's analysis, with acting being a "prehending," but it is nevertheless implicitly involved, for what is physically prehended is "from else-where/when," and since physical prehending is a relating, a form of extendedness is necessarily entailed. The main point is that in this philosophical position, as Whitehead explicitly maintained, extendedness is not an attribute inhering in a passive subject, but is the form of a *relation*, i.e., a feature of definiteness of relational acting. It is not difficult to see that "impenetrability" and "mass" are also readily interpretable as features of "acting." Impenetrability is analyzable as the "passive" concomitant of "acting," the "resistance" entailed in "reacting." The concept of "mass" has in the physics of this century come increasingly to lose its seventeenth-century connotation of "quantity of matter"; instead, it has come to be conceived as integrally bound up with physical "acting." Philosophically analyzed, it is to be conceived as a measurable feature of acting. The upshot of this analysis is that the physical existent, conceived as "acting," is necessarily "bodily," but this conception involves a different analysis of "bodiliness" from that which is still the dominant inherited presupposition.

VI

One further problem involved in the conception of the physical existent as acting needs to be discussed here, especially because of the continuation of the presuppositions inherited from the seventeenth century. This is the problem of "change."

The issue we have to face will perhaps most readily be appreciated from an examination of the inherited presuppositions. These are the conception of "change" involved in the theory of the physical existent as "matter." In terms of this theory, as we have noted earlier, only one kind of change is possible, namely, change in respect of place, i.e., locomotion. This conception admirably suited seventeenth-century physics, which was a pure mechanics. But philosophically the theory presented grave difficulties in respect of the problem of change. Since matter is completely without any principle of activity, as we have seen, this meant that the source of locomotive change was not found in the physical at all, and thinkers had to resort to the "meta-physical," i.e., God, as the principle or source of locomotive change. Leibniz strongly attacked this position as unsatisfactory, maintaining the necessity for finding the principle or source of locomotive change in the physical, and introduced a new conception of physics as a "dynamics." This conception of physics came to be adopted in the eighteenth century and onward, but without Leibniz's or any other philosophical foundation for it, by which the principle of change could be grounded in the physical—indeed, the philosophical issue involved in this conception of physics was completely ignored. This meant the continued acceptance of the presupposition of the conception of locomotion as the basic and only change in the realm of the physical.

This presupposition is, however, quite plainly inconsistent with the conception of the physical existent as "active," for acting per se is a kind of change, and since this acting is the source of locomotive change, the latter cannot be basic. This means that the conception of the physical as active necessitates a complete reexamination of the problem of change, and a reassessment of the status of locomotion. The seventeenth-century conception of the physical as matter had necessitated the extrusion from the physical of all the kinds of change which had previously been ascribed to it except locomotion. But with the rejection of the conception of the physical as matter, the ground for that extrusion has fallen away, and the case for the other kinds of change need to be reconsidered.

In the previous section we have seen that the fundamental "change" entailed by the conception of the physical existent as "acting" is that which constitutes the process of becoming. Aristotle had subjected this "process" (*kinesis*) involved in becoming to a detailed and penetrating examination, from which he concluded that this "process" is to be analyzed as manifesting three kinds of "change" (*metabole*): qualitative change, i.e., change in respect of kind or sort; quantitative change, i.e., change in respect of size and shape; and *phora*, i.e., locomotion, change in respect of place. The conception of physical acting as basically a "relating," it seems to me, necessitates readmitting both qualitative change and quantitative change to the physical. In the previous section I have argued for the rejection of the conception of the fundamental substrate recipient of definiteness as essentially passive, inert, and therewith also of the conception of the definiteness of the physical existent as an attribute passively inhering in that substrate. If instead we accept with Whitehead the contrary conception of the fundamental substrate recipient of definiteness, this entails, as we have seen, that it is "acting" which is defined by particular definiteness, and since acting is basically a relating, definiteness as "informing" the physical is the characterization of a relation. Thus, the qualitative definiteness is the quality of a relation, and this implies, as Whitehead has argued (e.g., in *Science and the Modern World*) that quality is misconceived when thought of as "simply located" as an attribute of an individual existent.

What is particularly relevant here is that with the conception of the physical as "acting," and with the definiteness being the definiteness of that acting, there is no ground for ascribing only some kinds of definiteness, e.g., the quantitative, to the physical and excluding qualitative definiteness, as was done in the seventeenth century-theory—an exclusion which still largely continues as a tacit presupposition. This implies that with the conception of the physical as "acting," qualitative change must be ascribed to the physical. Further, this conception of the physical existent necessitates, too, the admission of quantitative change in a respect importantly different from that involved in the conception of the physical existent as matter. Since matter is per se changeless, it can admit of no change of shape or magnitude; this theory could admit quantitative change only as a derivative of locomotive change. In the conception here advanced, as we have seen in the previous section, extensiveness is a quantitative determination of acting, and therewith quantitative change is readmitted to the physical existent per se—and not as a mere derivative of locomotive change. In terms of this conception, if any kind of change is to be accorded a derivative status, it would be locomotive change. This is indeed the status accorded it by Whitehead. This derivative status for locomotion seems to me, however, not to be necessarily entailed in the conception of the physical existent as acting; locomotive change could be conceived as involved in acting coordinately with the other two kinds of change.[10]

10. See chap. 16, below.

VII

One upshot of this philosophical analysis of change is that some inherited conceptions of the natural sciences need to be reexamined. For example, insofar as physics is conceived as concerned essentially with entities in respect of their locomotion, physics cannot be the fundamental science in the sense of that to which the others, such as chemistry, are ultimately reducible. The other kinds of change have at least an equal claim to be regarded as fundamental, and insofar as chemistry is concerned with these other kinds of change, it is to be considered as having a status coordinate with that of physics. On the other hand, insofar as the subatomic entities, which are the subject of inquiry of physics, are basically relevant to chemistry, physics has reason in this respect to be accorded a certain fundamental status.

The situation is, however, profoundly affected if the two inherited presuppositions, which we have found good reasons to regard as highly questionable, be rejected. The first is that the physical existent is to be identified only with the ultimate constituents of compounds. The rejection of this presupposition, it seems to me, deprives physics of the fundamental status which it had been accorded in terms of the seventeenth-century conception of the physical as matter. The rejection of this presupposition brings another question respecting physics: whether it can continue to investigate the subatomic entities essentially and simply in their individuality, or whether it needs to investigate them also explicitly as "constituents," i.e., as parts of organic wholes—this would entail that the entities are not to be understood as merely individual but as in relationship, and that the character and behavior of the entities will differ, depending upon the whole of which they are constituent parts.

The second presupposition we have seen reason to question is that of the ultimacy of locomotive change in the physical. If this be rejected; it raises the question whether the subatomic entities can continue to be satisfactorily investigated only in respect of their locomotive change. Do not the other kinds of change also require to be brought into consideration? It seems to me that these implications of the physical conceived as active are making themselves felt in contemporary physics, but that in the absence of a coherent philosophical theory to provide a foundation, it has not been possible to bring them adequately into effect in scientific theory. To bring these into effect, it seems to me, will require some far-reaching changes in theory in physics, and correspondingly also in the other natural sciences.

In the conception of this widened view of change for which I have argued as being necessarily involved in the physical existent as acting, the issue of the relation of the biological sciences to physics and chemistry becomes highly relevant. This brings up the problem of the nature of "life." This problem is related to that of "change." To make the connection we need to bring into consideration, together with the foregoing analysis of "change," a main point in my argument in this paper, namely, the necessity to reject the metaphysical dualism inherited from the seventeenth century. A principal consequence of this rejection is that mental functioning can be, and needs to be, readmitted as integral to physical existence as essentially involved in physical acting. Earlier, I dealt with one aspect of this in pointing out that "acting" entails a teleological factor, and that to this the mental is necessary. But this readmission of the mental as necessary to an adequate conception of the physical existent is not to be taken as implying that the physical existent is thereby to be conceived as "alive." To put this differently, the concept of "organism" is not synonymous with the concept of "life"—the phrase "living organism" is not a pleonasm. Certain particular features are requisite for an organism to be regarded as "living."

Whitehead has maintained that the fundamental feature involved in "life" is the "origination of novelty."[11] The acting of nonliving actual existents manifests a high degree of regularity which is formulated in the respective natural sciences as empirically discovered "laws." In Whitehead's theory, the ground for the regularity of the acting of an existent is the massive determination of its acting by its inherited past. In contrast with this situation dominantly prevalent in physical existence, Whitehead holds, "Life is a bid for freedom."[12] The fundamental requisite in this is the mental or conceptual origination and entertainment of teleological possibility divergent from that of the inherited determination.

The question of the reason for this conceptual origination now becomes crucial. Whitehead's general answer is that this is one possible mode of survival of a physical existent—in his theory, in this context a "structured society" of actual entities—through important changes in its environment. One possible response to this situation is for the existent itself to remain unchanged through the environmental change. The other possible response is for the existent to adjust itself to the environmental change by itself changing. The latter mode necessitates conceptual *initiative*, i.e., conceptual origination and "appeti-

---

11. *PR*, pt. 2, chap. 3: (C), 145; (M), 156.
12. Cf. *PR* (C), 145; (M), 159.

tion" (in its basic sense defined in the *OED* as "bent of the mind toward the attainment of an object of purpose").[13] This is the mode of response characterizing the existent as "living"; the former mode of response is that of "nonliving" existents.

Now, the change of the existent itself in response to environmental change can be one tending toward the maintenance of its distinctive character as different in relation to its environment, or toward the progressive elimination of that distinctive character, or toward the enhancement of that character. The last route is that requiring the highest degree of conceptual originality, which in turn would tend toward a greater complexity of the organism or existent. This would be the basis for an upward evolutionary development.

The complexity of an organism is not only in itself, however; its internal complexity is matched by the complexity of its relations with its environment—these two complexities are interdependent. The complexity of interrelations with the environment is not merely a complexity of "responses to" other existents, but consists also in a complexity of "interweaving with" its environmental existents. Most conspicuous in this "interweaving" is the "use" of environmental existents as "food"—both "non-living" existents as well as "living" ones. Details are beyond the scope of this paper; I am concerned with philosophical generalities only.

One of the most important of these is that organisms are not adequately understandable and analyzable when conceived only in terms of the interrelatedness of their parts or constituents to the organic whole; it is necessary to take equally into account the interrelatedness of the organic wholes to each other. This holds evidently for "living" organisms, but not exclusively for them. In other words, this interrelatedness is of great importance also to the nonbiological sciences. The difference is that in the biological sciences this interrelatedness is of greater complexity.

13. *PR* (C), 141; (M), 155.

14

MOTION, ACTION, AND PHYSICAL BEING

I

It has been widely recognized that the twentieth-century developments in physical science have profoundly affected the concepts of space and time, and these concepts have consequently been subjected to a good deal of philosophical scrutiny. The extent to which the concept of motion has also been affected by these developments has been far less appreciated, and this concept has not received the degree of philosophical attention which it merits. Yet the implications for the philosophy of the physical or nature of a change in the concept of motion are possibly even more far-reaching than in the case of the other two concepts. The reason for this is that, contrary to currently dominant presuppositions, there is an even closer connection between the concept of motion and that of physical being than has been revealed with respect to the other two concepts and the physical. This connection tends to be obscured at the present time because of tacit presuppositions concerning motion which have derived from the inheritance of philosophical doctrines respecting the physical developed in the seventeenth century. We need to start with an examination of the concept of motion in seventeenth-century thought.

By the end of the second decade of the seventeenth century a radically new concept of physical being began to establish itself as the outcome of scientific inquiry, more particularly into the problem of chemical combination. This had resulted in the rejection of the Aristotelian doctrine that physical being is metaphysically analyzable as composite of matter and form, and in its replacement by the conception of physical being as constituted by matter alone.[1] This conception received its first full metaphysical analysis by Descartes, and by the last

---

1. See my *NPE*, pt. 2, and particularly chap. 11, for an exposition of this development.

decades of the century, after the publication of Newton's *Principia*, this conception of the physical was dominant.

Metaphysically considered, this new conception of the physical as matter stood in the sharpest contrast with the Aristotelian conception, antecedently dominant since its revival in the Scholastic Middle Ages. Fundamental in the latter conception was that the physical is "in becoming." Now, the new seventeenth-century development of the conception of the physical as matter had occurred as an intrinsic part of the Renaissance revival of Neoplatonism. What is basically relevant in respect of the concept of the physical is the ontology of Neoplatonism, its conception of "being": this is that "being" excludes "becoming," that what fundamentally "is," is in itself changeless. This ontology is that in terms of which the physical was metaphysically understood in the seventeenth century: the "being" of the physical as *matter* entailed that matter is in itself changeless, that it excludes becoming.[2]

Adequately to appreciate the consequences of this new doctrine of physical being for the concept of motion, we need to see what the latter concept had been in the antecedent period. We are of course here concerned with the philosophical sense of the word "motion," but properly to grasp that, especially so at the present time, it is necessary to see it in its relation to the general range of meanings of the word. The English word *motion* derives, via the French in the thirteenth century, from the Latin *motus*—to which the English uses correspond.[3] The verb *moveo* derives from the I.-E. base *mou-, *meu-, *mu-, as does the Greek ἀμείβω ("to change"), and means "to change the position of, or one's position, to affect, stir, prompt"[4] (which is also the meaning of the German verb *bewegen*), from which derive a variety of specialized senses. The philosophical meaning of *motus* is one of the specialized senses of the word, one which was acquired by its use as the Latin rendering of a concept developed in Greek philosophy, and particularly of its use by Plato and Aristotle. The relevant Greek term used by Plato and Aristotle was κίνησις—and not that which is the etymological cognate of the Latin *moveo*, viz., ἀμείβω. This fact is of significance, for the meanings of κίνησις and *motus* do not exactly correspond, the word κίνησις including in its connotation that it is the opposite of στάσις, "rest," which is not the case with *motus* in its primary meaning, nor with ἀμείβω. The word κίνησις, in its philosophi-

---

2. For an analysis of this in Descartes, see my "The Ontology of Descartes," *Review of Metaphysics* 34, no. 2 (Dec., 1980).
3. Cf. *OED*.
4. Cf. *The Oxford Dictionary of English Etymology*.

cal use by Plato and Aristotle, meant "a process of change," being used sometimes as the inclusive term for all kinds of change, more particularly those specifiable as generation, decay, qualitative change, quantitative change, and change in respect of place ($\varphi o \rho \acute{a}$), Aristotle, however, frequently restricting the meaning of κίνησις to only the last three. It was to render this philosophical meaning that Aquinas and subsequent Scholasticism used the word *motus*, and this was the earlier philosophical sense of *motion* in English.

In Aristotle's philosophy, the physical, φύσις, entails "becoming" (γένεσις)—and correspondingly decay (φθορά)—and "becoming" involves a process of change (κίνησις) from potentiality (δύναμις) to actuality (ἐνέργεια), this process (κίνησις) being analyzable into three kinds of change, namely qualitative, quantitative, and change in respect of place. The new seventeenth-century philosophy of physical being as "matter," as we have noted, entailed that matter is in itself changeless, excluding "becoming." This meant that matter, in itself, involves no process of change, i.e., κίνησις or *motus*: it could involve neither qualitative change (since matter per se is completely devoid of the qualitative), nor quantitative change (i.e., augmentation or diminution, since matter is homogeneously matter). That is, in the new philosophical doctrine all the formerly distinguished kinds of "motion" (κίνησις)—including generation and decay—are excluded as applicable to physical being as matter, except the last: the only kind of change possible for matter is change in respect of place, i.e., locomotion. With locomotion as the only kind of change in the new conception of the physical, it is readily explicable that soon the term *motion* came to lose its wider sense and came to mean exclusively "locomotion," or change in respect of place.

This explains too, what has become a dominant presupposition at the present time, that there is no close connection between motion and physical being per se. For in the conception of the physical as matter there is indeed no close connection between the two; on the contrary, "motion" is in no respect entailed by "matter": matter cannot itself originate motion (for it is completely devoid of any internal principle of change) nor does it require to move, or to be moved. This was quite clear to the leading protagonists of the doctrine of the physical as matter (Descartes, Gassendi, and Newton are to be particularly instanced), who consistently could see no other source of the motion of matter than the act of God. This disconnection between matter and motion survived the eighteenth-century dismissal of the conception of a *deus ex machina*, this disconnection becoming enshrined in the post-Newtonian doctrine that physical science rests upon four ultimates—

space, time, matter, and motion—which are neither mutually entailed in, required by, nor derivable from each other.

The point particularly to be emphasized is that this entire conception of "motion" is the outcome of, since it is required by, the new conception of physical being as "matter," in itself changeless, devoid of all "becoming" and of any inherent principle of change.

II

With the conception of physical being as matter, the new seventeenth-century *science* of the physical or nature was the inquiry, not into matter per se—that being homogeneous, everywhere the same, and changeless—but into the motion, or more specifically the locomotion, of matter. In other words, the new physical science was a mechanics, i.e., an applied mathematics of motion. But this science early required the introduction of the notion of "force" as the cause of motion or change of motion; Newton introduces it at the very beginning of his *Principia*, in the first law of motion.

Now, this raised the philosophical issue as to the status of "force." Force could not be identified with motion, since it is that which "causes" or "produces" the motion. Further, since this "causing" or "producing" entails a "potency" or "power to do or effect," force could not be ascribed to matter, as a property of matter, since matter per se is entirely devoid of any principle of change. The attempt to conceive force in terms or "push" or "shove," i.e., as a resultant of motion, could not be successful since this confused "motion" with "action"—which both Descartes and Newton, as well as Leibniz, saw to be quite distinct.[5] "Motion" is the resultant of *action* and could thus not be identified with it. Through the eighteenth century, "force" remained an indispensable factor in the scientific scheme of thought, but without any adequate philosophical intelligibility.

In the nineteenth century, "energy" was introduced into physical theory as a fundamental concept, not replacing "force" but extending it. For, as we have noted, in the context of physical science *force* connoted a "power to do or effect," which is also indeed what was meant by *energy*—this term deriving from Aristotle's ἐνέργεια (compounded from ἐν, "in," and ἔργον, "work, action") meaning "in-work" or "in-

---

5. Cf., e.g., Descartes, *The Principles of Philosophy* (trans. Haldane & Ross, 1931), pt. 2, princ. 25: "And I say that it [motion] is the *transportation* and not either the force or the action which transports, in order to show that the motion is always in the mobile thing, not in that which moves; for these two do not seem to me to be accurately enough distinguished."

act." The term in modern physical theory meant the power of doing work possessed by a moving body by virtue of its motion and was later distinguished into "kinetic energy" when the body is actually moving, and "potential energy" when the body is at rest.

To be noted with respect to the concept of "energy" in nineteenth-century physical theory is that with it, scientific thought had introduced "action" into the physical realm—in contrast to the previous ascription of action solely to God, whereby it was transcendent of the physical. Now, this raised the problem of the metaphysical status of "energy." Though this philosophical issue might be, and indeed mostly was, ignored by scientists, the fact nevertheless is that scientific theory and concepts have metaphysical implications. In this case, since energy was not able to be ascribed to matter, implicitly it was accorded the status of an independent physical ultimate. In other words, as C. F. von Weizsäcker has pointed out, this meant that "in the nineteenth century there appeared to be two substances in physics, matter and energy."[6] That is to say, nineteenth-century physical science entailed a metaphysical dualism of two kinds of physical being, with no clarity as to how they could be coherently related.

The significant trend of the twentieth-century developments in physics has been to overcome this dualism. Relativity theory regards matter (mass) and energy as relativistically equivalent, and in microphysics energy has come to be conceived as fundamental, it being capable of transformation into matter. Werner Heisenberg has seen the metaphysical implication of these developments, stating it as follows in his Gifford Lectures: "The elementary particles in modern physics carry a mass. . . . Since mass and energy are, according to the theory of relativity, essentially the same concepts, we may say that all elementary particles consist of energy. This could be interpreted as defining energy as the primary substance of the world. It has indeed the essential property belonging to the term 'substance', that it is conserved."[7]

What is primarily relevant in these developments with respect to our topic is that insofar as it is held that elementary particles or matter "consist of energy," this entails a radical departure from the antecedent concept of "matter." For in this new theory nothing whatever of the antecedent connotation of "matter" remains. When in the seventeenth century the doctrine of physical being as matter was

---

6. C. F. von Weizsäcker, *Die Einheit der Natur* (München: Carl Hanser, 1971), 344 (English trans. *The Unity of Nature* [New York: Farrar, Straus, Giroux, 1980], 276).

7. Werner Heisenberg, *Physics and Philosophy* (New York: Harper and Row, 1958), 70–71.

introduced, the fundamental feature in the connotation of the term *matter*, which it had had since its inception with Aristotle, was retained, namely, that of "substrate." This doctrine also retained from the Neoplatonic concept of "matter," going back to Plotinus, the connotation of what is in itself unalterable (since it itself is without any form or definiteness) and entirely devoid of any principle of change (since in the Neoplatonic ontology form alone could constitute a principle of agency or change). The difference effected by the seventeenth-century doctrine was the ascription of "being" to matter itself, in entire disjunction from form. Since in the Neoplatonic ontology "being," as excluding "becoming," is changeless, the ascription of being to matter, as in itself changeless, was held to be entirely consistent.[8]

In twentieth-century physical theory the connotation of *substrate* has been transferred to *energy*, as Heisenberg has indicated in the passage above, and does not pertain to what continues to be called "matter" or "material particles." Further, since the particles of "matter" are held to "consist of energy," it is clear that what is called "matter" is no longer in itself changeless and devoid of any "principle of action"; quite the contrary is the case. In this theory, at least as interpreted by many such as Heisenberg, "matter" does not even retain the seventeenth-century connotation of its being the physical "substance"—i.e., what is philosophically considered as the ultimate entity or being. On the contrary, it is "energy" which is the ultimate "substance," from which so-called "matter" is derivative.

The upshot of the foregoing analysis is that physical being, in twentieth-century physics, is not "matter" or "material" in any previous sense of that word. Indeed, the continued use of the term *matter* at all, I would say, is questionable as implicitly importing connotations which are rejected in contemporary physical theory.[9]

III

One does not have to accept Heisenberg's analysis as metaphysically adequate—indeed, it is not—nevertheless to recognize what it brings out with respect to the development of thought in twentieth-century physics, namely, that it has completely destroyed the tenability of the

---

8. See my "The Ontology of Descartes."
9. It could be held that the term *matter* is now used to denote energy in particulate form. But at most this represents a weak analogical use of the term *matter*, with nothing of its previous connotation.

conception of physical being as "matter." Not only is this the case with respect to physics; it is equally so in chemistry and in the biological sciences—although most scientists in those fields have not yet adequately appreciated this.

The point in contemporary physical theory which is of special significance to us here is that in it "energy" is no longer regarded as extrinsic to physical entities—as it was in the nineteenth century—but is, rather, conceived as intrinsic to the physical entities. The issue is what philosophically is entailed in this position.

We have seen that in nineteenth-century physical theory *energy* meant a "power to effect," and that what was effected was motion or change of motion in physical entities. These entities, being "matter," could not be intrinsically affected because they were in themselves changeless, so that the only effect possible was in respect of their change of place, i.e., locomotion. Twentieth-century physical theory retains the connotation of *energy* as the "power to effect," and what is effected is motion or change of motion. But with energy intrinsic to the physical entities, what is entailed is that the effect is primarily in respect of each physical entity itself. This is to say that the intrinsic energy is a power to produce motion or change of motion in the entity itself; i.e., the entity is self-moving.

Now, the issue which must be raised here is how this "energy" or "power" is to be *philosophically* conceived. That is, what is the philosophical analysis of this concept? The notions of "force" and "power" cannot be accepted as philosophically ultimate; "force" or "power" must pertain to something, something which exercizes them—this is to say that these notions presuppose some subject. Since they are conceived as inherent in the physical entity, that entity itself must be the subject in question. This means that the philosophical analysis must be of the entity itself. The issue then is: what must be the nature of the entity such that it can exercise power or force? The force or power with which we are concerned here is not to be taken in a general or abstract sense; in the present context we are concerned with a particular force or power, namely, that which has "motion," or more precisely, locomotion, as its effect. This is not to say, however, that there might not be more than that involved in the concept of force or power as we are concerned with it.

To pursue our analysis, let us for the meantime confine the "effect" to motion, i.e., to locomotive change. Now, motion as the *effect* has to be distinguished from the *cause* of the effect. That is, this cause, the "power" entailed in "energy," is not itself "motion" or "a motion." Descartes, as we have seen, had insisted on this distinction between "motion" on the one hand, and "force" or "action" on the other.[10] This, too, is the distinction which Aristotle had made between κίνησις and ἐνέργεια—from which our modern terms were derived, as we have seen.

It is, however, not sufficient merely to distinguish these two; it is necessary also to specify that distinction, to indicate wherein it consists. It is evident that in the case of "motion" we are concerned with a *process*, in the general sense of a "going on or being carried on."[11] The question to be considered is whether in the case of "force" or "power" we are *not* concerned with a "process," that in these we have something quite else.

The word *force* means "strength, power," and *power* means "capability to do" something. But "capability" per se cannot produce an effect; capability per se is a "potentiality," which can be efficacious only by being "actualized"—literally, "made actual." Now, *actual* means "of or pertaining to acts," and *act* (from *actus*) means "a moving or doing; and a thing done; an action; a deed."

Philosophically what is entailed is that "force" or "power," in order to produce an effect, must issue in "action." The "action," however, is not to be identified with "motion"; on the contrary, it is the "action" which produces the effect, that "motion." The point is that "force" or "power" cannot "produce" or "cause" an effect without issuing in an "action," since "power" per se is "potential" and can affect only by "actualizing" its potentiality in an "action." Further to be noted is that the word *action* literally means "a process of acting or doing," and in a more abstract sense a "state of acting"—*acting* being defined as "the process of carrying out into action." The philosophical conclusion from this analysis is that "action" is a *process*. That is, there is a *process* involved in "action" as well as in "motion."

Now, the concept of "process" implies some kind of "change." In the case of "motion," in the sense in which we have been using the term, the change is that in respect of place. What is the change entailed in "action" or "acting"? Since the "action" which we are having under consideration is, as we have seen, that issuing from "force" or "power" as a "potentiality," it is clear that the change involved here is that from "potentiality" to "actuality," i.e., to a state or condition of being "actual," this state being that in which the end of the force or power is achieved or realized—what Aristotle expressed in his term ἐντελέχεια, literally, "having its end in itself."

---

10. See n. 5, above.
11. For this and all subsequent definitions, see *OED*.

But does this mean that the "change" in question is constituted by the "transition" or "passage" from one "state" or "condition" to another? What is entailed in this? That is, what is this "transition" or "passage"? Is it something different from the two "states" or "conditions"? This cannot be, for so to regard it would involve the introduction of a *tertium quid* with no intelligible connection with its terms, for it would be some other kind of entity different from those constituting the terms. It is important, on the contrary, to be clear that there is only one proper or real entity involved here, viz., the physical entity, and that both the "potentiality" and the "actuality" pertain to, and are grounded in, the physical entity in question as subject. The "transition" must likewise be grounded in that entity. That is, it is the entity, as subject, which is in transition from potentiality to actuality. And it is so by "acting": the "acting" is *the process of carrying its potentiality into actuality*, i.e., into realization. Now, the question is whether the "actuality," the "realization," is *beyond* the process of acting, existing when that process is complete and over? But what is this "actuality," i.e., this "state of being actual"? What is being referred to or denoted here? It is not the "motion"; it is the physical entity itself, as "actual." What does it mean to say that the physical entity is "actual" or in a "state of being actual"? Since the word *actual* means "of or pertaining to acts," and *act* means "a doing," what is entailed is that the state of being "actual" obtains only *in an act*, "in a doing." That is to say, "actual" entails being "in-act." The conclusion, that the actualization or realization of potentiality obtains "in-act," is what Aristotle expressed by his term ἐνέργεια.[12]

IV

The main point brought out in the foregoing analysis is that "action" is an internal process of change of the physical entity in question. The issue which must now be considered is the relation between this "action" and the "motion" of the entity—which earlier we had explicitly taken as a process which is the "effect" of the "action" (the motion under consideration being that of the physical entity itself, i.e., its process of change in respect of place). The question facing us is that of the connection between these two processes. Are these two processes

---

12. Literally, "in-act." In *Metaphysics*, 9.1048b18–34, Aristotle distinguishes ἐνέργεια as the kind of process that has its end present in (ἐνυπάρχει) itself (in contrast to beyond it): "the same thing at the same time is is seeing and has seen, is thinking and has thought" (1048b33–34).

The term ἐνέργεια is usually translated "actuality" and sometimes "activity"—the

distinct and different, the connection between them being that "motion," the process of changing from one place to another, is the resultant, the product, of the internal process of "action"?

But how is this to be understood? Is it the case that the process of motion is the resultant or product of action, in that the process which is "motion" is *beyond* the "action," i.e., that the "motion" comes into existence *at the termination* of the process of "acting," when the process involved in "action" is strictly over? This conception is, however, open to serious objections. It entails not only a difference between the two processes, but more particularly that they are temporally sequential, that of "motion" following upon the completion of the "action." But this implies that the physical entity in question, when in motion, is no longer "active," i.e., "in-act," in a process, but that on the contrary it must be considered as being *in a state of inactivity*. The question must be raised, however, whether the physical entity is able consistently to be conceived as being "in a state of inactivity." Could an entity in such a state be "actual," i.e., "really existing as such"? This would entail the conception of an actual physical being as in itself changeless. Now, this is indeed the conception which had been maintained from the seventeenth to nineteenth centuries, and that which twentieth-century scientific thought has rejected, as we have seen.

Metaphysically considered, the rejected doctrine is that an "actual being" is in itself changeless. But this, as has emerged from our analysis, is not only questionable, but has to be rejected, because the conception of "an *actual* being in itself changeless" involves a contradiction. For "actual," as we saw at the end of the previous section, entails "being in-act," i.e., in a process of activity, which is the opposite of "in itself changeless."

This means that although these two processes, that of "action" and that of "motion," are distinguishable, they are not to be separated, and especially not as being sequential. The connection between them requires to be differently conceived. For what is entailed is that the two processes must be in some respect coincident. The problem is, how precisely this is to be conceived.

---

former when the connotation of the term involves its contrast with δύναμις ("potentiality"), and the latter when its connotation involves its contrast with ἕξις ("disposition"). But both of these contrasts are involved for Aristotle in the meaning of the term, i.e., ἐνέργεια connotes both "actuality" and "activity," and not one to the exclusion of the other. This sense tends to be lost by taking "actuality" in its more abstract meaning of "existing in fact—as opposed to possibility or potentiality." The word *actuality* should rather be taken in its primary sense of "state of being actual," where *actual* means "of or pertaining to acts," and *act* means "a doing" or "action," i.e., "a process of doing or acting."

The first question to be considered is whether the "action" is one which is *solely* productive of "motion," or whether it is a more complex process, involving other results as well. Now, we have seen that "action" is a "process of acting," and that this "process" implies some kind of "change." Further, this "change" must be in respect of the physical entity itself, and that it must, in a basic sense, involve the "actualization" of the entity. In other words, its "process of acting" must be a process of *becoming actual*. The *fundamental question* which it is appropriate to raise concerning this "process of change" and its issue, viz., the entity as "actual," is: "of what kind or sort?"—the question which is expressed by the Greek interrogative ποῖος and the Latin *qualis*. For the quite fundamental consideration of the entity respecting its process and its emergent "actuality" is concerning "what" it is, "of what kind—among the possible kinds"; i.e., it is the question respecting its *quality*.

It will perhaps assist the appreciation of this point if we contrast this conception of physical being with that of the being conceived as "matter." In the latter conception there could be no question of "change in respect of kind or sort," for "matter," being simply "matter," is as such incapable of change into any other kind or sort; that is, there could be no question respecting any change of "quality." Equally, there could be no question of change in regard to "quantity," i.e., a question respecting a change in "size"; for a piece of matter is not, qua "matter," capable of either augmentation or diminution. The only capability remaining for "matter" is change in respect of place, i.e., locomotion. As opposed to this, with the conception of physical being as "active," as involving a "process of activity," both the two questions which were irrelevant with respect to "matter," become highly pertinent to this alternative conception of physical being. That is to say, with regard to this conception of physical being, the process of acting must involve change both in respect of quality and quantity.

The question now to be considered is what the connection is between these two species of change involved in the "process of acting" of a physical entity, on the one hand, and its change in respect of place, i.e., its locomotion, on the other. Is the latter to be regarded as a distinct and separate species of "change," not involved in the two former ones but quite distinct from them? When, however, we take account of the point made earlier, that "motion," or locomotive change, has to be the "effect" of the "action" of the physical entity, it becomes clear that this species of change cannot be separated from the other two species as having no connection with them. This is to say that the physical being is not to be conceived as having three distinct and different kinds of "action," i.e., three separate and simultaneous "acts" not involved in each other. Rather, the physical being as subject, i.e., as "agent," is to be conceived as involving *one* "process of acting," having three "aspects." This means that the "agency," the "process of acting," is analyzable as involving three distinct—but not separate or separable—outcomes or results. One of these is in respect of place, locomotion. This is to say that the "process" involved in "motion" (locomotion) is not a process separate from, and other than, the process involved in "action," but rather as an "aspect" of the "process of acting" of the entity in question. As such a distinct "aspect," "motion" (locomotion) is capable of being considered in abstraction from the total "process of acting" of the physical entity. This abstraction occurs in the science of mechanics, for example, and quite legitimately so for scientific purposes. But philosophically it is to be recognized as an *abstraction*, and not to be mistaken for a separate, concrete process.

V

Up to now we have been considering the "action" of a physical being insofar as it is an internal or immanent process, involving itself only. But science in the twentieth century has made clear not only that physical being is "active" in the sense of involving a "process of activity," but also that it is *interactive*, i.e., that it is in "interaction" with other physical beings. The problem is how this "interaction" is to be philosophically understood.

This "interaction" of physical entities entails that each entity is affected by other entities, and that each entity affects others. How is this to be analyzed? More specifically, how is this "interaction" to be conceived in relation to the internal process of action of a physical being?

It seems to me that there are three main possibilities as to this "interaction." Let us consider the interaction between two entities, A and B. One possibility is that A is "active," "acting on" B, and by this "acting on" affecting B, but that in this relationship B is "passive," i.e., "suffering action from without," or "being acted upon." The second possibility is that A, by its own acting, does not affect B at all, but that in the relationship it is B which is "active," itself "actively taking account of" the condition or state of A. A third possibility is that A and B both simultaneously mutually affect each other by "acting on" each other. This possibility is a more complex one than the others, and might turn out to involve features of the others, so they should be considered first.

The second of these has a long history; it is the classical Neoplatonic position, going back to Plotinus, which has been widely accepted in the modern period, from Descartes onward, consequent upon the introduction of the metaphysical dualism of matter and mind as two separate kinds of substances or beings. The ontological basis of this position, in classical Neoplatonism, is that since only form or soul is "being," this alone is "active" or a principle of agency. Accordingly, in the modern period, soul or mind—Descartes's *res cogitans*—is active, whereas the physical as "matter" is without any principle of agency. Consequently, in the perceptual relationship between the two, "matter" cannot affect soul: in perceiving, it is soul alone which "acts," "taking account" of motion in matter, the product of this "act of perceiving" being a "percept" in the soul. Further, it is to be noted that since matter is without any principle of agency, one material entity cannot affect another, even in impaction; this is why the notions of "force" and "energy" had been introduced, as we have seen earlier.

The special significance here of the introduction of the notions of force and energy into physical science, and in particular of the twentieth-century development resulting in the conception of energy as inherent in physical entities, is that it entailed the notion of "efficacy" being in the "cause," i.e., of a "power to produce" a change as "effect." Now, it seems to me that this notion of "efficacy in the cause" cannot adequately be accounted for in terms of the second possibility we are considering, namely, in terms solely of *an acting in the "effect,"* i.e., in entity B.[13]

This renders the first possibility peculiarly relevant, namely, that entity A "acts on" entity B, while B is "acted upon." This means that the "action" of physical entity A is not wholly immanent, but that, on the contrary, it is also transeunt.

There is, however, a question to be raised about entity B, which in this relationship is "acted upon," namely, how exactly this "being acted upon" is to be conceived as far as entity B is concerned. Earlier, I used the word "passive" as synonymous with "being acted upon"—this being indeed the primary meaning of "passive." But this word also has the meaning of "in a state of quiescence, inactive, inert." The question is whether the effect on B is to be conceived as a purely inert resultant of the acting of A? Or is it rather to be conceived as a "reception," a "response," a "reaction," on the part of B? It seems to me that the latter is the only tenable position. Since the entity B is essentially, i.e., in itself, "active," "in-act," the effect on it of being "acted on" by A would be by its own "action" constituting an "act of receiving, re-

---

13. This is Whitehead's position in his doctrine of "prehension."

sponding, reacting" to A—for these terms *reception, response, reaction,* all entail *act*, and do not connote a purely inert resultant.

This position also has a long history, going back to Aristotle at least. It seems to me that this is the only viable position with respect to the "action" of a physical being in the context of the present-day conception of physical being which is in accord with contemporary science. The "action" of a physical being must be "relational acting," which means that it must involve a "receiving or responding to" the transeunt acts of other physical entities—an immanent acting constituting a process of transition from potentiality to actuality, and a transeunt acting an "acting on" other entities. I suggest that the third possibility mentioned above, that of mutual "interaction," can be consistently understood only in terms of this Aristotelian position.

VI

I will conclude by briefly indicating a significant implication of the foregoing philosophical analysis for the science of nature. Physical science from the seventeenth century has been the understanding of nature in terms of the motion, i.e., locomotion, of its elementary entities—and this is still the dominantly accepted view of it. The other sciences of nature, chemistry and biology, have been conceived as ultimately reducible to physics, i.e., that their subject matters would be finally understood in terms of the motion of the elementary entities.

But if the elementary entities be seen as basically "active"—as opposed to being inert, as formerly conceived—then the science of nature is faced with a very different situation. For locomotive change must be seen as but *one aspect* of the change involved in the process of acting of physical entities, and not the most fundamental one at that. Primacy must be accorded to the process of acting as relational and to the internal change involved in the *process* of acting. I would submit that for chemistry and biology it is the relational aspect of acting which is most pertinent, and that in micro-physics this is also to a considerable extent the case. But in the end these two aspects, the locomotive and the relational, cannot be separated from the internal process of acting. That is, the adequate understanding of the relational and locomotive aspects is dependent upon the conception of the internal process. This will increasingly have to be taken into account in scientific theory and thought. This means that metaphysics will have to be taken into full and proper partnership in the inquiry into nature.

15

PLATONISM, ARISTOTELIANISM, AND MODERN SCIENCE

I

In the modern epoch the factor which has been determinative of the course of philosophical thought has been science, as in the medieval period the determinative factor had been religion and theology. Since the seventeenth century philosophical thought has been through two phases or periods of this influence of science. It is now, I shall argue, at the end of the second, and at the beginning of a third major phase.

The first period, extending from roughly the beginning of the second quarter of the seventeenth century till the end of the third quarter of the eighteenth, was one in which philosophy was close to science, one in which the philosophical preoccupation had been the elaboration, throughout its entire range, of the implications of the fundamentally new philosophical position which had emerged toward the end of the second quarter of the seventeenth century from scientific developments, the philosophical position which established itself as foundational to the new science of the modern era. This period ended with Kant's pre-critical work.

Kant's "Copernican revolution" inaugurated the second phase. This epoch-making change in Kant's thought marked the realization of the implications of the metaphysical dualism introduced in the seventeenth century, implications which had been determinative for Hume earlier than Kant, and which had in the eighteenth century, after the triumph of Newtonian physics, led to the division of fields of knowledge, natural science preempting the realm of physical nature, leaving philosophy to only the realm of mind. Henceforth, science and philosophy went their separate ways. The disconnection of philosophy from science was manifested in the two main philosophical movements of the nineteenth century, positivism and idealism, characterizing respectively two disparate philosophical attitudes toward science. The former accepted science as the only positive knowledge, whereas the latter rejected entirely that claim by science. Positivism, withdrawing philosophy from any positive contribution to the knowledge of the nature of things, eschewed metaphysics, while idealism asserted metaphysics as the only route to a true understanding. The positivistic attitude has become predominant in this century, but its earlier virile faith has noticeably dissipated; some acknowledgment of metaphysics has been creeping back, and "ontology" has been readmitted, albeit in a desiccated form in connection with logical theory. The other stream of thought has also run into the shallows; idealism has given way to phenomenology, in which philosophy is attempting to reestablish foundations and struggle back to metaphysics. But this stream has not been able to free itself from its inheritance grounded in the seventeenth-century dualism and its consequent separation from science.

We have today, I would urge, arrived at a turning point, at which it has become necessary to scrutinize critically our inherited presuppositions. This means that it has become necessary for us to take a careful look at our philosophical inheritance. We need to reassess the course of the modern philosophical development in order to be able to take our bearings for the future.

II

As a first step in this reassessment we should explicitly and finally reject the long dominant erroneous supposition that modern philosophy started in the seventeenth century by making a completely fresh start after a clean break with antecedent thought. It is important to acknowledge, too, that the beginning of modern science also did not constitute any such discontinuity. On the contrary, it is possible now to see more clearly the very definite continuity of seventeenth-century scientific thought with that of the preceding period, and it is of great importance now to give full weight to the features of that continuity. Further, science and philosophy were at that time not as separated as they subsequently became; seventeenth-century philosophy and science were two aspects of a single movement of thought going back to the fifteenth century, to the renascence of Neoplatonism after some centuries of the dominance of Aristotelianism.

The later sixteenth and early seventeenth centuries saw an increasing attack on Aristotelianism, accompanied by a growing acceptance of Neoplatonism. This revived Neoplatonism was no mere return to the Augustinian tradition; it went back to Plotinianism, and to the twelfth-century Platonism of the School of Chartres. The crucial thinker in this revived Neoplatonism was Nicolaus of Cusa in the fifteenth century; the determinative features for the scientific and philosophical development of the sixteenth and seventeenth centuries are to be traced back to him. His doctrine of the world as *explicatio Dei* gave a considerable impetus to the study of nature as a way to the understanding of God, and therewith to scientific thought in the next two centuries. But far more important for modern science and philosophy was the conception involved in this doctrine of God as unfolding his absolute infinity in the form of an infinite extension, for thereby Cusanus had inaugurated the epoch-making break with the inherited conception of the universe as finite.

Intrinsically connected with this, and of even greater import for modern thought, was Cusanus's revival of Plato's emphasis on mathematics, a side of Plato's thought which had been largely ignored in the intervening centuries. The outcome in Cusanus was his conception of the infinite extension of the universe as being fundamentally mathematical. This meant that the world is in its essence a geometrical structure, and thus the understanding of the world was to be achieved by a mathematical inquiry. This philosophical doctrine is what became foundational in modern thought, from Copernicus and Galileo, through Descartes, Leibniz, and Newton, to the mathematical physics of the present day. Descartes gave precise philosophical formulation to this doctrine in maintaining that in pure mathematics we have knowledge of the essence of the physical universe. In this respect, modern science and its implicit philosophy remains basically Platonic.

Another feature of Neoplatonic thought which became of considerable importance for the modern period was the resuscitation of the doctrine of a world soul. This doctrine had a major role in the philosophy of Nicolaus Cusanus. In the next century, in a combination with Stoic, Averroistic, and alchemistic influences, and the Aristotelian *aether*, the conception of a world soul became prominent in the doctrines of Agrippa of Nettesheim, Paracelsus, and other sixteenth-century thinkers, notably Bruno; then, in the seventeenth century, via Henry More, it became transformed by Newton into the conception of God as extended and active everywhere and everywhen.

But another, more profound consequence of this fifteenth-century resuscitation of the doctrine of the world soul was the role it played in recasting the earlier Neoplatonic conception of matter. For Plotinus matter was "not-being," an image of itself produced by soul;[1] for Augustine, matter was a *prope nihil*.[2] By the fifteenth century a marked influence of the Arab interpretation of matter had begun to affect Western thought, resulting in matter's being accorded a much more positive status, as having an essence of its own as matter, not derivative from form. Cusanus, following Thierry of Chartres, conceived matter as possibility. In God, absolute act and absolute possibility are coincident; by the *explicatio*, "unfolding," of God in the universe, the former becomes the world soul, while the latter becomes matter, equated with possibility. By a further contraction, the multiplicity of existent things result, as corporeal and ensouled. In Agrippa and Paracelsus matter is more definitely conceived as corporeal, in itself passive, soul constituting the principle of life and motion. This conception of ensouled corporeal matter became widely characteristic of sixteenth-century Neoplatonism.

This conception of matter was fundamental in Paracelsus' new theory of the elements as mercury, sulphur, and salt, in place of the traditional, Aristotelian elements, fire, air, water, earth. This new theory not only diminished the emphasis on the qualitative involved in the traditional conception but, of even greater moment, the Paracelsian theory maintained, contrary to the other conception, that the elements are not mutable, that they do not change into each other. This doctrine, spread by the influence of the Paracelsian medical school, was to have momentous consequences.

It was in respect of the theory of chemical combination that a direct consequence was seen by medical men, for whom this theory had special interest. In this theory traditionally—again going back to Aristotle—chemical combination proper, *mixis*, was distinguished from mere aggregation. But this presupposed that the constituents, ultimately the elements, undergo mutation in chemical combination or *mixis* whereby a new chemical entity emerges. But if the elements remain changeless in themselves, it implies that the presumed chemical combination is impossible; it is merely apparent, a *mistio ad sensum*.

This had enormous and far-reaching philosophical consequences. The ultimate constituents of chemical combination, i.e., aggregation, are, as noted, the elements, and these, philosophically considered, are the primary existents or substances. This entailed the rejection of the Aristotelian doctrine of a human or animal bodily being as a paradigm instance of a substance.[3] Such a being, on the contrary, does not

1. Plotinus, *Ennead* 3.9.3.10–16.
2. Augustine, *Confessions*, bk. 12, para. 6.
3. Cf. Aristotle, *Metaphysics*, 1032a17–20.

constitute one integral substance, but rather is an aggregation of very many substances.

III

It was the French medical man Sebastian Basso who, before the turn of the century, was the first to see with considerable clarity the philosophical implications of this development. The elements are in themselves changeless, but that which is in itself changeless is matter; therefore, the elements are matter. Further, to be in itself changeless entailed being devoid of form, for form is the principle of change. Therefore matter, without form, is substance. Thus was effected a series of identifications: the constituents of chemical aggregation are the elements; the elements are bodily matter; matter is physical substance.

Now if matter, shed of substantial form and soul, *anima*, is physical substance, it is evident that soul or mind is to be accorded the ontological status of a distinct and separate substance. Thus was introduced the metaphysical dualism which has so profoundly determined modern thought. It is particularly to be noted that this doctrine was the outcome in the seventeenth century of Renaissance Neoplatonism. What had occurred was that the traditional Neoplatonic distinction of form and matter had undergone a profound change, into a full metaphysical *separation* of form and matter. This was enabled by the fundamental alteration of the ontological status of matter, from not-being or a *prope nihil* as a recipient or substratum of form, to itself being or substance. While this metaphysical dualism is clearly a distinctively and indeed radically new philosophical position, it is most important to recognize the features of essential continuity, and to acknowledge this position as Neoplatonism in a new form or guise. I shall refer to it as "modern Neoplatonism."

The first large-scale published statement of the modern Neoplatonic position was Basso's book *Philosophia Naturalis* in 1621, its publication having been much delayed by the ban by the Church on all such doctrines. But Basso had clearly for many years in Paris been the leader of a circle of medical men and other thinkers vigorously interested in the new theory of nature. It was into Paris, in which the intellectual ferment had considerably mounted by the beginning of the third decade of the century, that Descartes came in 1625 and concentrated during that time on physical theory. When he left in 1629 he had the bases of his own physical theory worked out[4] but suppressed

---

4. Cf. Descartes's letter to Mersenne, Dec. 18, 1629.

the publication of *Le Monde* after the condemnation of Galileo. The first full philosophical development of modern Neoplatonism began to appear in Descartes's writings in the next decade, in his *Meditations on First Philosophy* (1641) and his *Principles of Philosophy* (1644).

In these treatises there is elaborated not only the new metaphysical dualism of *res extensa* and *res cogitans*, but also the essential Neoplatonic ontology. Although the physical *res* or substance is matter, matter retains the fundamental feature it has always had in Neoplatonism, namely, that of passivity. In Neoplatonism it is form alone, as the direct derivative from God, which is active. Thus, in the modern doctrine, although matter is held to be substance, it is substance without act. Therefore, in this doctrine the physical does not have, as it does have in the Aristotelian theory, the principle of its motion in itself; in the modern doctrine the physical as matter is in itself completely passive, i.e., able to be acted on—as Newton put it, it is mov*able*, but cannot move itself. The principle of motion of the physical, as all adherents of the new doctrine realized, must be God as the only available agent.

By contrast, the other kind of substance, the plurality of *res cogitantes*, are, as minds or souls, active in themselves, i.e., they are agents. This is particularly clearly, and indeed crucially, exemplified in perception. In perception there is the occurrence of locomotion in *res extensa*, including that portion of *res extensa* constituting the human body. But this locomotion does not directly affect the mind or soul, the *res cogitans*, for the fundamental reason in Neoplatonism—as was made quite clear by Plotinus and appreciated in medieval Neoplatonism—that mind or soul is without passivity ($\pi\acute{\alpha}\theta$os, *passio*), i.e., of being able to be acted on. On the contrary, mind is wholly active. In perception the mind *acts* correlatively to a motion in the body. That is, sensation is not a passion undergone by the mind, but an action of the mind. This is particularly clear in the modern metaphysical dualism, for matter is wholly devoid of any of the qualitative features antecedently assumed to inhere in the physical. A color, for example, cannot derive from a material thing; a color can only be an "idea" in the mind of a perceiver, as was clear to Descartes and to Locke—for the former the qualitative features were "adventitious ideas," for the latter they were "simple ideas of sensation."

IV

This doctrine of "ideas" is a distinctive feature of modern Neoplatonism in the seventeenth century. The adequate appreciation of this doctrine requires its being seen in contrast both with the antecedent Aristotelian position and with that of earlier Neoplatonism. In the Aristotelian theory the perceiver is initially passive, i.e., acted on by the perceived thing. Crucial here is that this *passio* is essentially that of the soul, and not of the body in contrast with the soul. Thereby the perceiver receives the form which is the essence of the perceived individual thing. Thus in this theory there is an identity of the form in the *psyche* or soul of the perceiver with the form of the perceived thing. Aristotle is therefore able to maintain that strictly it is an individual being which is the object in perception.

For the earlier Neoplatonic theory Augustine can be taken as most adequately representative. He maintained the Platonic mind-body dualism and accordingly clearly distinguished between the bodily sense organs and the activity of the soul in perception. In an interaction with a perceived thing, the sense organ is acted on, "suffering" an impress. The mind or soul is "aware" of this, its awareness being an act, not a *passio*, since mind cannot be affected by, i.e., acted on by, an inferior substance. This mental act of perceiving is the producing of a form or idea as an image of the form or *species* of the perceived thing.

That the idea in the mind is truly an *image* of the perceived thing was in this Neoplatonic theory considered to be assured by the basic doctrine that all forms are derivative from God, both those which inform things and those in the mind as ideas, both alike having ultimately a single paradigm in God. This ground for assurance was carried over into modern Neoplatonism by Descartes and Locke, among others, but strengthened now by the conception, first formulated by Cusanus in his doctrine of the universe as *explicatio Dei*, the conception that the universe is fundamentally mathematical, so that we are assured that our mathematical thinking accurately images the structure of the universe.

But there was involved in modern Neoplatonism a most important difference from the earlier in respect of the "ideas" because of the modern metaphysical dualism. Since by this doctrine sensible forms were eliminated from physical matter, sensible ideas could be only "representative," and not strictly "images," of forms in things. Both Descartes and Locke maintained that the quantitative ideas, on the other hand, were true images of the real nature of the physical, Locke supposing this to be grounded in these ideas having been "caused" by the physical things. That Locke's supposition was untenable came to be clearly appreciated, by Berkeley and Leibniz among others. The quantitative ideas are no less purely subjective than are the qualitative; if the latter be "representations," and thereby phenomenal, then the quantitative ideas must be equally phenomenal—this is entailed in the basic Neoplatonic position to which all those thinkers were committed. The only way, Leibniz saw, in which any correspondence of any ideas in the mind with the nature of physical things could be maintained was by recourse to God, as had been Descartes's procedure; Leibniz stated this position as his principle of preestablished harmony.

It is important to recognize that the empiricism deriving from Locke is no less an exemplification of modern Neoplatonism than is the rationalism deriving from Descartes. This is the ineluctable consequence of the modern metaphysical dualism. In proclaiming empiricism in opposition to rationalism, Locke was clearly under the influence of the medieval Aristotelian doctrine that all knowledge is grounded in perception. But his acceptance of the dualism deprived Locke of the metaphysical basis for claiming an identity of the ideas in the mind with the forms of things perceived. Matter is capable only of locomotion, and any effect on the body—sense organ or brain—is only locomotion of the matter constituting the body, which, as Locke was indeed clear, cannot affect the mind. However much thinkers might attempt to hedge on this, on the basis of the metaphysical dualism there is no way in which mental "experience" can be initially a *passio*, a being acted on.

Kant's critical philosophy was truly epoch-making in its determinative influence on subsequent philosophy. In his new philosophical development Kant turned from his earlier preoccupation with the philosophy of nature to the metaphysics of knowledge. This turn had been instigated by profound difficulties he had run into by reason of the fundamental relativity involved in his physical monadology, difficulties affecting the very basis of knowledge of the physical, particularly the basis of measurement and of the applicability of mathematics to the physical. The resolution of these difficulties was to be achieved by a "Copernican revolution." Previously he had been implicity proceeding on the inherited Aristotelian position that knowledge is determined by physical things; his revolutionary new position grounded knowledge instead in the structure of mind. In particular, space and time, the basis of measurement, and mathematics itself, were grounded in the mind and not in physical things. In this new position Kant was working out consistently the implications of the modern metaphysical dualism, which previously he had indeed accepted but without appreciating adequately the implications of that doctrine. In fact, the full implications became clear to Kant only gradually over the years of work on his new doctrine, as a consequence of which his statements on many crucial points continued to manifest a certain amount of ambiguity.

One such area of ambiguity was in respect of sensation. A continuation of Aristotelian presuppositions is displayed at the very beginning of the *Critique of Pure Reason*, in section 1 of the "Transcendental Aesthetic," in which he says that "*intuition* [*Anschauung*] takes place only in so far as the object is given to us," that this is only possible "in so far as the mind is affected in a certain way." *Sensibility* (*Sinnlichkeit*) he defines as "The capacity (receptivity) for receiving representations [*Vorstellungen*]," and *sensation* (*Empfindung*) as "The effect of an object upon the faculty of representation, so far as we are affected by it."[5] These statements might seem to mean that sensibility is a *passio*, a being acted on. However, the very terms *intuition* (*Anschauung*) and *representation* (*Vorstellung*) entail the contrary. To "intuit," i.e., "look on or at," as also to "represent," are *acts* of mind; neither can be a *passio*. Further, in Kant's doctrine, the "content" or "matter"—as opposed to the "form"—of the intuition and representation is a "sense-content," such as color, sound, taste, etc.; the "form" is constituted by "space" and "time." Now, as Kant explicitly holds, in accordance with the metaphysical dualism, sensible qualities such as color, taste, etc., "cannot be rightly regarded as properties of things, but only as changes in the subject."[6] That is, the sensible content, as well as the spatial and temporal form, derive from the mind, and not from the physical thing. Thus Kant's position is as completely essentially Neoplatonic as is that of Hume and of their seventeenth-century predecessors.

The fundamental reason for the enormous influence Kant's philosophy had on subsequent philosophical thought is that it rescued modern Neoplatonism from what came increasingly to be appreciated as a most troublesome defect and dilemma. This was that the subjectivism entailed in the modern metaphysical dualism drove either to the Scylla of scepticism with Hume or to the Charybdis of a divine preestablished harmony with Leibniz, the latter coming increasingly, especially in the eighteenth century, to be felt to be objectionable as a *deus ex machina*. Kant demonstrated that a full and consistent subjectivism is able to avoid both these unpalatable consequences. This was done by showing that it could not be the physical thing in itself which is the object in knowledge. The object known is necessarily an *appear-*

---

5. I. Kant, *Kritik der reinen Vernunft*, A20, B34: "Die Wirkung eines Gegenstandes auf die Vorstellungsfähigkeit, so fern wir von demselben affiziert werden" (English trans. by Norman Kemp Smith).
6. Ibid., B45.

ance of the physical thing in the mind, all features of that appearance being necessarily grounded in the mind. Thus, what Kant did was fully to confirm the subjectivism which arose with Descartes as a consequence of the metaphysical dualism, and to work it out consistently into a coherent philosophy.

The major influence of Kant on subsequent philosophy has been the overwhelming acceptance of subjectivism, thus securing the predominant continuation of modern Neoplatonism. Opposing features of Aristotelianism which had tended to linger have been largely eliminated. That this is the situation today, two centuries after Kant, is signified by the extent to which subjectivism has come now to be held as a tacit presupposition, one so obvious that a contrary position is not only not taken seriously but often presents difficulty in being able to be conceived at all.

V

One of the most important consequences of Kant's thought has been the complete abandonment of the philosophy of nature as it had antecedently been engaged in. This is significant of the essential difference between what at the beginning of this chapter I distinguished as the first two phases of modern philosophy, the second beginning with Kant's critical doctrine. In the first phase the fundamental concern of philosophy had been nature; from Descartes to the pre-critical Kant the metaphysics of nature had been basic in philosophy, because these thinkers saw that the new conception of nature fundamentally affected the entire range of philosophical problems and conceptions. In this phase not only was philosophical thinking closely associated with science—indeed the major philosophers were also scientists—but crucial was that philosophy had nature or the physical as its primary object. This is exemplified by Kant in his pre-critical period, in which he developed a "physical monadology"; his preoccupation was the nature of physical being and of the relations of physical existents, what this entailed for causality, for the nature and status of extension, and thus for the problem of the relation of the mathematical and the physical.

Kant's critical doctrine fundamentally changed the stance of philosophy with regard to nature. This comes out clearly in the contrast between Kant's pre-critical dissertation *Monadologia Physica* (1756) and his *Metaphysische Anfangsgründe der Naturwissenschaft* of 1786. The former, as its full title indicates, is concerned with "the employment of metaphysics, in its connection with geometry, in the philosophy of nature."[7] Part 1, according to its heading, "explains the existence of physical monads as involving geometry,"[8] and part 2 "explicates the most general properties of physical monads in so far as they are diversified in the different monads, and as thus rendering intelligible the nature of body"[9]—body being a composite of monads. The later treatise deals, as its title states, with "the metaphysical foundations of natural science"—natural *science* and not natural or physical *existents*. Here "metaphysical foundations," as Kant explains in the preface, means "the principles of the construction of concepts that belong to the possibility of matter in general."[10] According to the critical position, a physical existent is not knowable in itself; the object known is the subjective response to the motion of the physical thing. That is, the physical existent is not in itself given in knowing; on the contrary, as Kant puts it in this treatise, "The fundamental determination of a something that it be an object of the external senses is motion, for thereby only can these senses be affected. The understanding leads all other predicates back to motion."[11]

Here we have the crucial difference between Kant's pre-critical and critical positions. Motion can only be known in terms of place, motion *meaning* change in respect of place. In his earlier period Kant maintained that place was knowable only in terms of the acting of the physical monads on each other, for there could *be* no place or space at all without the monads' acting on each other. Thus knowing motion entailed knowing physical monads in themselves, i.e., in their acting. Now, the essence of the critical position is the denial of the knowability of physical things in themselves. Thus to render motion knowable—and this is the sine qua non of scientific knowledge—Kant held that place or space must be grounded in the mind and not in things. Accordingly, as he states it in his later treatise, "space in general does not belong to the properties or relations of things in themselves, . . . but belongs merely to the subjective form of our sensible intuition of things and relations, these [things and relations] remaining wholly

---

7. I. Kant, *Metaphysicae cum geometria iunctae usus in philosophia naturali, cuius specimen I. continet Monadologiam Physicam.*

8. "Monadum physicarum exsistentiam geometriae consentaneam declarans."

9. "Affectiones monadum physicarum generalissimas, quatenus in diversis diversae ad naturam corporum intelligendam faciunt, explicans."

10. I. Kant, *Metaphysische Anfangsgründe der Naturwissenschaften* (vol. 4 of the edition of the Königliche Preussische Akademie der Wissenschaften): "Prinzipien der Konstruktion der Begriffe, welche zur Möglichkeit der Materie überhaupt gehören"; Eng. trans. by J. Ellington, as *Metaphysical Foundations of Natural Science* (New York: Bobbs-Merrill, 1970), 9.

11. Ibid., 13–14.

unknown to us as regards what they may be in themselves."[12] Further, mathematics, in terms of which there is knowledge in the strict sense of motion, is itself a mental construct in Kant's doctrine; thus the seventeenth-century conception of Descartes, Galileo, Leibniz, and Newton of the physical as in itself mathematical is untenable. Accordingly, nature or the physical, as known in science, and as in principle knowable at all, is necessarily phenomenal, that is, an appearance in the mind; nature in itself remains on the other side of the metaphysical divide, unknowable.

This epistemological subjectivism—which is nothing but the essential Neoplatonic position—is carried to its metaphysical consequences in Idealism, particularly in the doctrine of Hegel. Kant's metaphysical dualism is rejected; nature is not a material thing in itself. *Being* for Hegel is *Geist*, and this ontology is accordingly determinative for nature. In Hegel's doctrine, as he puts it the Introduction to his *Philosophy of Nature*, "nature has presented itself as the Idea in the form of *otherness*."[13] In this century modern Neoplatonism has also manifested itself particularly prominently in the dominant positivistic philosophy of science in its variety of forms such as "scientific empiricism," "operationalism," etc. The epistemology of these theories is fundamentally subjectivistic. Basically like the Kantian position, in these theories it is not the physical things in themselves which are the objects in scientific knowledge; scientific knowledge is in terms of mental "models," "operations," or "behavior," such as "language."

VI

To both the Hegelian and the positivistic positions, a "realist" reaction has occurred, to the former in the early twentieth century, to the latter more recently. But both these realist reactions have been primarily epistemological—Hegelianism had resulted in a long-lasting revulsion against metaphysics. And because they have avoided metaphysics, both these movements have failed to develop a definite alternative to modern Neoplatonism; for example, the metaphysical dualism has continued on the whole to be half-heartedly maintained or

12. Ibid.: "dass der Raum überhaupt nicht zu den Eigenschaften oder Verhältnissen der *Dinge an sich selbst*, die sich notwendig auf objektive Begriffe müssten bringen lassen, sondern bloss zu der subjektiven Form unserer sinnlichen Anschauung von Dingen oder Verhältnissen, die uns, nach dem, was sie an sich sein mögen, völlig unbekannt bleiben, gehöre" (English trans., 23–24).
13. Hegel's *Philosophy of Nature*, English trans. by A. V. Miller (Oxford: Clarendon Press, 1970), B, The Notion of Nature, sect. 9, p. 13.

acquiesced in. A. N. Whitehead and Nicolai Hartmann are the two notable exceptions in the earlier realistic movement, but neither has gained any considerable following.

But it is not sufficient merely to *assert* an epistemological realism; it is necessary that this position be based upon a metaphysics in terms of which it can be explicable how it is possible for physical things in themselves to be the objects in knowledge. The necessity of such a metaphysical foundation for a realist epistemology was most fully recognized by Whitehead, a recognition to which he was gradually forced by his concern, after the completion of *Principia Mathematica* with Bertrand Russell, expressed in the title of his next major book, *An Enquiry into the Principles of Natural Knowledge*. In this he was involved in those basic issues which had been Kant's concern in the works I discussed earlier, namely, how there is scientific knowledge of physical entities in motion, that is, how this motion is mathematically understood. The fundamental problems are those of the nature and status of place and of the foundations of geometry. The problem concerning place is intrinsically bound up with the issue of the physical existent, and the problem concerning geometry is intrinsically bound up with the issue of the relation of mind to the physical. The fundamental question is, therefore, what is the nature of the physical such that it can be known, such that the physical can be the object in knowledge? Whitehead, from his background as a logician as well as an epistemologist, saw that it is indispensable, if there is to be knowledge of the physical in itself, that physical entities themselves be the subjects of propositions. A metaphysical theory is thus necessary in terms of which to explain how physical things in themselves can be the subjects of propositions.

For the solution to this issue Whitehead was driven to the opposite direction to that taken by Kant, who had sought the solution in a more consistent subjectivism; Whitehead was forced to abandon the subjectivism of modern Neoplatonism which had been his inheritance through British empiricism, and to accept instead the essentially Aristotelian position. In Aristotle's doctrine it is the individual form of the entity perceived which is received by the perceiver; thereby the object of perception is the physical entity in itself. In Whitehead's theory too there is an initial reception of the physical entity in itself as object; he terms this reception the "physical prehension" of the datum. What is essential in this Aristotelian position by contrast with the Neoplatonic one is that the object is a thing received, and not, as Whitehead has put it, "either a *mode* of reception or a thing *generated*" in the perception.[14] In this position therefore it is the physical in itself which is essentially knowable and known. Further, this position implies the rejection of the modern ontological dualism of the physical and the mental and of their metaphysical separation, which is the other basic aspect of modern Neoplatonism. By contrast with this, Whitehead's position is in this respect also fundamentally Aristotelian.

Now, the significance of this development does not lie in the epistemology as such. The reason for my singling out Whitehead is not that he was a scientist who became interested in the epistemology of science. It is also not that he was a scientist who came to appreciate with particular clarity the extent of the revolutionary change in scientific theory in this century, although both these considerations are far from irrelevant. The reason is that he had seen more clearly than most that this change entailed the complete rejection of the metaphysics upon which modern science had been based since the seventeenth century, that a new metaphysics is accordingly now necessary as a basis for science, and that he has gone further than any other thinker in elaborating such a metaphysics. In saying this I am not seeking to urge the acceptance of Whitehead's particular metaphysics. My point is that science has in our time come up against quite fundamental problems which involve more than essentially scientific issues, which involve philosophical issues of the utmost difficulty and complexity: the ultimate issues of first principles, of what is, of being and becoming, of continuity and discreteness, the ultimate issues of the nature and status of motion, of place, time, extension, of the mathematical, of mental functioning in its relation to the physical. Scientific thought today requires these philosophical issues to be investigated, an investigation needing considerable philosophical sophistication. That is to say, philosophy is today being required to turn again to those fundamental issues of the philosophy of nature which preoccupied thinkers in the first phase of modern philosophy.

Now, this task which philosophy is required to undertake demands a profound change in contemporary philosophy, not only in respect of subject matter but also in respect of fundamental theory. For the philosophy of nature entails that nature or the physical be in itself the object of philosophical inquiry, and this it is unable to be on the Neoplatonic subjectivistic basis. This inquiry, in other words, can be undertaken only on an essentially Aristotelian basis. Because of the predominant influence of science in the modern period, philosophy

---

14. *AI*, 229.

will increasingly be compelled to fulfill its role in respect of the need of science for a metaphysical foundation. On this ground I see philosophy now beginning to enter upon a new phase, one which will be distinctively different from that of the last two centuries, one which will involve the abandonment of modern Neoplatonism and the turn to an essential Aristotelianism.

Let me in conclusion make a few brief comments respecting the Aristotelianism of the third phase of modern philosophy. Of course it cannot constitute a wholehearted adoption and adaptation of Aristotle as had occurred in the Scholastic period; modern scientific development precludes that. Further, developments of scientific thought in this century have presented a challenge to philosophy more profound than any it has had to face since late Hellenistic times, far more profound than that of the seventeenth century. At that time it was possible for philosophy to carry over intact from the preceding epoch the entire range of basic philosophical categories and concepts, whence modern philosophy could be the continuation it was of Neoplatonism. But contemporary scientific development has thrown into question in an extremely fundamental way all our inherited philosophical concepts, categories, and basic presuppositions. Nothing like this has happened since Parmenides. Philosophy is being faced in our time with the necessity for a more thoroughgoing rethinking of the fundamental philosophical problems, concepts, and categories throughout its entire range, than philosophy has undertaken since the time of Plato and Aristotle. This rethinking will affect science no less deeply than it will philosophy itself. And the consequences for human life will be no less great than were those of the new science and philosophy of the seventeenth century. In Greek times Aristotle had brought philosophy back to a necessary concentration upon *physis*, nature, as the object of philosophical inquiry. The profundity of the Aristotelian insights into the philosophical issues involved are unsurpassed. We need today to come back to this source, more particularly in respect of the fundamental issues and problems.

Index

Act: analysis of, 88; of becoming, 140; of unifying, 136; acts, 90
Acting, 9, 11, 32, 166; analysis of, 171; as becoming, 175; concept of, 55; of physical existents, 40, 148; entails potency, power, 173; purposive, 167; qualitative and quantitative, 176; as relational, 40, 148, 150, 158, 159, 171, 174, 176, 193; as involving teleology, 178
Action, 8; introduced into modern physics, 184; not motion, 183; as process, 189, 190
Active force, 89, 90; necessity for motion, 88
Activity, 89; of physical, 33, 43
Actuality, 40, 41, 79, 89, 137; of compounds, 128; meaning of, 187, 188; connection with potentiality, 32, 132
Actualization, 21, 37; analysis of, 190
Aether, 81; *aether*, Aristotelian, 99
Agency: analysis of, 191; of compounds, 128
Agrippa of Nettesheim, 51, 108, 196; physical entities as ensouled, 197
Albertus Magnus, 111
Alchemism, 196
Anaxagoras, 108
Anima, 48
Antitypy in Leibniz, 87, 174
Appearance, characters as, 115
Appetition, analysis of, 179
Archai, theory of three, 47
Arche, 21
Archimedes, 108
Aristarchos, 108

Aristotelianism, 13, 44, 54, 66, 108, 153, 156, 195, 208
Aristotle, 10, 13, 20, 21, 22, 23, 24, 25, 26, 31, 37, 38, 42, 44, 45, 48, 61, 68 n.6, 80, 86, 171, 208; theory of active intellect, 50; on actuality and potentiality, 42, 64, 128; concept of *aether*, 196; being used in many senses, 33, 45; beings as active, 32, 52, 118; analysis of becoming, 182; becoming as actualizing, 171; concept of body, 74; doctrine of categories, 145; *Categories*, 144; theory of chemical combination, 53, 110–12, 115, 134, 180, 197; on chemical change, 78; on coming-into-being, 134; status of compounds, 122; *De anima*, 50 n.5; *De generatione et corruptione*, 110 nn.1, 2, 3, 134 n.3, 134 n.4, 137 n.7; divisibility, 37; theory of elements, 60, 108, 126, 135, 197; theory of changing elements, 58, 109; epistemological realism, 201; *hyle*, concept of, 76, identified with *dynamis*, 173; ideas, conception of, 200; *kinesis*, analysis of, 38, 89, 154, 175, 181, 182; κίνησις and ἐνέργεια, distinction between, 187; knowledge grounded in perception, 201; knowledge of the physical, 207; matter, conception of, 52; matter-form, analysis of, 172; *Metaphysics*, 45 n.1, 60 n.4, 76 n.2, 78 n.4, 112 n.4, 132 n.2, 133, 170 n.7, 188 n.12, 197 n.3; on mind and body, 45, 46; misinterpretations of, 172; on motion, 37; motion, principle of, 199,

Aristotle (*continued*)
  theory of, 78–79; nature, theory of, 20–21, 130; contrast with Neoplatonism, 47; passivity in, 193; perception, theory of, 50, 200, 206, 207; physics dependent upon metaphysics, 38; *Physics*, 25, 79 n.5, 92; on physical being, 112, 140; the physical, concept of, 152, 182, theory of, 132, as involving potentiality and actuality, 42, as involving potentiality-actuality distinction, 126, 127, 135, 136, 137; place, definition of, 92, 98, 99, 101, not physical, 32; potentiality, concept of, 135; predication, concept of, 144; sensation, theory of, 48, 49; soul-body relation, rejection of Plato on, 49; soul, theory of, 51; criticism of Plato's theory of soul, 48; on substance, 132, 133, concept of, 197, in becoming, 132; no substance composed of substances, 132, 133; substance, single, unitary, 133; substantial forms, 88, 109; substrate, theory of, 185; unity, concept of, 132; unity of being, 133; on universal, 170; three ultimate sources, 144; on the void, 69, 80–81, concept of, 98, 99
Asklepiades, 108
Atom: concept of, 81; atoms, 9; material, 90, as changeless, 118
Atomism, 22, 56–74; corporeal, 36, 37, 38, 60, 61; material, 3, 15, 22, 25, 26, 32, 33, 36, 42, 55, 107, 115, 116, 117, 118, 121, 124, 130, 131, 142, 148, 149, 150, 161, theory of, 36, 54, 65; mathematical, 65; theory of, 22, 25, 109, 122, 128, 129, 130
Augustine, Bishop of Hippo, 48, 51, 144; *Confessions*, 145 n.5, 197 n.2; matter, conception of, 197; mind-body dualism, 200; perception, theory of, 200; seminal reasons, 77; soul, doctrine of, 46
Augustinianism, 172

Averroes, 20, 50, 76–77, 111, 196; Averroism, 172
Avicenna, 20, 52, 111; form of corporeity, 77

Bacon, Francis, 3, 109; on motion, 79; *Novum Organum*, 53, 79 n.6
Bacon, Roger: on matter, 77; *Opera hactenus inedita fratris Rogeri Baconis*, 77 n.3
Basso, Sebastian, 3, 4, 23, 25, 54, 58, 59, 78, 79, 80, 81; atomism, material, 116; body, as aggregation, 53, 109, 115; chemical combination, theory of, 134; matter, as changeless, 198, as the physical, 54; molecule, concept of, 122; *Philosophia naturalis adversus Aristotelem Libri XII*, 23, 53, 198; on the void, 99
Becoming, 5, 8, 9, 21, 37, 38; in Aristotle, 24, 140; contrast with being, 154; exclusion from matter, 185; problem of, 107; process of, 23, 154
Being, 5, 9, 20, 21, 33, 45; contrast with becoming, 154; as changeless, 181; coming into, 119; many senses for Aristotle, 33, 45; as matter, 4; in Neoplatonism, 48; as one, 133; problem of, 207
Bentley, Richard, 6; *Works of Richard Bentley*, 7 n.1
Berkeley, George, 95, 200
Bodiliness, new analysis of, 174
Bodin, Jean, 109
Body, 6, 32, 165–79; as aggregate, 132; as composite, 10, 36; as compound, 119; concept of, 6, 7, 9, 37, 45, 132, as relative, 32; features of, 174, as derivative, 39; as matter, 10, 80; nature of, 204; ontological status of, 37, 38, 42, 61, 122, 174; ontologically derivative, 37; passive or active, 48; as phenomenal, 115, 116; as plurality in relation, 32; as potentiality, 49; in Renaissance Neoplatonism, 51; no effect on soul, 55

Body-mind relation, 201
Bonds, chemical, 159, 167; valency, 157
Boyle, Robert, 3
Bruno, Johannes, 51, 81, 109, 196; atomism of, 69, 71; *De la causa*, 70n.11; corpuscular theory, 81; mathematical atomism, 65; universe as mathematical, 70; on void, 99
Burtt, E. A., *The Metaphysical Foundations of Modern Science*, 58n.1

Cabbalism, 108
Campanella, T., 108
Čapek, Milič: "Leibniz on Matter and Memory," 119n.9; *The Philosophical Impact of Contemporary Physics*, 12, 90
Cardano, G., 51, 78, 108
Category, meaning of, 144
Causality: problem of, 203; in Whitehead, 162
Cause: concept of, 186; the four causes, 21
Change, 165–79; analysis of, 174–79; concept of, 188; kinds of, 11, 23; locomotive, 176; in respect of place, relative, 30
Changeability, defining, 158, 159
Changeability of sub-atomic entities, 8
Characteristic, defining, 158, 159
Chemical change, theory of, 78
Chemical combination, 59, 122; theory of, 52, 53, 108, 109–12, 197; problem of, 180
Chemistry, 10; status of, 177
Cicero, 108
Clarke, Samuel, 29, 94; on space, 101
Coming-into-being, 134
Composites, 10; as acting, 160, 161; features of, 42
Compound actuality, theory of, 129, 130–38
Compounds, 10, 165–79; as acting, 165, 166; agency of, characters of, in modern science, 123; theory of, 125; unity of, 127, 136
Conception, meaning of, 170
Conceptual origination, 178
Constituents, ultimate, 159, 160
Continuity: divisibility of, 25, 37, 81; of motion, 10; problem of, 207
Copernicus, world as mathematical, 196
Corporeality derivative from matter, 24
Corpuscula, 78
Cosmology, 13
Cosmos, 21
Creativity, 175

Democritus, 22, 23, 53, 66, 80, 108, 113n.5
Des Bosses, 113n.5, 117
Descartes, Rene, 3, 4, 6, 8, 14, 16, 20, 27, 28, 29, 31, 37, 39, 40, 42, 54, 55, 83, 88, 113, 153, 164, 169, 181n.2, 198, 200, 205; action is not motion, 183; atomism, rejection of, 65; bodies as derivative, 36; body, concept of, 149, theory of, 71; category of quantity, 146; distinction between action and motion, 186, 187; God as source of ideas, 200; God as source of motion, 84; ideas, subjective, 199, theory of, 200; on mathematical and physical, 15, 27, 37, 39, 69, 71, 72; matter, concept of, 27, 62, as extensive, 27, 37, 81, as full, 27, 82, as physical, 27, 145, 180, as quantitative, 145; *Meditations*, 199; letter to Mersenne, 198n.4; *Le Monde*, 54, 199; motion, conception of, 93; Neoplatonism of, 192, 201; object of geometry, 96; ontology of, 199; philosophy of nature, 28; physics as mechanics, 28, 142; physics in, 28, 80; connection between physics and metaphysics, 38–39; on place, 100, definition of, 101; *Principles of Philosophy*, 3, 70nn.7, 8, 70n.10, 93nn.3, 4, 100, 183n.5,

Descartes, Rene (*continued*)
199; relativity of place and time, *Reply to Objections*, I, 70n.9; solidity, concept of, 115; soul as active, 192; space and matter, 96; subjectivism, 203; universe as mathematical, 70, 196; on the void, 69, 93
Deus ex machina, 15, 24, 31, 40, 71, 83
De Volder, B., 73, 85, 113n.5, 119n.9
Ding an sich, 12, 30, 41
Discreteness, problem of, 207
Divisibility, 33
Dualism: metaphysical, 4, 14, 149, 169, 178, 194, 198, 199, 200, 201, 202, 205, 207; ontological, 47, 55, in Kant, 42; in Renaissance Neoplatonism, of mind and body, 56, 200
Dynamics, 6, 84; science of, 175
Dynamis (δύναμις), 42, 79, 134, 182

Earley, Joseph E., 164n.3, 168n.5; dissipative structures, 168
Effect, concept of, 186
Eidos, 21, 76, 170, 173
Einai, 89
Einstein, Albert, 7, 8, 9; relativity theory of, 139, 141
Elements: atomic, 114; as changeless, 53, 57, 58, 79, 109; quantitative, 58; theory of, 52, 57, 62, 78, 108; as ultimate constituents of compounds, 57
Emergence: of compound entities, 167; concept of, 158; of organisms, 168
Emotion, 47
Empedocles, 108
Empirical inquiry, 32
Empirical verification, 42
Empiricism, 201; British, 206; Neoplatonic, 201
Energeia (ἐνέργεια), 21, 42, 79, 89, 134, 182, 183, 187, 188; in Neoplatonism, 47
Energy, 115, 192; concept of, 33, 125, 134, 183; as fundamental, 184; meaning of, in modern physics, 183–84; metaphysical status of, 184; theory of, 186; as substance, 184; as substrate, 185
Ens reale, 117
Entities, changeability of, 10
Epicurus, 6, 66, 108
Epistemology, 4
d'Espagnet, Jean, 109
Eternal objects, Whitehead's, 173
Ether, 7
Euclid, 108
Existent: as active, 9; as changeless, 125; as unitary, 22
Explicatio Dei, 196, 197
Extension, 32; analysis of, 30, 39; as attribute, 31; not attribute of single existent, 30, 39; concept of, 6, 25; divisibility of, 27, 65; infinite divisibility, 63; as inhering quality, 85; as relation, 30, 39, 85; as relational, 39, 41; and space, 8; ontological status of, 27, 203, 207; as ultimate, 85
Extensive continuum, Whitehead's theory of, 41
Extensiveness, 14, 174; as form, 174; as fundamental, 36

Fallacy of misplaced concreteness, 119
Faraday, Michael, 7
Feeling, 47
Field, electrodynamic, 7; concept of, 125, 134; theory of, 15, 43
Finite, 33
Food, status of, 179
Force, 80, 81, 167, 192; concept of, 6, 7, 31, 39, 148, 157, 166, 183; in Leibniz and Kant, 102; meaning of, 187; necessary in acting, 173; ontological status of, 157; primitive, 89; strong, 159; theory of, 186
Ford, Lewis S., 166
Form, 21, 23, 47, 57, 109; active, 199; as being, 192; of corporeity, 77; correlative to matter, 23, 36, 80, 152; of extensiveness, 174; substantial, 60, 88, 107–8, 109;

Index

substantial, Aristotelian concept of, 57; theory of, 128
Forma, 170
Forms: of compounds, 137; eduction of, 77; from God in Neoplatonism, 200; in Neoplatonism, 47, 48; Platonic, 47; sensible, 200; as souls, 48
Fracastoro, G., 51, 78, 109

Galen, 108
Galileo, 3, 4, 14, 20, 25, 26, 37, 42, 54, 58, 67, 116, 153, 205; and atomism, 71; *atomi non quanti*, 25, 27, 37, 63, 64, 68; atoms and motion, 63, 64; matter, concept of, 36, 62; mathematical and body, 72; on mathematical and physical, 69, 73; mathematical atomism, 66; matter as mathematical, 26, 37, 63, 65; mechanical concept of nature, 80; physics as mechanics, 142; qualitative subjective, 59; *Opere, Edizione Nazionale*, 58 n.1, 59 n.2; void untenable, 63; universe as mathematical, 70, 196
Gassendi, Pierre, 4, 14, 15, 54, 79, 80, 83, 88, 93, 115; and atomism, 26, 71; matter, concept of, 37, 62; concept of molecule, 122, 149; corpuscular theory, 81; God as source of motion, 84; material atomism, 26, 116; on mathematical and physical, 67, 68, 69; matter as solid, 26, 66, 82; *Opera Omnia: Syntagmatis Philosophici*, 68 n.5; separation of mathematical and physical, 26, 37, 65; solid atoms, 26; theory of atomism, 26, 65; theory of atomism and void, 27, 67; theory of void, 66
Genesis, 21, 79
Gent, Werner, *Die Philosophie des Raumes und die Zeit*, 119 n.9
Geometry: foundations of, 206; non-Euclidean, 15
Gilbert, William, 78, 109
Gilson, Etienne, *History of Christian Philosophy in the Middle Ages*, 77 n.3
God, 38, 113; as absolutely infinite, 196; as acting, 88; as active, 29, 31, 38; activity of, 15; as *actus purus*, 172; as agent, 199; as being, 145; as cause of motion, 24, 71; as *coincidentia oppositorum*, 197; as creator, 28, 83, 94; in Cusanus, 196; for Descartes, 113; eduction of forms, 77; as extended, for Newton, 28, 29, 38, 196; extended spirit, 29, 38; in Gassendi's system, 67; as infinite, 70; in Leibniz's theory, 131; in Neoplatonism, 199; Newton's conception, 84, 100; in Newton's concept of place, 101; perpetual recreation by, 119; as principle of change, 175; as principle of concretion, 161, 162; as principle of motion, 24, 28, 39, 71, 172; relation to world soul, 51; source of forms in Neoplatonism, 200; as source of motion, 81, 82, 184; and concept of space, 94; subjective aim, 132; as transcendent, 47; and truth of ideas, 201; in Whitehead's theory, 131, 132
Gorlaeus, David, 3, 58, 78, 79, 80, 109, 112; *Exercitationes Philosophicae*, 53, 53 n.6; on void, 99
Gravity, innate, 6
Greenberg, J., *Bruno's Philosophy of the Infinite*, 70 n.11

Hartmann, Nicolai, epistemological realism, 206
Hartshorne, Charles, on panpsychism, 169
Hegel, G. W. F., 205; ontology of, 205; *Philosophy of Nature*, 205; *Philosophy of Nature*, Eng. trans. by A. V. Miller, 205 n.13
Heisenberg, Werner, 184, 185; concept of potentiality, 126, 135; *Physics and Philosophy*, 126 n.18, 127 n.19, 135 nn.5, 6, 184 n.7; *Zwei Vorträge*, 127 n.19, 135 n.6
Henry of Ghent on matter, 77

214 Index

Heron of Alexandria, 108
Historical inquiry, 10
Hobbes, Thomas, 3, 14, 169; *De Corpore*, 3; fluidity theory of matter, 72
Homer, 46
Hume, David, 95, 194; Neoplatonism of, 202; scepticism of, 202
Huygens, Christiaan, 6, 84, 115, 153; corpuscular theory of, 81; mechanical concept of nature, 80; physics as mechanics, 142
Hyle, 21, 47, 76
Hypokeimenon, 173

Idea, Hegelian, 205
ἰδέα, 170
Idealism, 194, 195, 205
Ideas in Neoplatonism, 199, 200; as phenomenal, 200, 201; as representative, 200; ontological status of, 200; as subjective, 199
Impenetrability, 33
Impetus, 200; in Gassendi's system, 67
Individuation, principle of, 68
Infinite, 33
Inquisition, 54
Intellection, act of soul alone, 49
Interacting of constituents, 167
Interaction, analysis of, 191
Intuition in Kant, 202

Kant, Immanuel, 8, 12, 15, 39, 90, 166, 206; on acting of monads, 102; ambiguity in doctrine, 202; body as phenomenal, 115; matter, conception of, 84; "Copernican revolution," 194, 201; critical philosophy, 204; *Critique of Pure Reason*, 12, 29, 95, 95 n.10, 101, 104, 202; *De mundi sensibilis*, 104; "Distinction of Regions in Space," 103; epistemological idealism, 201; *Inaugural Dissertation*, 95 nn.9, 11, 101; influence of, 41, 203; knowledge of the physical, 41; mathematics as a construct, 15, 205; mathematics a mental construct, 30; *Metaphysische Anfangsgründe der Naturwissenschaft*, 203, 204 nn.10, 11; *Metaphysical Foundations of Natural Science*, Eng. trans. by J. Ellington, 96 n.12, 204 n.10; metaphysical dualism, 42, 102; metaphysics of knowledge, 201; *Monadologia Physica*, 102, 103, 203, 204 n.7; theory of monads, 101, 102; Neoplatonism of, 202; object as phenomenal, 147; ontological status of space, 96; physical monadology, 203; pre-critical philosophy, 104, 194; on relations, 41, 102, 103; space, 97–104, as absolute, 95, concept of, 94, 95, the meaning of "space," 100, subjective, 41, 95, as *Unding*, 8, 29; subjectivism of, 202, 203, 206; *True Estimation of Living Forces*, 101, 102 n.7
Kepler, Johannes: matter as inert, 153; mechanical concept of nature, 80
Kinematics, 80
Kinesis, 20, 23, 24, 78, 79, 80; analysis of, 89, 175; Aristotle's concept of, 38; meaning of in Greeks, 181
κίνησις in Aristotle, 187; change from potentiality to actuality, 182
Kinetics, 6, 28, 38, 80
Knowledge in Kant, 204; metaphysics of, 201; of physical, problem of, 41
Koyré, Alexandre, *From the Closed World to the Infinite Universe*, 100 n.5

Laws, empirical verification of, 42; of motion, 9, 43; of nature, 42
Leclerc, Ivor, *The Nature of Physical Existence*, 13, 39 n.1, 41 n.6, 106, 146 n.7, 166, 180 n.1; "Ontology of Descartes," 181 n.2, 185 n.8; ed., *The Philosophy of Leibniz and the Modern World*, 119 n.9
Leibniz, G. W., 3, 4, 6, 10, 14, 30, 33, 34, 39, 40, 41, 42, 83, 113, 113 n.5, 153, 166, 169, 200, 202,

205; acting as perception, 30; action not motion, 183; on active force, 84; antitypy, 174; body, attributes derivative, 40, 42; on body, 40, 62, concept of, 120, 121, 129, ontological status of, 114, 122, 130–31, as phenomenal, 74, theory of, 72, 73; continuum, labyrinth of, 82; De Volder, letters to, 84 n.11, 85 nn.12, 13; dynamics, science of, 175; extension, 28, analysis of, 146, as relation, 39, 146, theory of, 73, not ultimate, 85, finite and infinite, 33; force, concept of, 102; God, 84, as principle of motion, 24, 71; groups, basis for concepts of, 124, status of, 131; ideas, status of, 201; *Journal des Savants*, 72 n.12; material atomism rejected, 30; on matter, 62; monads, as souls, 73, 127, 130, unity of, 136; monadism, spiritual, 116; *Monadology*, 89, 89 n.16, 113 n.5, 119 n.9; motion, 75–90, analysis of, 87, concept of, 40, as relational, 146; in Neoplatonic tradition, 146; "New System of Nature," 40 n.5, 44, 73 n.13, 89 n.15, 118 n.7, 173 n.8; ontological difference between constituents and body, 65; perception, 32, 40; perpetual re-creation, 119; *phenomenon bene fundatum*, 117; on physical existents, 31; physical as matter, rejection of, 31; place, definition of, 101, rejection of Newton's concept of, 94; power fundamental to acting, 173; preestablished harmony, 131, 161 n.2; *Principles of Nature and Grace*, 113 n.5; relatedness of constituents, 162; relation, primary category, 149; on relation and possibility, 31; relations, mathematical, 146, grounded in the physical, 41, phenomenal, 147, phenomenality of, 118; space, concept of, 94, 95, 96, 100, 101; "Specimen Dynamicum,"

86 n.14; substance, not changeless, 125, not material, 86; unity, as phenomenal, 121, status of, 132; world as mathematical, 196; *vinculum substantiale*, 117, 118

Leucippus, 23, 108

Life, analysis of, 178

Locke, John, 166; category of quantity, 146; *Essay Concerning Human Understanding*, 82 n.7, 145 n.6; God as source of ideas, 200; ideas as subjective, 199; ideas, theory of, 200; on perception, 201; primary and secondary qualities, 145; solidity and extension of matter, 82

Locomotion, 6, 10, 11, 24, 38, 39, 43, 190; concept of, 182, 183; as continuous, as discontinuous, 10; pertains to plurality, 89; status of, 175; vibratory, 11

Locomotive change as ultimate, 177

Logic, 4

Lowe, Victor, 15

Lubin, Eilhard, 81, 109, 122

Lucretius, 108

Magnenus, J. C., 122

Man, conception of, and universe, 5

Mass, a feature of body, 174

Materia, 76

Mathematical, 38; continuum, infinite divisibility of, 27, 82; as mental, 37, 41; ontological status of, 14, 26, 27, 30, 38, 207; and the physical, 14, 15, 29, 33, 38, 40, 41, 68, 72, 203, 204, 206; pertains to possibility, 41

Mathematics, 14; applied, 183; foundations of, 14, 15; as mental construct in Kant, 15; object of, 96, in Kant, 205; and the physical, 38, 96, 201; pure, 14, 49; status of, 200

Matter, 4, 6, 7, 9, 21, 22, 23, 27, 28, 43, 47, 75; as actual being, 23, 37; as being, 5, 9, 185, 190; as body, 9, 24, 71, 72; and change, 5; as changeless, 23, 92, 176, 181, 183, 198; as composite, 10; con-

Matter (*continued*)

cept of, 5, 7, 61, 62, 63, 109, 141, 153, 177; connotation of term, 154; as corporeality, 27, 36; correlative to form, 4, 36; as derivative, 8, 185; devoid of becoming, 37, 140; devoid of sensible forms, 200; as ensouled, 78, 80; essence of its own, 197; as essentially extensive, 27, 38; as extension, 69; and form, 4; homogeneity of, 42; how to be understood, 35; identified with body, 59; as inert, 33, 134, 140, 142, 148, 153, 175; locomotion of, 92, 201; as mathematical, 25, 26, 63; and mind, 44–56; in modern Neoplatonism, 55; and motion, 37, 75–90, 140; nature as, 92; in Neoplatonic conception, 48, 196; ontological status for Leibniz, 86; as particulate energy, 85 n.9; passivity of, 199; as the physical, 23, 36, 57, 58, 140, 152, 164, 169, 180, 181, 184; as physical being, 145; as physical existent, 23, 25, 36, 172; as possibility, 197; potentiality of, 77; presupposition of, 163; not explicative of relations, 158; Renaissance concept of, 84; in Renaissance Neoplatonism, 52; as solid bulk, 26, 27, 66; as substance, 4, 78, 198; as substrate, 184, 185; as ultimate, 141, 183; unchangeable, 5; without becoming, 5, 39, 153; without power and activity, 82–83; without principle of agency, 192

Measurability, 6; foundation of, 26
Mechanics, 6; quantum, 10, 90; science of, 113, 191
Mechanism, 24; concept of, 124, 143; theory of, 163
Mental, relation to physical, 207
Mental pole, 170
Metaphysics, 38, 195, 205; and physics, 45
Mind, 4; conception of, 44; ontological status of, 46, 169
Mind and body, problem of, 45
Modern science, 35, 45; basically Platonic, 196
Molecule: character of group, 123; concept of, 122, 131, 149
Monadology, Kant's physical, 201
Monads, 86, 87, 89, 90, 101; active for Kant, 102; enduring entities, 119; as simple constituents of compounds, 118; theory of, 127; as unitary, 133; unity of, 136; windowless, 118
More, Henry, 83, 196
Motion, 5, 6, 7, 11, 14, 204; as absolute, 141; not active, 183; analysis of, 86; Aristotelian concept of, 24; of atoms, 64, 67; change of place, 5; concept of, 37, 38, 140, 141, 180–83, 187, 188; laws of, 9, 42, 113; as locomotion, 78; and matter, 55, 70, 71, 75–90; meaning of word, 181; and concept of place, 32, 98; principle of, 197; analyzed as relation, 146; as relative concept, 32; source of, 24, 40; status of, 207; as ultimate, 183
Motus, concept of, 5, 182

Nature: conception of, 4, 5, 19, 20, 21, 35, 80; as ensouled, 52; as mechanism, 5, 80; in modern conception, 19–34, 37; as phenomenal, 205; as object of philosophical inquiry, 30, 203, 207; as philosophical concept, 30; philosophy of, 19, 30, 203; as totality, 21
Neoplatonism, 14, 45, 46, 48, 58, 66, 77, 108, 153, 205; concept of agency, 191, 192; Augustinian, 51, 196; doctrine of categories, 145, 146, 147; doctrine of, 47; form as active, 199, as principle of activity, 173; forms, derivative from God, 200; of Hume, 202; ideas, doctrine of, 199, 200, ontological status of, 200; inheritance from, 172; of Kant, 202; matter in, 185; matter, conception of, 196, 197, as passive potentiality, 173; on mind-body dualism, 47; modern, 198, 200,

201, 203, 205, 206, 207, 208; ontology of, 169, 181; perception, theory of, 50, 200; priority of quality, 144; relations, doctrine of, 147; in Renaissance, 51, 55, 58, 59, 198; Renaissance ontology, dualistic, 54; resuscitation of, 44, 195; in sixteenth-century thought, 197; soul, as active, 50, whether with passivity, 199; subjectivism of, 207; world soul, conception of, 196

Newton, Isaac, 3, 4, 5, 6, 7, 8, 14, 15, 25, 38, 39, 40, 54, 61, 88, 141, 146, 153, 205; action not motion, 183; on active force, 84; atomism, material, 116; atoms, as bodily, 28, 114; body, characters of, 74; force, concept of, 31; God, conception of, 84, as active, 29, 31, as extended, 29, 38, 196, foundation of measurability, 29; matter, characters of, 62, as passive, 199; nature, mechanical concept of, 80; *Opticks*, 4, 28 n.2, 33, 83 nn.8, 9, 84 n.10, 141 n.3; *Philosophiae Naturalis Principia Mathematica*, 3, 59, 60 n.3, 92, 93 nn.5, 6, 100, 112, 114 n.6, 181, 183; physics of, 194; physics as mechanics, 142; physics and metaphysics, 38; place as absolute, 93, 140, not relative, 93; "Rules of Reasoning," 3, 59; solidity, concept of, 115; space, concept of, 96, 100, 101, meaning of, 94, ontological status of, 99; theology of, 26; world as mathematical, 196

Newtonian doctrine, misconception of, 94

Nicolaus Cusanus, 14, 58, 67, 196; *explicatio Dei*, 200; matter as possibility, 197; Neoplatonism of, 51

Nous, 46, 50; in Neoplatonism, 47

Ontology, 195; Neoplatonic, 199
Ontos on, to, 23
Operationalism, 205
Order, 21
Organism, 24; concept of, 124, 125, 138, 143, 167; not synonymous with life, 178; ontological status of, 167; relational wholes, 177; relations, complexity of, 179

Ousia (οὐσία), 61, 78, 79, 89, 122; as substance, 172; as unitary, 133

Oxford Dictionary of English Etymology, 18 n.4

Oxford English Dictionary, 181 n.3, 187 n.11

Paracelsus, 51, 78, 108, 196; elements, theory of, 52, 197; physical entities as ensouled, 197

Parmenides, 23, 80, 208; concept of being, 133

Particles, 7, 9; atomic, 9; elementary, 9

Passivity, analysis of, 192, 193
Patrizzi, Francesco, 51, 109
Perceiver, passive in Aristotle, 200
Perceptio, 89
Perception, 32, 40; of motion in matter, 192; as relation, 32
Perishing, 119
Phenomenology, 195
Philo, 47 n.3
Philosophia naturalis, 3, 19, 35, 43
Philosophical problems of scientific entities, 155, 156
Philosophy: and science, 4; disconnected from science, 194; separation from science, 195
Philosophy, first, 25, 45
Philosophy of nature, 3–16, 30, 44, 45; problematic of, 11, 12, 13, 16, 30; and science, 43; in seventeenth century, 35–43
Philosophy of organism, 40
Philosophy of science, science as object of, 4
Phoronomy, 6, 80; physics as, 28, 37
Physical: as active, 42, 148; as in becoming, 140, 181; as body, 168; as changeless, 135; as full, 80; as not inert, 141; as matter, 35–43, 142, 145, 152; relation to mathematical, 33, 40; mental, 207
Physical acting, problem of, 166
Physical being: as active, 190; nature of, 203
Physical existent: as acting, 44, 172,

Physical (*continued*)
178; as body, 28; concept of, 12, 15, 35, 152–64; as matter, 22, 35, 36; primary constituent of compound, 132; as *res extensa*, 11
Physical existents: as active, 153, 164, 172, 175; identity of, 22, 30, 155; as primary, 23; as ultimate constituents, 22–23, 177
Physical pole, 170
Physics, 9, 42; as kinetics, 28, 38, 80; for Leibniz, 86; as mathematical analysis of motion, 38, 42; as mechanistic, 6; as quantum mechanics, 10; science of, 27, 183; science of nature, 80; other sciences reducible to, 193; status of, 177
Physicus, 52
Physis, 20, 21, 78
Place, 5, 6, 37, 92; absolute, 38, 39, 93, 140; distinct from body, 101; change of, 5, 6, 10, 24, 32, 38, 175; concept of, 39, 93; concept of, in Aristotle, 98, in Leibniz, 42, in sixteenth and seventeenth century, 98, as relative concept, 32, relativity of, for Descartes, 29; ontological status of, 87, 94, 101; status of, 140, 206, 207
Plato, 46, 68, 68 n.5, 108, 170, 173, 208; on acting, 166; on body-soul relation, 49; conception of true being, 23; meaning of *kinesis*, 181, 182; emphasis on mathematics, 196; on mind and body, 200; contrasted with Neoplatonism, 47; *Parmenides*, 133; *Republic*, soul in, 46; *Sophist*, 133, 173 n.9; *Theaetetus*, 166, 166 n.3; three ultimate sources, 144
Platonism, 108, 194–208; School of Chartres, 196; of modern science, 196
Plotinianism, 196
Plotinus, 47 n.3, 192; doctrine of, 47; *Enneads*, 197 n.1; matter in, 185; conception of matter, 196, 197
ποῖος, 190
Positivism, 25, 194, 195; an error, 33; Neoplatonic, 205; in philosophy of science, 205
Possibility, 33, 42; order of, 42
Potency, 137; necessary in acting, 173
Potentiality, 21, 33, 41, 137; connection with actuality, 33, 37, 40, 42, 132; of compounds, 128; meaning of, 187, 188; ontological status of, 33
Potentiality and actuality, distinction of, 126, 127, 135
Power, 80, 81; concept of, 138; lost to matter, 82; necessary in acting, 173; theory of, 186
Predication, concept of, 144
Preestablished harmony, 15, 41, 117, 131, 147, 161 n.2, 201, 202
Prehension: conceptual, meaning of, 170; physical, 170, 206; as relational, 118, 119; Whitehead's theory analyzed, 192
Prehensive acting, 170
Presuppositions, philosophical, 163, 195
Prigogine, Ilya: dissipative structures, 168; *From Being to Becoming, Order out of Chaos*, 168 n.4
Probability, statistical, 9
Process, concept of, 187, 188
Propositions, theory of, 206
Prote hyle, 76
Psyche, 46, 48, 50
Ptolemy, 108
Purpose, 167
Pythagoreanism, 108

Qualis, 190
Qualitative features, ontological status of, 58
Qualities: as inhering, 145; primary and secondary, 145
Quality: category of, 144, 145, 149, 158; change in respect to, 190; as relational, 176
Quantity: category of, 144, 145, 146, 149; change in respect of, 190

Raphson, Joseph: *Analysis Aequationem Universalis*, 100 n.5; on space, 100
Rationalism, 201
Reacting, 166
Realism, epistemological, 205, 206

Relating, act of, 40
Relation: by virtue of acting, 158; of mind and body, 201; category of, 144, 145, 146; concept of, 33, 39, 40, 141; as inhering, 145; of mathematical and physical, 31; nature of, 39, 41, 171; perception as, 32; phenomenal, 41; primary category, 149; reciprocal interacting, 174
Relational acting, 42, 193; relational wholes, 177
Relations, 12, 13, 139–51; complexity of, 179; integrating, 137; for Kant, 102; as mathematical, 146, 147, 148, 149; no explanation of, in matter, 158; nature of, 12, 32, 33; as phenomenal, 40, 90, 118, 147; of physical existents, 203; structural problem of, 156, 157
Relationships, problem of, 12, 13, 157
Relativity: general theory, 7; special theory, 7; theory of, 184
Renaissance, 44, 50
Res cogitans, 14, 54, 192, 199
Res extensa, 8, 14, 27, 28, 39, 54, 70, 71, 81, 93, 113, 199
Res, space as a, 8
Richard of Middleton, 77
Russell, B. A. W., and Whitehead, A. N., *Principia Mathematica*, 15, 206

Scaliger, Julius Caesar, 51, 78, 109; concept of space, 98; *Exotericarum exercitationum*, 98 nn.1, 3
Scepticism in Hume, 202
Science, 9; and philosophy, distinction between, 4
Scientific empiricism, 205
Scotus, John Duns, on matter, 77
Seminal reasons, 77
Seneca, 108
Sennert, Daniel, 3, 25, 58, 59, 78, 109, 122; *De Chymicorum*, 53; on void, 99
Sensation, 47, 48
Simple location, Whitehead's criticism of, 176

Society: defining characteristic, 119; ontological status of, 119, 120, 121, 122; theory of, 132
Solidity, in body, 26, 27, 32, 37, 115
Soma, 46, 46 n.2
Soul, 46; as active, 48, 50; as alone active, 55; as being, 192; not affected by body, 55; immortality of, 50; ontologically distinct, 198; ontological status of, 46; without passivity in Neoplatonism, 199; as principle of activity, 77; as principle of agency, 192; principle of life and motion, 197; as principle of motion, 50; in Neoplatonism, 48; in Renaissance Neoplatonism, 51
Space, 5, 6, 7, 8, 25, 75; concept of, 8, 139, 140, 141, 180; concepts of, 91–96; development of new meaning of, 92; etymology of word, 91; as extended area, 99; where God active, 29; as internal place, 93; meaning of word, 97; object of geometry, 14; as physical object, 8; ontological status of, 27, 96; subjectivity of, in Kant, 40, 201, 202, 204; as substance, 8; as totality of places, 38, 100; as ultimate, 141, 183; as *Unding*, 8, 29
Spinoza, 113
Stoicism, 196
Structure: concept of, 42, 131; of groups, 124
Subjective aim: from God, 131, 132; in Whitehead's theory, 131, 132, 161
Subjectivism, epistemological, 205
Substance, 6; Aristotelian concept of, 197; as changeless, not changeless, 125; as changeless, 126, 132; as constituents of compounds, 130, 132; material, 5, 8; material changeless, 5; physical, 109; as unitary, 22, 133
Substrate as passive, 176
Supersession, 119

Teleology in acting, 178
Telesio, Bernardino, 51, 80, 109; concept of space, 98; *De rerum natura*, 98 n.2

Theobald, D. W., 142; concept of relation, 147; "Some Considerations on the Philosophy of Chemistry," 142 n.4

Theory, testing of, 162, 163

Thierry of Chartres, 197

Thomas Aquinas, 48, 111; *Commentary on Aristotle's De anima*, 49 n.4; inheritance from, 172; matter, as extended stuff, 173, as passive substrate, 172, theory of, 77; *motus* in, 182

Thymos, 46

Time, 5, 6, 7, 25, 75; absolute, 38, 39, 142; concept of, 139, 140, 141, 180; when God active, 26; for Newton, 94; status of, 27, 207; subjective in Kant, 201, 202; as ultimate, 183

Transition, analysis of, 88

Unity: of composites, 167; of compounds, 136; ontological status of, 121, 132; as phenomenal, 121

Universal, concept of, 170

Universal entities, data of pure mathematics, 49

Universe: as indefinite, 70; as infinite, 70; mathematical, 14, 200

Vacuum, 6

Velocity, 6

Vis inertiae, 83

Void, 27, 37; concept of, 63; extensive, 82; meaning of, 93; and place, 99; problem of, 66; in Scaliger's concept, 98; theory of, 8

Weizsäcker, C. F. von, 7, 8; *Die Einheit der Natur*, 7 nn.2, 3, 12, 184 n.6; on matter and energy, 184

Whewell, W., *Philosophy of the Inductive Sciences*, 91 n.1

Whitehead, A. N., 11, 12, 16, 30, 39, 40, 42, 114, 164, 164 n.3; acting, as mental, 169, as relating, 158, 159, as relational, 159, 174, 176; actual entities as primary constituents of compounds, 118, 119, 130; *Adventures of Ideas*, 13 n.4, 207 n.14; extreme atomism, 119; on bifurcation of nature, 169; *Concept of Nature*, 9; concept of causality, 162; *An Enquiry into the Principles of Natural Knowledge*, 12, 206; epistemological realism, 206, 207; extension as relation, 30, 31, 85; extensive continuum, 42; extensiveness in, 174; form rejected as principle of activity, 173; basis for concept of groups, 124; on status of groups, 131; laws as statistical, 42; analysis of life, 178; locomotive change, status of, 176; on mathematical and physical, 15; on mental and physical, 171; ontological principle, 120; philosophy of organism, 167; theory of organism, 124, 125; panpsychist, seen as, 169; physical as active, 154; physical existent as active, 173; *Process and Reality*, 13, 15, 33, 40 nn.3, 4, 42 n.8, 44, 118 n.8, 119, 119 nn.10, 11, 120 nn.12–15, 125, 149 n.8, 154 n.1, 160, 161 n.2, 165, 169 n.6, 171, 178 n.11, 178 n.12, 179 n.13; concept of process, 154; process as coming into being, 171; relatedness of constituents, 162; relations, primary, 149; relations, real, 118; theory of prehension, 192 n.13; theory of propositions, 206; *Science and the Modern World*, 11, 12, 43 n.9, 44, 124, 125 n.16, 126, 161 n.2, 176; concept of society, 178; status of society, 122; theory of society, 119, 129, 132, 160, 161, 168; theory of subjective aim, 161; substrate activity, 173; status of unity, 121, 132

Wiener, P. P., *Leibniz Selections*, 72 n.12

World: as infinitely extended, 196; as mathematical structure, 14, 196

World soul, 196; Plotinian, 51; in Renaissance, 51; in Cusanus, 197

www.ingramcontent.com/pod-product-compliance
Lightning Source LLC
Chambersburg PA
CBHW031413290426
44110CB00011B/369